"Ehrenberg has produced a beautifully written interdisciplinary study of Trump's racism that is based on profound political insight and scholarly acumen. It should become a standard work."

Stephen Eric Bronner, *Board of Governors Distinguished Professor Emeritus of Political Science, Rutgers University*

WHITE NATIONALISM AND THE REPUBLICAN PARTY

In this book, John Ehrenberg argues that Donald Trump, as both candidate and president, represents a qualitatively new stage in the evolution of the Republican Party's willingness to exploit American racial tensions.

Works on Trump's use of race have tended to be fragmentary or subsidiary to a larger purpose. Ehrenberg concentrates his investigation on Trump's weaponized use of race, contextualized through historical and theoretical details, demonstrating that while Trump draws on previous Republican strategies, he stands apart through his explicit intention to convert the Republican Party into a political instrument of a threatened racial order. The book traces the Grand Old Party's (GOP) approach to racial matters from Goldwater's "constitutional" objection to federal activity in the South to George W. Bush's overtures to Black citizens. Ehrenberg examines the role of racial animus in prying loose a significant portion of the Democratic Party's electoral coalition and making possible Trump's overt flirtation with white nationalism. He concludes that the Republican Party will find it difficult to jettison its 50-year history of embracing and amplifying white racial animus and resentment.

White Nationalism and the Republican Party will be of interest to academics and students of American politics, voting behavior, American party politics, race and American politics, twentieth-century American history, political leadership, politics of inequality, race and public policy.

John Ehrenberg is Senior Professor of Political Science Emeritus and former Chair of the Political Science Department at Long Island University. Professor Ehrenberg has devoted a lifetime to research and writing on political ideologies and the history of political thought. His works have been translated into languages including Chinese, Japanese, Korean, Turkish, and Egyptian, while he has also been the recipient of many awards, including the Alfred McCoy Award for Lifetime Achievement from the American Political Science Association's Caucus for a New Political Science. Some of his previous works include *Civil Society: The Critical History of an Idea*, *Israel and Palestine: Alternate Perspectives on Statehood* (co-edited with Yoav Peled), *The Iraq Papers* (edited with J. Patrice McSherry, José Ramón Sánchez, and Caroleen Marji Sayej), and *Servants of Wealth: The Right's Assault on Equality*.

WHITE NATIONALISM AND THE REPUBLICAN PARTY

Toward Minority Rule in America

John Ehrenberg

NEW YORK AND LONDON

Cover image: enjoynz

First published 2022
by Routledge
605 Third Avenue, New York, NY 10158

and by Routledge
4 Park Square, Milton Park, Abingdon, Oxon, OX14 4RN

Routledge is an imprint of the Taylor & Francis Group, an informa business

© 2022 John Ehrenberg

The right of John Ehrenberg to be identified as author of this work has been asserted in accordance with sections 77 and 78 of the Copyright, Designs and Patents Act 1988.

All rights reserved. No part of this book may be reprinted or reproduced or utilised in any form or by any electronic, mechanical, or other means, now known or hereafter invented, including photocopying and recording, or in any information storage or retrieval system, without permission in writing from the publishers.

Trademark notice: Product or corporate names may be trademarks or registered trademarks, and are used only for identification and explanation without intent to infringe.

Library of Congress Cataloging-in-Publication Data
A catalog record for this title has been requested

ISBN: 978-1-032-02342-7 (hbk)
ISBN: 978-1-032-02341-0 (pbk)
ISBN: 978-1-003-18296-2 (ebk)

DOI: 10.4324/9781003182962

Typeset in Bembo
by Newgen Publishing UK

CONTENTS

Preface ix

    Introduction: Trumped 1

1 Barry and George Go Fishing 12

2 Dick's Trick 26

3 Whistling for Plutocracy 43

4 The Wrecker and the Warrior Throw a Party 64

5 The Tribune Rides Forth 90

6 Toward White Minority Rule 106

Bibliography *127*
Index *136*

PREFACE

As soon as Donald Trump was declared the winner of the 2016 presidential vote, an army of pundits, columnists, social scientists, and ordinary citizens set about trying to understand what had happened. The election's surprising result required an explanation.

I'm a political scientist by training, and, like many others, I followed the professional literature as colleagues tried to tease out the elements of Trump's triumph. Two sets of explanations quickly emerged.

One of them focused on the profound changes that have been transforming the American economy. Decades of deindustrialization and the disappearance of millions of manufacturing jobs have hollowed out vast swaths of the country's industrial heartland, areas that were home to some of the world's most powerful companies and whose communities were shining examples of American economic prowess. Decades of economic decline have produced unemployment, disinvestment, poverty, and an assortment of social ills that have devastated once-thriving regions and made their voters open to Trump's promise to revive industry, get tough with China, and "Make America Great Again." There was considerable evidence to support the view that stagnant economic prospects for millions of working- and lower-middle-class families lay at the bottom of Trump's victory.

A second set looked at the way Trump had mobilized the old demons of American racism and xenophobia during his campaign. A sharp uptick in measures of racial prejudice, hostility to immigrants, and anti-Muslim rhetoric correlated with areas of strength for the Trump campaign. His core message of American restoration had a bright white color. Here too, millions of Republican and independent voters responded to Trump's overt appeals to racial animus and his calls for restoration.

Were these two impulses connected? Did Trump's dark vision of American economic decline reinforce his appeals to white racial conservatives who had been hammered by decades of crisis? Or was it the other way around: was his appeal primarily a racist one to which millions of white voters rallied in an era of economic restructuring and a narrowing of their life chances? Several influential studies looked at the relationship between the economic and ideological forces that had upended decades of moderate, centrist American political history. The overwhelming consensus was that economic distress and racial animus were related, but that the Republican candidate had benefited mightily from the GOP's identification as the "white man's party."

Other forces were at work, and several played prominent roles in further attempts to understand what had produced President Trump. If the candidate had positioned himself as the champion of vulnerable white voters, he certainly added overt appeals to men of all social classes. Promising to restore them to their accustomed place of power and respect, he reviled "political correctness," contemptuously called his opponent a "nasty woman," and strutted around as an unreconstructed supermale from an earlier period of American history. Attacks on *Roe v. Wade*, boasts about the size of his penis and high testosterone levels, and promises of a chest-thumping foreign policy conveyed the message that here was a tough guy who would appeal to insecure men threatened by changes in gender roles. White men have been the Republican Party's most reliable source of electoral support for decades, and Trump certainly worked to amplify the GOP's appeal to masculinity.

Calls to resentful white men were amplified by appeals to conservative Christians convinced that they were under assault by the ungodly agents of secularism. Attacks on scientists, promises to appoint Supreme Court justices who would overturn *Roe* and strengthen religious liberty rights, full-throated support for Israel, and ostentatious appearances with the Christian Right's celebrities carried Trump, never known for his religious devotion, to an 80–20 margin of victory over Hillary Clinton among white evangelical voters. Religious conservatives who were alarmed at how politicians were turning their backs on God were as attracted to Trump's promises of restoration as were other constituencies convinced that they were being persecuted by forces they could neither understand nor control.

Powerful demographic forces certainly magnified white voters' fears that the future might be different from what they had come to expect. Large-scale immigration set off alarm bells as hundreds of American communities saw rapid increases in non-white populations. From Tea Party activists to Sheriff Joe Arpaio, immigration politics took center stage as Spanish-speaking communities took root in areas far away from the country's coastal centers of immigration, Somali migrants settled in Minnesota, and Vietnamese communities appeared in South Texas. Old patterns of xenophobia harkened back to movements that sought to restrict immigration as Trump's promise to "Make America Great Again" spoke to an imaginary America that was white and native-born.

Trump channeled old American patterns of racism, male supremacy, xenophobia, religious grievance, and populist rage during his campaign. They figured prominently in his appeal to millions of disenchanted voters, and it's often difficult to tease them out from one another. But distinctions have to be made if we are to understand the forces that are shaping contemporary American politics.

This book analyzes how Trump used, changed, and profited from the Republican Party's long flirtation with racial animus. Its focus is broader than a single individual, for the GOP has moved from a conventional racial conservatism to an implicit white nationalism. As the party's racial politics changed, it moved from promising white voters that it would hold the line and protect the foundations of the racial status quo to the position that political power should be used in the interests of white people. Trump's campaign and presidency were nodal points in this evolution. Justifications for racial discrimination began to appear in official administration policies as white nationalism began to migrate into the halls of power.

This didn't happen in a vacuum. Trump marched forward as the defender of beleaguered white people, but he was also the pied piper of a fast-congealing plutocracy. As millions of American families continued to suffer stagnant incomes and decreasing wealth, their "American dream" became an unattainable fantasy. The country's history made it easy for Republican candidates to racialize white families' declining standards of living and convince them to blame their situation on communities of color. Old currents of American history worked to reinforce the combination of concentrated wealth and concentrated political power. A new American plutocracy whose economic and political domination rivaled that of the Gilded Age and the Roaring Twenties took shape amid heightened talk of racial discord and continuous economic upheaval.

In concentrating on Trump's appeal to racially conservative whites, I don't mean to imply that his misogyny, hostility to immigrants, or promises to restore American industry were unimportant. Social science has convinced me that his ability to tap into racial animus and his developing white nationalism resonated with millions of white Americans who faced a future of continuing economic turmoil and changing demographics. This is not intended to be an exhaustive account of his rise to power. I leave it to others to account for the other dimensions of his candidacy and presidency.

Brooklyn, New York
December 2021

INTRODUCTION

Trumped

Hundreds of millions of people around the world were astonished when Donald Trump won the 2016 presidential election. It seemed like a bolt out of the blue, a sudden interruption of all that was normal and a radical break with a dependable American past that had been responsible, orderly, and moderate. How had this happened? What did it mean?

It was Trump's explicit appeal to white Americans' xenophobia and racial animus that made his campaign stand out. But what appeared to be simply an electoral tactic had two sides to it. On the one hand, it was an intensification of long-established trends that had been maturing for decades inside the Republican Party. At the same time, it was a sharp break with conservative orthodoxy on racial affairs. This contradictory situation has made it difficult to locate Trump in the racial history of recent American politics – particularly since he had gone beyond simply using race in a bid for electoral advantage. He is tightly connected to the last 50 years of Republican political development and has deployed long-established arguments that are now congealing into a conscious political movement supported by a mass base. His candidacy and presidency traced an arc from the white resentment initially retailed by Barry Goldwater and George Wallace through Richard Nixon's dog whistling and the claims of color blindness adopted by Ronald Reagan and both George Bushes. On the other hand, his open attacks on minorities and immigrants represented a new phase in the development of an American Right that has risen to power on the strength of half a century's worth of appeals to racial resentment, white fear, and demographic anxiety. His predecessors were not above aiming specific appeals to white voters as an electoral strategy, but they governed as normal racial conservatives. The Trump moment is a qualitatively different one. It results from, and accelerates, the radicalization of a Republican Party that is fast becoming the political apparatus of white minority rule.

DOI: 10.4324/9781003182962-1

Trump stood apart from other Republican political figures in his overt embrace of racism as both an electoral strategy *and* a governing principle. American history has long featured the implicit assumptions and explicit assertions that membership in its civic community is absolute for white people and conditional for everyone else. After all, it was only in 1965 that all citizens attained formal membership in the national political community. The civil rights movement's successful struggle for a nonracial civic nationalism that was founded on Enlightenment principles of universalism has long been locked in struggle with powerful impulses that animated slavery, attacks on immigrants, Jim Crow, and the use of racism for political gain. These impulses were there long before Trump became president; economic decline and demographic changes have brought them to the surface in a particularly concentrated, explicit, and virulent form. Trump gave them shape and substance and used them to galvanize his 2016 campaign, organize his presidency, and set the conditions for his 2020 run. He was astute enough to recognize them, cynical enough to use them, skilled enough to intensify them, and successful enough to see them through to completion. He surpassed his predecessors by clarifying these inchoate impulses and deploying them as instruments of political combat and governance. His reactionary chant of "Make America Great Again" announced the *herrenvolk* conception of democracy to which he subscribes.

Having ridden racial animus and hatred of immigrants to the presidency, Trump set about remaking the Grand Old Party (GOP) into something that broke from much of its past. Although they were always willing to exploit racial division for immediate political gains, even the most conservative Republicans accepted an inclusive conception of citizenship that reached across racial, religious, and ethnic lines. Trump moved past this implicit understanding and systematically attacked the long effort to fashion a comprehensive democracy. It took a civil war and the Fourteenth Amendment to overturn an explicit assumption that slaves and their descendants were incapable of living with white people in conditions of freedom and equality. The Dred Scott announcement that people "of the African race" were not citizens whether they were slave or free found its modern echo in Donald Trump's MAGA promise. His 2016 campaign was Chief Justice Roger Taney's delayed triumph.

Although the success of this call for racial restoration was shocking to many, it was prepared by a generation's worth of ideological development. The story begins 50 years ago when the Republican Party saw an opportunity for electoral advantage. As the national Democrats broke with their "solid" base, their support of the civil rights movement triggered a mass exodus of white Southerners. It wasn't long before the Republicans became the champions of an aggrieved regional white population. Barry Goldwater announced this phase with his opposition to the Civil Rights Act in the name of "states' rights," a stance that propelled him to victory in the Deep South and Arizona – his only victories in 1964. Optimistic expectations that his candidacy represented the end of the hard right were soon dashed on the rock of American race relations. As George Wallace demonstrated that a racially tinged populist conservatism could succeed on the national stage, Richard Nixon deepened the assault on the New Deal coalition by driving a wedge between Black and the lower-middle- and working-class white voters that had been the foundation of Democratic supremacy.

The story is a mixed bag of forward movement and backward regression, of attempts to embrace the future and nostalgia for a vanishing past. The Civil Rights and Voting Rights Acts of 1964 and 1965 – two signature pieces of congressional legislation that enjoyed wide popular and much Republican support – did away with legalized white supremacy. But a multiracial democracy required more than these important steps toward formal democracy and equality before the law. The next phase of the civil rights movement made it clear that substantive social and economic changes were required to address deeper racial issues. A white population that had been generally supportive of formal equality rebelled. Fed by deepening anxieties about crime, urban uprisings, and Black political activity, widespread resistance to busing, open housing, affirmative action, welfare, and other programs provided an opportunity that the GOP was quick to exploit.

A very real sense of economic, cultural, and social insecurity motivated millions of white voters during this period, pushing them to the right and into the arms of a Republican Party that began moving away from its support of the civil rights movement. American racial hierarchy delivered material rewards to its beneficiaries, and wide segments of the white lower-middle and working classes responded to its incentives by delivering their votes to the party that promised to defend them. With race as the pivot of political reaction, the stage was set for a generalized assault on the democratic upsurge of the Sixties and early Seventies. Wallace and Nixon were careful not to call the fundamental institutions of the New Deal into question, but Reagan broadened the conservative attack on Keynesian redistribution into a generalized assault on political liberalism and the welfare state. His election opened a Pandora's box of counterrevolution as his administration demonstrated its hostility to urban life, racial justice, gender equality, and the democratic gains against which he had campaigned. From its friendliness to antiabortion activists to its indifference to the spread of AIDS, crack cocaine, crime, and poverty, Washington declared an end to the Sixties. A national government that had a brief career as the unreliable agent of equity quickly became its enemy. Racial resentment had paved the way for the Right's ascendancy, but much more was at stake than race. The forward motion of an earlier period came to a screeching halt in 1980 as white America announced that it had had enough social reform.

Reagan's rhetorical anti-statism was the contradictory side of his administration's very energetic work to paralyze the federal government's regulatory and redistributive functions. But even as Washington showed no real interest in civilizing the market, Reagan never explicitly renounced the gains of the civil rights movement. He continued Nixon's policy of defending formal equality before the law and generally declined to stoke racial tension as president. But his relative orthodoxy in racial matters and defense of civic nationalism were undermined by the beginning of an historic upward redistribution of wealth. The terms of the implicit bargain that was struck between a nascent oligarchy and the mass of its aggrieved electoral supporters were elevated to a central role during his presidency. Corporations and the rich got deregulation, lower taxes, privatization, and a general assault on the redistributionist welfare state. Lower-income whites received protection for jobs, housing and education, rhetorical support, and reinforcement of their status as hard-working, tax-paying Americans who were being oppressed by parasitical minorities, contemptuous elites, greedy "special interests," and the bureaucratic liberal state that was in thrall to all of them. Reagan was able to mobilize a mass base of working-class and lower-middle-class white voters around an economic program that benefited corporations and the rich. His solution would echo in the administrations of both Bushes and was carried forward, this time without the pretense of racial neutrality, by Trump.

Reagan established the policies and the ideological foundations for a new American oligarchy. The 40-year process that he set in motion has dramatically intensified the central political dynamic of Republican politics. Accelerating economic inequality has radicalized an American Right whose political foundation is solidified by increasingly overt appeals to racial animus and calls for white solidarity. The tried-and-true strategy of pitting lower-income whites against Black progress has made possible the unprecedented transfer of wealth upward and suffocating pressure on the same petty bourgeois and working-class whites who have been its foot soldiers. In the absence of credible leadership, severe economic distress has prevented the development of a cross-racial class movement that could resist conservative hegemony. Fed by deindustrialization and globalization, unprecedented economic inequality has created a new ideological dynamic – but it's one that rests on the old foundation of racial resentment. A deep history made it easy for Trump to convince many beleaguered white voters that immigrants and minorities are responsible for their troubles. In doing so, he effectively neutered a badly weakened Republican current that had declined to use racial appeals for political gain. George W. Bush and other mainstream Republicans came to believe that their party had to embrace immigration reform, move away from overt appeals to racial animus, and reach out to Latino voters if it was to survive. John McCain tried to broker immigration reform before running for president and forbade his campaign staff from using the Reverend Jeremiah Wright in his race against Barack Obama. Republican National Committee chair Ken Mehlmann actually apologized in 2005 for the Republican Party's decades-long use of the "Southern strategy." Seven years later, the Republican National Committee commissioned a 100-page report that urgently recommended a more inclusive approach to voter in future elections – but it was immediately attacked by party officials and activists who would later rally to Trump. By 2016, this position was so enervated that it was relatively easy for the candidate to administer the *coup de grâce*.

Obama's election and far-reaching demographic changes fed the subsequent rise of the Tea Party amid intensified white anxieties about demographic change, economic decline, racial "extinction," and cultural loss. The radicalization of the Republican Party's electoral base has created the most right-wing national political formation in the industrialized world and has profoundly reshaped contemporary American politics. Trump recognized an opportunity to sharpen this weapon and targeted immigrants, women, and virtually all communities of color. An American president was willing to identify whiteness as the operative requirement for full membership and citizenship. His sneering hostility to immigrants from "shithole countries" and stated preference for Norwegians was only one sign of how the politics of race has continued to shape American politics – but now in unprecedented conditions. A rapidly hardening and increasingly overt commitment to white minority rule characterized his public rhetoric and rested at the center of his strategy for reelection in 2020. Defeat does not mean the end of this poisonous legacy. Trump's visceral embrace of racial animus will shape the country's politics for as long as the Republican coalition of the wealthy and the resentful endures.

Obama's election provided the gasoline to feed simmering white resentment, but it took someone to toss the match. Trump was happy to be the arsonist. He'd come a long way from the moment he decided that New York needed to hear his now-infamous view of the 1989 Central Park Five affair. Thirty years ago, he eagerly helped to poison race relations in the city, and this foray into local politics marked his first public embrace of racism for personal gain. Recent developments amplified his influence even as his worldview remained as narrow as ever. The Great Recession exposed the effects of a hollowed-out industrial core and historic levels of inequality. Obama's response was enough to escape the worst but did not address the crisis's root causes. Eight years of political paralysis and hysterical Republican opposition set the stage for the arrival of a candidate who was more than willing to enlist racism in his project of American restoration.

Trump's rise to the presidency was made possible by the "legitimate" parties' inability to address the deep causes of political dysfunction, social crisis, and economic decline. He arose out of the wreckage of a hollowed-out economy, and his grandiose claim that "only I can fix this" announced his intention to organize an economic program of protectionism, regressive tax cuts, privatization, and deregulation that would only exacerbate the inequality to which it was allegedly addressed. But his political program maintained an uneasy alliance with the polemical appeal to xenophobia, racism, culture war, and white nationalism that propelled his rise to power. Widespread apprehension about the future fueled his rise, but Trump's narrow electoral base was an unstable one. It became increasingly difficult for his administration to develop a coherent approach to the pressing issues of the day. As it lurched from crisis to crisis, it quickly wore out its welcome, leaving the country more divided than it had been when he assumed office.

Trump's manifest failures notwithstanding, the present moment is marked by how rapidly he legitimized overt appeals to white racial anxiety – and how accurately he has come to personify the historical moment in the process. He's not alone. From the Philippines to Brazil and Italy through Hungary and Great

Britain, unprecedented challenges to the existing order have generated an international tendency that draws on national, ethnic, and racial chauvinism in the service of plutocracy and reaction. Ever the salesman, Trump marketed specifically American themes at mass rallies of whiteness, but he drew on traditions of European fascism that target individuals and communities of color for polemical and physical attack. A quintessentially American racial context served to crystallize international tension, racial history, and class conflict. But underneath the chaos one can discern a certain logic. The Republican Party has become a party of rural, conservative, older white voters in a country whose demographics are rapidly slipping away from it. Donald Trump is its pied piper who looks backward to a vanishing past. Having remade the Republican Party in his own image, he will leave a reactionary political apparatus whose appeal to racial animus and white grievance will persist long after he is gone. Even in defeat, it is unwilling to act like a normal political formation and change its leader's unpopular program to bring it closer to public opinion. Its policies of voter suppression, immigration restrictions, deportations, and "the wall" are not really about fighting voter fraud, halting illegal immigration, and protecting American workers from low-wage competition. They're about delaying the demographic realities. The damage they've done will be serious, but it can't last. Even in the medium run, fighting the future is doomed to fail.

Since the Republicans have been the nation's dominant political party for the past 40 years, the evolution of their racial positions has been particularly important in shaping American public life as a whole. It's a 50-year history whose main contours are plain, even if they developed unevenly. By 1964, Goldwater had seen that the South was available to Republican presidential candidates, but he knew that this would require a break with the GOP's earlier support for civil rights and occasional federal intervention in support of racial equity. Wallace demonstrated to subsequent Republican and Democratic political figures that racial politics were becoming nationalized, that white resistance to substantive measures to address racial inequality was deep and wide, and that, as he put it, "the whole United States is Southern." Nixon, Reagan, and the Bushes were not above using racial appeals and "dog whistles" to win elections, but in general they stayed within the boundaries of conventional racial conservatism.

This is where Trump is different. He went beyond Reagan's rhetoric of racial neutrality and colorblind policy and openly embraced rhetorical racism and elements of white nationalism as both an electoral strategy and a principle of governance. There's a qualitative difference between him and his Republican predecessors, a difference that has developed alongside a dramatic radicalization of the Republican electoral base. Amid a series of economic and political crises, Trump has overseen the process by which the GOP has become the political guardian of a racial order that is being undermined by globalization, immigration, demographics, and a rapidly changing set of social mores.

Accelerating economic inequality has precipitated powerful currents that have radicalized millions of Republican voters. From 1980, the year of Reagan's election, to the 2016 events that produced President Trump, the share of national income that flowed to the richest 1 percent of American households doubled, going from just over 10 percent to 20 percent. During that same period, the share of income going to the bottom half of American households has been cut in half, falling from just over 20 percent to around 10 percent. The two have switched places, another way of saying that the richest one percent now have what the bottom half used to have. A developing class of plutocrats has literally enriched itself at the expense of half the population. The United States stands alone among similar societies in the extent and rapidity of this upward transfer of wealth, an important reason why our society is so divided and our politics are so virulent.

Unlike the postwar period that Paul Krugman has called the "golden age" of American capitalism, the distribution of wealth has become a zero-sum game in which the winnings of some come at the direct expense of others. It's not surprising that these dramatic economic changes should be paralleled by corresponding ideological and institutional ones. Deindustrialization and globalization have marched in lockstep with governmental policies to accelerate the effective fusion of economic and political power. Wealth shapes politics, and politics strengthens wealth, in a self-perpetuating loop that becomes ever more entrenched and resistant to democratic regulation. Aristotle saw how dangerous this was two and a half millennia ago, and his warnings about the twin evils of unrestrained cupidity and political decay are echoed every day in the morning newspapers.

There was nothing automatic or inevitable about the development of American plutocracy. It required a specific set of policy decisions, institutional developments, and ideological changes. Indeed, the current environment is radically different from the 30 years of broad white middle-class prosperity and the accompanying ethos of moderate social reform, political consensus, and Keynesian expertise that marked the "golden age." Its American Dream is now out of reach for millions, and as it fades out of sight it plays its role as a nostalgic slogan rather than as a description of reality. "Making America Great Again" just gives the fantasy a name.

Trump's administration laid bare the basic dilemma of the American Right. The contradiction that rests at its heart isn't about to go away any time soon. It rests at the heart of the strategic choices made by the GOP half a century ago and illustrates a general problem. Any conservative political party that seeks to win competitive elections is faced with a complicated and difficult task. It must assemble an electoral coalition that can enable it to deliver rewards to corporations and the rich. That coalition has to rest on the loyalty of a working- and lower-middle-class voting base that will be most injured by these rewards. The contradictions of this alliance often make it difficult to sustain, but the Republicans' 50-year hegemony has been remarkably stable because it has tapped into a long history.

Racism, xenophobia, and nativism have provided the glue for the alliance that rests at the heart of Republican power. Both partners in this arrangement have benefited, which is precisely why it has been so durable. Corporations and the rich have gotten the tax breaks, regressive financial policies, deregulation, and privatization that have been their most important priorities for decades. The mass of white voters has gotten protection of their neighborhoods, housing values, schools, and jobs from competition and repeated assurances that the national government would go no further than enforcing the minimal requirements of equality before the law. Rhetorical nods to the "middle class," commitments to "family values," and support for "hard-working, tax-paying Americans" serve to reassure anxious white people that Washington will not abandon them. Trump's signature hostility to immigrants and communities of color built on an historical foundation of racism that has become more poisonous as the country has become more diverse and cosmopolitan.

The path from Goldwater to Trump is long and full of detours, but its main trajectory is clear. Following his defeat of the Eastern Republican establishment by building support in the South and West, the Arizona senator organized his 1964 campaign around attacks on the liberal reformist state. Goldwater was personally opposed to segregation and had voted for the 1957 and 1960 civil rights bills. But he abandoned the Republican Party's often-successful attempts to attract Black voters and decided, as he put it, to "go hunting where the ducks are." The ducks quacked with a pronounced Southern drawl, and Goldwater explained his "constitutional" opposition to the 1964 Civil Rights Act as a defense of private property-owners to do what they wanted with what was theirs. His campaign broke with his party's racial history and provided an early sign that the country's political affairs were about to be reshaped. Indeed, it wasn't long before the politics of race would spill out of the South and come to shape much of the country. The 1948 rebellion by the Dixiecrats had been limited to the Democratic Party and seemed to have little to do with a GOP that was largely absent from the region. Unencumbered by the South, the "party of Lincoln" had supported legislative action to codify civil rights and was more progressive than the Democrats on issues of race. The Democrats, hobbled by their reliance on Dixie's electoral votes and congressional seniority, were the party of Jim Crow. But Goldwater recognized that the region was ready to move away from its automatic support for the Democrats. So complete was the exodus of Southern whites that no Democratic presidential candidate has won a majority of the party's former stronghold since 1972. Goldwater's attacks on the New Deal failed to gain much support and many Southern voters returned to the party of their parents in subsequent elections. But his embrace of states' rights and hostility to federal support of racial reform would gather momentum in the country as it became clear that more was needed than formal equality before the law. The process that began with Goldwater has benefited every successful Republican presidential candidate since. In 2016, 73% of white voters in the South voted for Trump.

George Wallace took Goldwater's position to a national audience by broadening Southern resistance to civil rights. By the time he began to run for president, the campaign of "massive resistance" that had swept over the South in the wake of the Supreme Court's 1954 *Brown* decision had spread to the North. Wallace's successful appeals to Northern whites served notice that racial politics were not limited to Dixie. He avoided Goldwater's unpopular attacks on the New Deal and focused his efforts on housing, education, and jobs in a successful effort to mobilize white voters who were fed up with Black demands. He defended Jim Crow in the South but echoed Goldwater's claim that segregation was a regional custom and that different parts of the country had to figure out how to manage racial matters in accordance with the fundamental principles of limited federal power and states' rights. The authentic language of American protest, populism had long spoken for the middle stratum of free, propertied white men whose labor, it was said, provided the foundation for republican self-government and political democracy. Wallace was on familiar ground when he took this position to a national audience. Even as he avoided the explicit racism that had marked his earlier career, everyone knew whom he meant when he attacked the lazy parasites who lived at the expense of the productive classes. Aiming his rhetorical barbs at the elites above and the "bums" below, he claimed to speak for the millions of white voters who believed that federal enforcement of civil rights measures threatened their housing values, the integrity of their neighborhoods, their investment in their childrens' education, and their seniority on the job. As millions of white voters hardened their opposition to substantive measures that they feared might threaten their new-found prosperity, opposition to open housing, affirmative action, racial preferences, and quotas in hiring and promotions bound them to the Republican Party.

Nixon got the message. The New Deal coalition of Northern workers, white Southerners, and racial and ethnic minorities had rested at the base of Democratic hegemony since the Depression. But it was vulnerable to attack, and Nixon figured out how to institutionalize and legitimize Wallace's assault. Claiming to speak for the white "silent majority" during a period of acute social and political unrest, he peeled off substantial numbers from the Democratic Party even as he defended the New Deal, Keynesianism macroeconomic policy, and equality before the law. By promising not to introduce any new initiatives to address substantive racial inequality and largely ignoring those that were in place, his "law and order" rhetoric revealed a fault line in postwar American politics that the Republican Party was able to exploit. Populism had come to require defending hardworking white male American property-owners whose taxes were being used to support both the idle rich and the parasitical poor. Nixon racialized this position and used it to electoral advantage. It was made possible by the visceral white rage that accompanied riots and uprisings in cities, court-ordered school busing, the emergence and widespread adoption of race-based affirmative action, and protests against the Vietnam War. Wallace had begun to unambiguously express those discontents a few years earlier, but Nixon saw that he was on to something. The dialectic of history produced a 1968 presidential election that was simultaneously the high point of the Sixties and the beginning of the counterrevolution.

Reagan amplified conservative attacks on the New Deal coalition and went further than Eisenhower and Nixon by attacking the welfare state that had been inaugurated with the Roosevelt's New Deal and extended by Johnson's Great Society. His disingenuous repetition of Martin Luther King's desire that the content of character replaces color of skin announced that the work of the civil rights movement was done. Government would henceforth be indifferent to racial disparities that were not the result of formal legislation. Hardworking, tax-paying Americans should not be called upon to support government programs that did not benefit them. The "magic of the market" will raise all boats and wealth will "trickle down," making Washington's intervention both unnecessary and counterproductive. Reagan's fidelity to the conservative program of tax cuts, deregulation, and privatization began the upward distribution of wealth and income that has continued for the past 40 years. His rhetorical and programmatic hostility to federal activity and social reform obscured his fierce commitment to federal activity in the service of wealth. He wasn't above using white racial anxiety in talking about welfare, Food Stamps, taxes, and crime but did preserve Social Security and Medicare because they were important to broad swaths of his white electoral base. Like Nixon, he accepted the basic premises of a cosmopolitan, multicultural social order and generally stayed away from stoking racial tension as president. Both Bushes continued this policy as they focused their attention on the white suburbs; the infamous Willie Horton advertisement helped get George H.W. Bush elected, but Nixon, Reagan, and the Bushes governed as ordinary civic nationalists.

Trump was already elevating the GOP's flirtation with elements of white nationalism to an active courtship before he decided to run for president. He had embraced "birtherism" during the Obama presidency, using it to speak directly to the question of who belongs in the United States – and, more importantly, who doesn't. When Trump, then the Tea Party, and important elements of the GOP electoral coalition mainstreamed the claims that Obama had been born in Kenya, they were going further than suggesting that he was ineligible to be president. The suggestion that Obama wasn't a "real" American quickly developed into the claim that he was a secret Muslim, that he was a terrorist seeking to undermine the United States from within, and that he was sympathetic to foreign anti-American conspiracies. Extreme claims from the fringe found their way into the mainstream of a Republican Party that was becoming the defender of white minority rule. By 2011, about half of Republican voters believed that Obama had been born in Kenya. The net effect of Trump's "birtherism" was to place Obama, and the Democratic Party that had nominated and elected him, outside the boundaries of legitimate American citizenship.

Trump's *herrenvolk* republicanism implied that full membership in the country's civic community should be reserved for white people. This version of white nationalism is likely to persist even after Biden's victory. Widespread fear of demographic change was reflected in Trump's stated preference for immigrants from Nordic societies, his repeated denigration of "shithole countries," his distaste for the Fourteenth Amendment's protection of birthright citizenship, his embrace of birtherism, his attempted Muslim ban, his ominous warnings about invading Latino "caravans," and other elements of his governing style. The GOP is not about to abandon these positions. The oft-repeated claim that the country is under siege and that a moral breakdown is accelerating the decline of American "culture" has become a staple of the Republican Party's appeal to its diminishing core of electoral support. Republican senator Lindsey Graham's twists and turns illustrate what has happened. In the middle of the GOP's 2012 nominating convention, he acknowledged that "the demographics race we're losing badly. We're not generating enough angry white guys to stay in business for the long term." It's one of the great ironies of contemporary American political history, and a fitting commentary about what has happened to his party, that Graham's recognition that the future president was a "race-baiting, xenophobic, religious bigot" didn't prevent him from becoming one of Trump's most loyal allies. The man who had once worked with John McCain to reform the nation's cruel and arbitrary immigration codes and urgently warned his party about the demographic cliff that awaited it has spent a lot of time defending a figure who rode to power on a tide of white racial animus and resentment. In yet another irony, it's Trump himself who made an indispensable contribution to Black Lives Matter, the largest mass movement against American racism in recent history. Graham's warnings are even more prescient now than they were four years ago. It's not entirely clear that his party will make the adjustment that history is demanding, but that doesn't change the fact that the writing is on the wall.

1
BARRY AND GEORGE GO FISHING

There was no border wall to speak of when Barry Goldwater was organizing his 1964 run for national office. The country was in the middle of the long economic expansion that had begun after World War II and had brought a measure of prosperity to millions of families. Unionized workers enjoyed unprecedented job security, steady employment, high wages, and generous benefits. Economic growth anticipated the "consumer republic" that would usher in Henry Luce's 1944 announcement of an "American century." John Kenneth Galbraith would coin the phrase "the affluent society" in his influential 1958 book, and it seemed that the bipartisan commitment to moderate reform and Keynesian economic planning would deliver social peace and economic growth for years. A productive and peaceful country would mean endless prosperity, mute class conflict, and make good on Woodrow Wilson's earlier promise to "make the world safe for democracy."

There was only one potential problem for this optimistic future. The Swedish economist and Nobel laureate Gunnar Myrdal had been asked by the Carnegie Corporation to write a report about the challenges facing American society in the postwar period. His 1944 examination of the "American Dilemma" was a comprehensive examination of the country's persistent problem of race relations – the very same phenomenon that we now call "systemic racism" almost 80 years later. The book's subtitle announced that "the Negro Problem and Modern Democracy" would continue to confront the country until it was addressed in a serious and honest fashion. Myrdal's examination of how the "problem" limited democratic participation in American society, politics, and economics proved more prescient than anyone imagined. Barely 11 years after his massive study appeared, Rosa Parks's refusal to give up her seat on that Montgomery bus precipitated the greatest mass movement for racial equality in the country's history. As Jim

DOI: 10.4324/9781003182962-2

Crow came under direct assault throughout the South, a tumultuous period of social activity, political conflict, and racial tension tested the limits of the country's optimism and ushered in a period of profound change. It turned out that much more was at stake than the future of a particular region. As it became clear that the "Negro problem" was a national one, a series of blows would shatter political liberalism's sunny confidence about the future.

Although the politics of race were most overt in the South, events would soon disabuse Northern whites of their belief that they were racially innocent. George Wallace's presidential campaigns would reveal the national dimensions of American racial discrimination, segregation, and exploitation, providing bitter evidence for Malcolm X's observation that "as long as you are south of the Canadian border, you are south." It turned out that Wallace was the perfect figure to demonstrate the links between the long Southern history of white privilege and racial supremacy and those of its Northern cousin. Slavery and Jim Crow were rooted in Dixie, but Southern racial politics have always had national implications. Indeed, much of American political history has been shaped by white Southern power that shaped national institutions before Lincoln's election and persisted despite a lost civil war and the subsequent transformation of its social order. Neither major party has been immune. From the Hayes–Tilden compromise of 1876 that ended Reconstruction and signaled national acceptance of Jim Crow until Barry Goldwater's 1964 presidential candidacy, the South exercised nationwide power through the Democratic Party. So durable has this power been that it is now expressed by Republican politicians. Even the advent of the broadest reformist regime in the country's history had to make its peace with Dixie's monolithic white voting bloc.

Despite FDR's sweeping victory in 1932 and overwhelming Democratic congressional majorities, the South exercised a national veto on race policy throughout the New Deal. Even though it was a minority in the Democratic Party, the region's senators and representatives held legislative power by virtue of their seniority and the systematic disenfranchisement of Black citizens. Their overriding goal was to protect the South's racial order from outside interference, particularly from Washington. This arrangement forced Roosevelt to stay away from a congressional effort to pass an anti-lynching law and affected the way the most important New Deal programs were structured. Formally race-neutral, the Social Security Act excluded agricultural workers, domestics, teachers, librarians, and social workers from receiving benefits, rendering 90 percent of Black workers ineligible for the New Deal's signature piece of social protection. The same was true of the Wagner Act, which created the conditions for the massive unionization of white workers in the North but excluded the same categories of workers left out of the Social Security system. After the war, the country's powerful industrial unions were able to negotiate private medical insurance, generous pensions, job security, cost of living adjustments, unemployment compensation during layoffs, and regular wage increases that worked to the advantage of their overwhelmingly white rank and file. The third foundational piece of New Deal legislation – the Federal Housing Act of 1934 – brought homeownership within the reach of millions of families by placing the credit of the federal government behind the private lending that made mortgages possible. But the Federal Housing Agency's determination to protect segregated neighborhoods in its "confidential" city surveys and appraisers' manuals channeled almost all lending to whites. Washington's encouragement of segregated suburbs was supported by massive direct federal spending and support for road construction, sewer lines, water supplies, schools, electricity transmission, and other infrastructure. Federal support for de facto residential segregation in the North continued after the war and extended past financial support for suburban single-family houses. Levittown, Long Island's pioneering postwar experiment in mass housing production for returning soldiers, was open to any veteran who could take advantage of federal lending programs, the vast majority of the veterans being white. The same was true of Parkchester in the Bronx, Stuyvesant Town in Manhattan, and dozens of other housing complexes in Northern cities. The GI Bill of 1944, which aimed to reintegrate veterans into the nation's society after the war, offered low-interest housing loans to all vets regardless of race but delegated implementation to local authorities, who responded to intense pressure from white neighborhood organizations. Restrictive covenants excluded non-whites from homeownership until the Supreme Court outlawed them in 1948, after which those same covenants remained by informal agreement. But even as they cemented white privilege into federal policy, the New Deal and World War II also broke the sharecropping system and brought millions of Black citizens into the national economy. The industrialization of Southern agriculture, made possible by federal support, freed millions of sharecroppers and farm workers to find industrial work in Northern cities like Chicago, Detroit, St. Louis, New York, Philadelphia, Baltimore, and Pittsburgh. Blacks also benefited from the Works Progress Administration, the Federal Writers Project, the segregated Civilian Conservation Corps, and other New Deal programs that provided work relief. Black soldiers returned from war with a newfound claim to full citizenship. In many cases, this involved broadening and deepening the rights they enjoyed in the North. Despite the widespread residential segregation and social isolation they experienced, they could vote, serve on juries, testify against whites, use public accommodations, and enjoy other public and private rights – benefits that were denied them in the Jim Crow South. Buoyed by massive Black participation in Northern industry during and after the war, civil rights organizations and many industrial unions brought pressure on Washington to begin moving away from its embrace of the South. The Social Security exemptions were changed beginning in the early 1950s, and by the middle of the decade, the non-South Democrats were clearly more progressive on racial issues than their Republican counterparts, whose dependence on Chambers of Commerce, business lobbies, and farm organizations made them reluctant to support federal intrusion into employment policies. Black voters outside the South began moving toward the Democrats in greater numbers. The New Deal's contradictory legacy empowered Black citizens in many areas even as it reinforced segregation and discrimination in others.

Despite the structural changes that were transforming the wider American economy, political life in the South remained white. The bargain that had brought an end to Reconstruction and installed Rutherford B. Hayes as President in 1876 still held sway: the federal government would not meddle with the South in matters of race, in return for which Northern finance and industry would be free to organize the national economy. This bargain held politics and the Democratic Party together until the civil rights movement forced a reckoning and compelled Northern Democrats to make a choice. The time-honored arrangement that had structured American politics for decades started to disintegrate as early as 1948 – years before Barry Goldwater discovered that he could pry loose white votes from Dixie and construct a new alliance of Southern Democrats and conservative Republicans.

The first hint of trouble came when that year's Democratic National Convention committed itself to "continuing efforts to eradicate all racial, religious, and economic discrimination." President Truman issued an executive order integrating the armed forces two weeks later, and a group of Southern Democrats immediately revolted. Rebels seized control of the Democratic Party apparatus in several Southern states and organized the "States' Rights Democratic Party," soon known as the Dixiecrats. Opposed to any hint of racial integration and determined to protect Jim Crow and white supremacy from federal intervention, the rebels invoked the Tenth Amendment, Hayes–Tilden, states' rights, local control, and a selective reading of American history as their slogans. South Carolina Democratic senator Strom Thurmond ran for president as a Dixiecrat in hopes of preserving Southern power by splitting the national party but was unable to prevent Truman's reelection. The Dixiecrats faded away after the election, but the end of the "solid" Democratic South was in sight. The fight to protect Jim Crow was largely fought inside the Democratic Party, but Southern leaders phrased their struggle in broad apocalyptic terms. Trumpeting their opposition to both parties, the Dixiecrats announced that "we call upon all Democrats and upon all other loyal Americans who are opposed to totalitarianism at home and abroad to unite with us in ignominiously defeating Harry S. Truman, Thomas E. Dewey and every other candidate for public office who would establish a Police Nation in the United States of America." They weren't the first to deploy states' rights in support of racial discrimination and white supremacy, and they wouldn't be the last.

Opposition to Washington would become the rallying cry for defenders of the "Southern way of life." As the national Democrats reluctantly began supporting a measure of racial democracy, the South summoned its familiar language of regional grievance. Events would soon give it the opportunity to assume the role of oppressed victim. The Supreme Court's 1954 decision in *Brown v. Board of Education* was a powerful sign that the rest of the country had finally decided that Jim Crow was no longer acceptable. In a nod to sensitive opponents, a second decision ordered desegregation "with all deliberate speed."

"Deliberate" meant "slow," and the white South exploded with violent rage, self-pity, and a near-universal desire to defend itself. Summoning up anti-Washington sentiment from the Confederacy, politicians and their allies announced a campaign of "massive resistance" to tyranny and repression. Riots and violence accompanied efforts to integrate the schools, and they found a theoretical expression in the so-called Declaration of Constitutional Principles. Written by Democratic senators Richard Russell of Georgia and the former Dixiecrat Strom Thurmond in 1956, the Southern Manifesto developed the "constitutionalist" objections to *Brown* that Barry Goldwater would take to a national audience.

The basic argument was that the Supreme Court had overstepped its bounds and arbitrarily imposed its will on a South that had organized its racial affairs to everyone's advantage. It claimed that the region's Black and white citizens lived together under a system that had evolved over decades, reflected Southern culture, was widely accepted, and ensured social peace. Signed by 19 Senators and 82 Representatives, the Manifesto invoked states' rights against a creeping judicial march toward totalitarianism. The Supreme Court was guilty of a "clear abuse of judicial power" and the Manifesto pledged to organize a legal effort to overturn *Brown*. It invoked the Tenth Amendment's limitation of the federal government's power to those that are specifically granted by the Constitution to support its contention that the Supreme Court had misinterpreted constitutional law and that its *Brown* decision was illegitimate.

Barry Goldwater was neither a segregationist nor a racist in his personal views, but he provided cover for them in his public life. His own twists and turns illustrated the contradictions of the moment. Even as he opposed the *Brown* decision and decried judicial overreach, he said that he was in favor of the decision's objectives. He thought school integration a worthy public policy, had voted for the 1957 and 1960 civil rights bills in the Senate, and took public positions against Jim Crow. But he opposed the Civil Rights Bill of 1964, objecting to its provisions outlawing racial discrimination in public accommodations and employment. They were a usurpation of power by the federal government, he said, the first steps on a road that would require a police state for enforcement. The Southern Manifesto had a new champion. The federal government had no business telling people what they could or could not do with their property.

Goldwater's candidacy was an important step in the Republican Party's abandonment of civil rights, but the process had begun four years earlier. Richard Nixon had developed a more progressive record on racial issues than John F. Kennedy, and the Republican platform of 1960 went further than the Democrats'. Three years later, Nixon himself had warned that if the Republicans nominated Goldwater "our party would eventually become the first major all-white political party." *The Chicago Defender* – the most important Black newspaper of the era – agreed, observing that the GOP was on the road to becoming "a white man's party."[1]

Despite lingering Black loyalty for the "party of Lincoln," Kennedy was able to assemble a coalition of Northern Blacks, ethnic blue-collar workers, and the white South to win the election. For the Republicans, the lesson was that competing with the Democrats for Black votes was probably a waste of time. The GOP's evolution into a white party began before Goldwater decided to run, but his 1964 candidacy solidified it and gave it a clear direction. After the Kennedy administration had used federal troops to break the University of Mississippi's violent resistance to integration, the Arizona senator demanded that the South have a voice in any matter that affected it. His embrace of Dixie began the process that would culminate in Donald Trump.

Written in 1960, *The Conscience of a Conservative* was Goldwater's statement of principles and survived his electoral drubbing to serve as a point of reference for all subsequent Republican political figures. It was ghostwritten by his speechwriter and adviser L. Brent Bozell and published in 1960 under Goldwater's name; the Arizona senator was always happy to pretend that he had written it. It was anchored in the same bedrock of rhetorical hostility to central government that has animated Republican Party politics ever since. Even conventional Republican politicians like Richard Nixon found it necessary to pay homage to the antistatism that runs throughout the book.

All governmental power, Goldwater declared, has a tendency to expand and threaten individual freedom as it does so. Since the New Deal vastly expanded the scope of the national government, Washington has become the most dangerous enemy of liberty. Goldwater was no anarchist; acknowledging that the state performs many vital functions, he simply argued that the function of wise government is to restrict its power. The whole point of the American Constitution is that it is "a system of restraints against the natural tendency of government to expand in the direction of absolutism."[2] The document's protection of states' rights is the cornerstone of those restraints. And nowhere was the power of the states clearer than in education.

Civil rights, Goldwater declared, are those that are embodied in laws, such as the right to vote or hold property. But integrated education is not a civil right, and the federal government has no business forcing it upon the states. Integration might be wise, it might be humane, it might be desirable – but it is emphatically *not* a civil right. The Fourteenth Amendment's provision about equal protection does not apply to education and cannot be used as a hammer with which to break down local practices. Under those circumstances, Goldwater argued that education policy is reserved to the states and the Tenth Amendment must carry the day. This criticism of *Brown* stands as an early version of the constitutional "originalism" that later became a bedrock principle of much conservative jurisprudence. The statesmen who wrote and passed the Fourteenth Amendment certainly did not intend to outlaw segregated schools or authorize federal intervention in education, said Goldwater. The *Brown* decision, he went on, violates the requirement that the intention of the Constitution be respected and that the

Supreme Court not substitute its will for the document's plain language. Neither the Supreme Court nor any other federal institution should be able to override local practices, laws, and history. Goldwater's critique was identical to that of the South and its "Manifesto."

He declared that he was in support of *Brown*'s objectives. School integration is right and proper, but he was not prepared to impose his views on the people of Mississippi or South Carolina. Education of children in their states is their business, not his and certainly not the court's.

> I believe that the problem of race relations, like all social and cultural problems, is best handled by the people directly concerned. Social and cultural change, however desirable, should not be effected by the engines of national power. Let us, through persuasion and education, seek to improve institutions we deem defective. But let us, in doing so, respect the orderly processes of the law. Any other course enthrones tyrants and dooms freedom.[3]

This would become a fundamental principle of American conservatism, repeated by some Democrats and almost all Republicans alike from George Wallace to Donald Trump. *The Conscience of a Conservative* sold hundreds of thousands of copies, helped establish a rhetorical foundation for the Right, and made Goldwater a star. It also had an immediate impact in the South, setting the conditions for his 1964 success in the region. He would win 55 percent of the Southern white vote that year, the first Republican to ever win a majority of white Southerners. He was fishing where the votes were, and there were plenty of them.

Even though he was careful to stay away from overtly racial themes during his campaign, Goldwater's "constitutional" objection to federal activity made it clear to millions of Southern whites that he was their ally in the fight against the civil rights movement. And, even as he refused to exploit the violent reaction to the *Brown* decision, he provided cover for moderate Southern whites who were redirecting their segregationist energies into concern about good schools, stable housing values, and safe neighborhoods. *The Conscience of a Conservative* helped make conservative opposition to further gains for Blacks acceptable to the moderate suburbanizing white middle class.

The 1964 election turned out to be a critical moment in the evolution of American racial politics. It was the first step in the Republican Party's courtship of racially resentful white voters, and Goldwater's success in the South would soon be mirrored when Wallace took his message to the North. A racial, cultural, and economic backlash to the civil rights movement was brewing among millions of white voters and the Republicans began pivoting toward them. Where Nixon had tried to appeal to both Southern whites and Northern Blacks in 1960, Goldwater had begun to crack open the South. His victories in Louisiana, Mississippi, Alabama, Georgia, and South Carolina showed that the white South was up for grabs. Much of the region would return to the Democrats in fits and starts during subsequent elections, but the process by which the GOP became a white party began with Goldwater's refusal to press the South to abandon its legalized racial regime. His public commitment to weakening the federal government masked his private commitment to equality. Even as he abandoned the overt race-baiting that had marked Southern politics for generations, it became clear that a national backlash to the civil rights movement was taking shape.

Goldwater's evolution expressed many of the contradictions that would characterize the country as a whole. Even as he endorsed states' rights in matters of education, he criticized Robert Kennedy's Justice Department for not prosecuting voting rights violations and supported a constitutional amendment to abolish the poll tax. These positions were consistent with his preference for state power over that of the central government and were evidence of an historical process that was under way but had not yet consolidated. As the GOP's geographical center of gravity shifted from the Northeast and Midwest to the South and Southwest, it became the vehicle for white backlash against Blacks and their Democratic allies. Much more was involved than the racial history of the American South. The mass base for the nationalization of Southern resistance was the anxiety of Northern whites who worried that their material interests were being threatened by the civil rights movement's turn toward substantive matters of economic redistribution and the Democratic Party's openness to policies like open housing and integrated schools. Developing this line of attack and taking it to a national audience would be left to George Wallace, who exchanged Goldwater's polite country club racial conservatism for a hard-edged populism. Although the source of his appeal was no secret, the Alabama governor would also avoid explicitly racist appeals and would focus on the material benefits of racism and white supremacy. He hoped that talking about housing values, job security, and neighborhood safety would ally him with a white population in the North that had just acquired a measure of wealth, a middle-class lifestyle, and the added psychological benefit of knowing they could not fall below their Black fellow citizens.

Wallace had made his national reputation as a rigid, demagogic segregationist and race-baiting Southern governor. He hadn't started out that way, carving out an early stance as something of a racial moderate. But he learned from his 1958 gubernatorial defeat at the hands of John Patterson that overt racial appeals could work in Alabama. Patterson had amplified his fear-driven message to white working-class and lower middle-class voters with apocalyptic warnings about crime, the breakdown of morality, and threats to their livelihood with overt appeals to racial solidarity. Wallace's lesson from his loss was that "I was outniggered and I will never be outniggered again." It didn't take long for him to change his public stance. After winning the governorship as a hardcore segregationist in 1963, he delivered his famous inaugural speech in which he promised "segregation now, segregation tomorrow, segregation forever." Months later, he gained national attention with his defiant "stand in the schoolhouse door" to prevent the integration of the University of Alabama. Wallace claimed that he really wanted to talk about roads and schools when he ran for governor but only got attention when he talked about race. In any event, the label stuck. No one who looked at the dynamics of his national campaigns could have had any doubt about their fundamental impulses.

Wallace crafted a conservative, antistatist plebeian populism whose racial undertone could appeal to both Southern whites and Northern ethnics. Jim Crow had appealed to many on largely psychological grounds but disenfranchised almost as many whites as Blacks. Whatever gains Southern whites imagined they gained from not being Black were offset by their isolation from the trade union movement and their availability as a source of cheap labor. But Wallace's appeal was no longer limited to his Alabama base. Northern white support for him was partly a nationalization of the South but also fed on regional issues. Wallace provided new rhetoric and a measure of legitimacy in a campaign to preserve white workers' access to employment, education, and housing. The mass base for his forays into national politics was created by the anxiety of Northern whites who became convinced that their material interests were being threatened by the civil rights movement's turn toward substantive matters of economic redistribution. Once the formal issues of equality before the law had been settled by the Civil Rights Act of 1964 and the Voting Rights Act a year later, the national Democratic Party began to support open housing, busing, affirmative action, and other measures. The Republicans became the institutional carrier of white backlash. Goldwater had set the conditions for this development, but it was Wallace who carried it to the North. His attacks on Washington's forays into "social engineering" was phrased in the dog whistles of racial grievance. His own biography charts the evolution of race-baiting from overt appeals to white solidarity to concern about property values, union seniority, safe neighborhoods, and good schools. His formula for success would last until Donald Trump.

It was his carefully scripted stand in Tuscaloosa that propelled Wallace to national prominence. He delivered a defiant speech that was heavy with populist themes of governmental oppression and invoked the Tenth Amendment to defend state sovereignty and the integrity of the University of Alabama. "I stand before you here today in place of thousands of other Alabamians whose presence would have confronted you had I been derelict and neglected to fulfill the responsibilities of my office," he announced.

> It is the right of every citizen, however humble he may be, through his chosen officials of representative government to stand courageously against whatever he believes to be the exercise of power beyond the Constitutional rights conferred upon our Federal Government. It is this right which I assert for the people of Alabama by my presence here today.[4]

Wallace drew on a deep well of Southern populism as he turned his attention to the North. Much of that populism had a decidedly racial slant. He had received hundreds of letters and telegrams from supporters outside the South, and they had a dramatic effect on him – and on the future of American politics. All of a sudden, he realized that explicit appeals to white fear could generate a national audience. "They all hate black people, all of them," he exclaimed to his aides. "They're all afraid, all of them! Great God! That's it! They're all Southern! The whole United States is Southern!"[5] He had been thinking of a national race for some time, but the broad reaction to his Tuscaloosa performance convinced him that he might have a future.

There was a lot to work with, for populism has long been the authentic language of American protest. It conceives of "the people" as a hardworking, productive mass of nobility and rectitude who are being exploited and oppressed by a shadowy "elite." Its language is one of victimization and often expresses a strong paranoid streak, since it doesn't always express its grievances in terms of institutions and is often given to moralistic denunciation.[6] Its veneration of "the people" is buttressed by the unstated conviction that the virtuous producer is male, white, and native-born. Those who create wealth are sandwiched between the idle, parasitic rich above them and the equally idle, parasitic poor below. This middle stratum needs to be defended from those who would tax its hard-earned wealth to support those who do not work. Populism's long respect for modest property-owners stems from the conviction that American nationhood, democracy, and membership required people with the resources and orientation to be useful republican citizens. This position was articulated by Aristotle and Cicero, was deeply influential at the Constitutional Convention, and has been expressed in American political language from Thomas Jefferson to Donald Trump. It provided the key to Wallace's successful appeal to white working people outside the South. Central to his argument was the claim that a small elite lived off the labor of the great white middle. A larger mass lived below, condemned to poverty by its lack of discipline, refusal to defer gratification, rejection of the work ethic, aversion to education, and disorganized domestic life. This position provided Wallace with a deep well from which to draw, for American populism tends to be a populism for white people.

Wallace's cultural conservativism expressed the populist turn from a criticism of business and Wall Street to an attack on an "elitist" Democratic establishment that was exercising its oppressive power through government.[7] Rhetorical support for the productive, tax-paying "middle class" could now be deployed in the new conditions of racial strife, antiwar protest, feminist agitation, and changing sexual mores. Wallace anticipated Nixon by speaking for the tax-paying, law-abiding, hardworking middle Americans who were being exploited and regulated by Washington to support unproductive hippies, long-haired protestors, promiscuous women, and lawless Blacks. It was Wallace who developed the Republican origin story of a sovereign white middle class squeezed by wealthy elites and bureaucrats from above and idle youth, Black criminals, and the free-loading poor from below. Richard Nixon would coin the "silent majority" as his slogan, but its modern version began with Wallace.

As monumental as the civil rights movement was in reshaping and democratizing American life, it also set off a sweeping counteroffensive that gathered steam through the Sixties. From fights over public accommodations to voting, busing, housing, education, quotas, affirmative action, and employment, racial politics were at the center of American public life for years. Even as Wallace's forays into the North demonstrated the power of the backlash, he remained an economic populist. The white South had benefited mightily from the New Deal, and Wallace had no interest in dismantling it. Indeed, he stayed true to his moderate roots in economic matters throughout his career. As a state legislator, he supported increased funding for health and education, attacked the state's regressive tax structure, and voted for improved roads and infrastructure spending. Goldwater had attacked the core propositions of the New Deal, but his economic radicalism prevented him from becoming an authentic spokesman for the bulk of the white working class. Wallace understood this and avoided Goldwater's brand of libertarian conservatism. He knew that Southern whites were looking for an enforcer and punisher, and his emotional appeal to a race-tinged populism rescued conservatism from Goldwater's unpopular hostility to measures that would bring economic benefits to his white constituency. He painted a picture of a society in crisis, beset from the outside by communist enemies and from the inside by moral decay, drugs, protest, sexual degeneracy, and demanding minorities – all tolerated by cowardly bureaucrats, judges, politicians, and intellectuals. Cultural nostalgia mixed easily with material concerns. For all his support of the New Deal and his refusal to attack unions, the core of his appeal lay in his suggestion that it was in the material interests of Northern white workers and small businessmen to resist housing integration and extending welfare state protections to their Black neighbors and coworkers. Always careful to avoid overt racism when he went national, Wallace talked about states' right, local traditions, resistance to a tyrannical central government, and scorn for incompetent "do-gooders."

Much of the dynamism behind his campaigns came from the upheavals of the Sixties, but Wallace didn't have to invent anything when he took his candidacy to the North. He simply recognized what was there and built on it. A powerful backlash against open housing and integrated schools had been developing for years, animated by attachment to the substantial material benefits that white families were getting from the exclusion and segregation of Blacks from the housing market. Hundreds of thousands of white families had struggled for years, often without the benefit of mortgages or loans, to build their own homes in Detroit and Chicago. Deeply attached to the American creed of homeownership and its promise of economic independence and stability, they insisted on government protection of the life they had labored to construct. When the Federal Housing Administration (FHA) began supporting mortgages and loans, white working-class and petty-bourgeois homeowners finally had a measure of security and respect that had eluded them for years. The FHA, the Homeowners' Loan Corporation, local bankers, developers, and realtors made it possible for many of them to get mortgages and benefit from the economic security of white neighborhoods in Northern cities and suburbs. Federal support for segregation lay in Washington's insistence that its lending protect the "character" of racially homogenous neighborhoods and support increasing property values. Since their homes represented the great majority of their wealth, a mass constituency for stability and segregation arose in dozens of other Northern cities. As millions of Southern Blacks migrated North to find work and escape Jim Crow, industrial cities organized a pervasive system of residential segregation that was backed up and amplified by federal policy. Cemented in place during the 1940s, a solid constituency of white homeowners successfully resisted integration and open housing for decades. The earliest manifestation of racial inequality in Northern industrial cities, this system of residential segregation has organized urban life for decades and continues to do so. Homeownership was the visible sign of middle-class status, the key to social stability, economic security, college education, and national membership. It was a fundamental prerequisite of democratic citizenship in the American "consumers' republic."[8]

Wallace recognized this enormous material stake in residential segregation and used it to drive a wedge into the heart of the New Deal coalition. There was nothing for him to invent. All he had to do was recognize and name what had been policy for years in Detroit, St. Louis, Baltimore, Chicago, and other cities. Civil rights were going national. The core imperative of Southern politics, as V.O. Key famously pointed out, has always been to sabotage the possibility of poor whites and poor Blacks coming together in defense of their common class interests.[9] The two essential cores of Southern politics – white supremacy and resistance to outside interference – formed the foundation for Southern politics. But there was a large, powerful, active, and experienced mass base for Wallace's appeal in the North, and he was nimble enough to take advantage of it. He got 264,000 votes in the 1964 Wisconsin Democratic presidential primary, followed by almost a third of the total in Indiana and over 250,000 in Maryland a few weeks later. Small property-owners and blue-collar workers were his strongest supporters, and Wallace was under no illusions about why they liked him. He may have warned them about federal tyranny, but it was his talk of Black crime and slovenliness that really got their attention. Invoking "law and order" and "neighborhood schools" would soon become Nixon's slogans, but it was Wallace who demonstrated their power.

The Sixties merely amplified Northern trends that had been present for decades. Working-class and petty-bourgeois whites were the most important voting blocs in cities from Chicago and Detroit to St. Louis and Boston, and they had been deeply opposed to residential integration long before Martin Luther King organized his campaign for open housing. Wallace's attacks on the liberal state found a ready-made audience in Northern constituencies that had been loyal to the New Deal, but they resonated most strongly with a Republican Party that was in transition. When the transplanted George H.W. Bush decided to run against liberal Texas Democratic senator Ralph Yarborough in 1964, he had to shed his upper-class Connecticut patrician aura and pretend to be a dependable conservative Republican. The state was reliably Democratic, and Bush's foray into West Texas's oil industry had brought him into contact with the low-tax, low-regulation ethos that later became central to the national Republican Party. Taking note of Goldwater's criticisms of federal legislation and of Wallace's burgeoning appeal in the North, Bush opposed the Civil Rights Bill and echoed Goldwater's claim that its provisions for fair employment practices and access to public accommodations were unconstitutional infringements on private property. "I hate to see [the] Constitution trampled on in the process of trying to solve civil rights problems," said one of the Republican Party's last "moderates." Bush lost the election, but his candidacy turned out to be an important step in the political biography that would bring him to Reagan's side and then to the presidency in his own right. Wallace was instrumental to this transition, and Bush knew it. The Wallace vote, he said, "indicates to me that there must be a general concern from many responsible people over the civil rights bill all over the nation."[10]

Wallace's campaigns made it clear that race was the bedrock for conservative populism's hostility to Washington. Republican rhetorical antistatism went all the way back to the nineteenth century, of course, and had deep roots in both the political economy of small-scale, dispersed smallholdings and the economic libertarianism of the Gilded Age. But Lincoln's stewardship of the country during the Civil War saw a massive project of state-building, and the same was true of Theodore Roosevelt's presidency. This contradictory legacy made it possible for the GOP to take advantage of the federal government's slow pivot toward support for the courts and for national legislation around civil rights. The long, successful Republican courtship of the South and of Northern whites found a recent echo in the massive white resentment that elected Donald Trump. Attack on immigrants who steal jobs and public benefits, liberals who assist them and look down on hardworking, tax-paying real Americans, and Blacks who live off the dole and refuse to play by the rules of an orderly society are merely the contemporary versions of Wallace's successes.

The basic contours of Republican political domination were taking shape during the 16 years that separate Wallace from Ronald Reagan. Richard Nixon studied Wallace's conservative populist appeal and institutionalized it, framing the Republican Party as the defender of the "silent American" and his opposition to open housing, street crime, urban disorder, and school busing. And it was Ronald Reagan who pulled everything together into a rhetorical hostility to Washington that avoided overt racial appeals and instead invoked the principle of a "colorblind" society to guide his administration's antipathy to affirmative action. It was Wallace who pioneered all this. The old upper-class, business-friendly conservatism of an earlier period had yielded to a right wing that encouraged the belief that white people were in danger and that the country had to stop rewarding Black misbehavior. When the Watts Rebellion broke out just five days after the

Voting Rights Act was signed and Newark, Detroit, and other Northern cities went up in flames soon after, it looked like violence, street crime, insurrection, and open race war were making a mockery of earlier assumptions that the country's race "problem" was limited to the South. Wallace had repeatedly reminded his listeners that the North was every bit as racist as the South. Now events had caught up with the rhetoric. A nationwide white backlash quickly gathered steam, and it was Richard Nixon who rode the tiger all the way to the White House. His Republican successors would go on to win five of the next six presidential elections. Their alliance with the South made it possible for them to divide the national Democratic Party and shatter its New Deal coalition. Anchored by the growing conviction that liberals had forgotten the mass of productive, tax-paying white citizens as they embraced the Black and the poor, millions of voters came to believe that their "middle-class" incomes and lifestyles were no longer safe. They were supported by a Republican Party that promised to protect them from irresponsible politicians and angry minorities who were unwilling to play by the rules that had made possible their newfound security. It was Wallace who helped the Right shed its identity as the genteel friend of privilege and enemy of progress by claiming to speak for ordinary white Americans who were under attack. Ironically, it was Richard Nixon who made him a Republican.

Notes

1. Jelani Cobb, "What Is Happening to the Republican Party?" *The New Yorker*, March 8, 2021.
2. Barry Goldwater, *The Conscience of a Conservative* (Shepardsville, KY: Victor Publishing, 1960), p. 18.
3. Goldwater, *The Conscience of a Conservative*, p. 37.
4. Statement and Proclamation of Governor George C. Wallace, University of Alabama, June 11, 1963. Alabama Department of Archives and History. https://archives.alabama.gov/govs_list/schooldoor.html.
5. Quoted in Charles M. Payne, "The Whole United States is Southern!": *Brown v. Board* and the Mystification of Race. *Journal of American History*, June 2004, 83. See also Dan Carter, *The Politics of Rage: George Wallace, the Origins of the New Conservatism, and the Transformation of American Politics* (Baton Rouge: LSU Press), p. 6.
6. The great essay examining this theme is Richard Hofstadter's "The Paranoid Style in American Politics," *Harper's*, November 1964.
7. Michael Kazin, *The Populist Persuasion* (Ithaca, NY: Cornell University Press, 1995).
8. Tom Sugrue, *The Origins of the Urban Crisis: Race and Inequality in Postwar Detroit* (Princeton, NJ: Princeton University Press, 2005).
9. V.O. Key, *Southern Politics* (New York: Vintage, 1963).
10. Quoted in Stephan Lesher, *George Wallace: American Populist* (Boston: Da Capo Press, 1995), p. 313.

2
DICK'S TRICK

George Wallace changed American politics with a hard-edged conservative populism that retained its racial appeal by casting itself as the champion of whites who themselves felt economically insecure and culturally threatened. Many lower-middle- and working-class voters were open to his claims that those above them scorned their religion, their food, their work, their ethnic identification, and other aspects of their identity. They were equally drawn to his suggestion that those below them were envious of their success and determined to take their property and their jobs. Wallace was perceptive enough to see that he could take Southern populism to a national audience by racializing the insecurities of the beleaguered white middle and working classes while moving away from over race-baiting. It soon became clear that a mass base for backlash in the North was taking shape independently of what was going on in Dixie – and that it had deep roots in many of the country's most important industrial cities. But as daring as Wallace was and as accurate in his diagnosis as he turned out to be, his regional past proved too great a burden for his presidential ambitions. It took Richard Nixon, just the sort of career politician that Wallace often denigrated, to bring millions of aggrieved whites toward the Republican Party and begin cementing a new and durable political coalition. Nixon's appeal to the white "silent majority" during his 1968 campaign for "law and order" focused their anger on disorderly Blacks, protesting youth, and an opportunistic liberal elite that encouraged both. These appeals enabled the GOP to organize a "Southern strategy" that placed Dixie at the center of conservative politics.

Despite his public denials, Wallace knew as well as everyone else that he was articulating – and stimulating – a powerful white backlash with his attacks on Washington. His contemptuous assaults on bicycle-riding bureaucrats, "pointy-headed" intellectuals, cowardly judges, and whining journalists were aimed at a

DOI: 10.4324/9781003182962-3

liberalism that had moved from New Deal regulative and redistributionist economics to "social engineering" on behalf of Blacks and the poor. As the national Democratic Party began to reluctantly embrace desegregation and integration in the North, Wallace's focus on racial threat made him a national force. He became a master at talking about Blacks when he pretended that he wasn't, and Nixon followed in his footsteps. The politics of race had become so engrained that its "dog whistles" were inaudible and yet widely recognized.

Nixon succeeded by expressing a much wider political, racial, and cultural resentment than Wallace. After 1965, the challenges of fighting Jim Crow had moved beyond the struggle for equality before the law. They had begun to call into question the entire country's racial order, much of which had been concealed behind the overt discrimination and state violence required to maintain the South's social structure. As racial politics flooded out of Dixie into the great industrial cities of the North, they gave rise to a period of broad and divisive conflict. It turned out that many whites all over the country had a vested interest in maintaining the existing structure. Coming just days after President Johnson signed the Voting Rights Act that signaled the end of Jim Crow, the Watts Rebellion meant arson, looting, and death despite what many whites considered the country's honest effort to address racial issues. Things went from bad to worse as city after city erupted in violence and disorder during the "long hot summers" of the mid-Sixties. When conservatives suggested that liberals were using the chaos to extort resources from the hardworking white "silent majority," the stage was set for Nixon to appear as the well-meaning figure trying to do the best thing for the country but being hounded by the same forces that were harassing "normal" citizens. He became the tribune for the misunderstood white lower middle class and was able to pose as the defender of order and sobriety during a period of unprecedented disorder and instability. As the focus of racial politics changed from legal equality and access to public accommodations to jobs, housing, incomes, and wealth, the stability of a broad swath of American society seemed to come under direct attack. Just as the movement brought civil rights to the national stage, so it brought the pushback. Just as white resistance to integration had shaped local urban politics in the North, Nixon helped shape it into a national force.

More was involved than racist ideas and local habits. The hollowing out of the nation's industrial core and a sense of genuine crisis in Northern cities prompted a wide reevaluation of earlier attitudes about the future. Detroit, the heart of the American auto industry for decades, suffered though successive bouts of recession, closed plants, and unemployment as the industry reorganized itself, tried and failed to respond to foreign competition, and moved production to other parts of the country and overseas. The city lost 134,000 manufacturing jobs from 1947 to 1963, jobs that had established the material conditions for the integration of Black labor into the national workforce and for the creation of a relatively prosperous and secure white working class. White resistance to residential integration had begun immediately after the war, but economic dislocation amplified the sense of siege and danger. Layoffs and downsizing hurt hundreds of industrial businesses that were dependent on auto production and many others that relied on the spending of auto workers. Advances in automation, communication and technology, new railroads to open up the South, the passage of the anti-labor Taft–Hartley Act in 1947 and the subsequent adoption of "right-to-work" laws in the South and Southwest, federal spending on highways, the rise of a Sunbelt-dominated military–industrial complex, and competition from a resurgent Japan began to decimate the older industrial cities of the Northeast and Midwest long before Nixon's 1968 success. Detroit, New York, Chicago, St. Louis, Philadelphia, Trenton, Camden, Buffalo, and dozens of other once-thriving, productive cities got hammered as firms reduced employment, closed factories, replaced workers with machines, and constructed new factories in suburban and rural areas and overseas. It took a while for a pervasive economic crisis to develop into an ideological and political one, but develop it did. In a bitter irony, the developing crisis of the American city fatefully coincided with the northern migration of millions of Southern Blacks looking to escape Jim Crow and find work. They found white residents in a decidedly unwelcoming mood, not much different from what it had been during the prosperous 1940s but now intensified by unmistakable economic contraction and a resulting social crisis.

It all came to a head in 1968. Martin Luther King had been a heroic figure during the struggle against Jim Clark and Bull Connor. By the time he made the turn to the Poor People's Campaign, his standing among white people had changed for the worse. Nixon took note of the shift in public opinion and was adept at using what Wallace had unearthed. He navigated the thin line of acceptable racial politics with a minimal strategy that threaded the needle between supporting the segregationist South and courting racist Northerners. Nixon vowed to respect the courts and promised to do no more than that, assuring Southern delegates to the nominating convention in Miami Beach that he would not enforce the Voting Rights Act and Civil Rights Act unless directly ordered to do so by "activist judges." Northern white backlash was predicated on the claim that the absence of Jim Crow's legal apparatus of white supremacy exempted the North from charges of systemic racism. But by the summer of 1966, urban uprisings and Martin Luther King's campaign for open housing began to precipitate a massive white reaction outside Dixie. Since the Democrats were still dependent on the South, and the Republicans were announcing themselves as the "law and order" party and opposing open housing and busing, it was clear that millions of white people were getting ready to abandon their support for substantive racial reform. The election of 1968 was the beginning of the end for New Deal racial liberalism. As important as the Vietnam War was that year, 68 was the backlash election.

If Wallace reveled in the role of outsider, Nixon was the consummate insider who modified Wallace's success in the North and brought it into the Republican Party. He saw that Goldwater had successfully appealed to hardcore segregationists in the Deep South, but he understood that he couldn't win with a strategy that pandered to the heart of the old Confederacy. Instead, he pivoted toward the Upper South and toward racial moderates in the North, both of whom were fed up with continuous Black demands. He also knew that this was a safe strategy, since millions of white voters in the Deep South would move toward the GOP as the Democrats aligned themselves with Northern Blacks and their organizations. The trick was to appeal to racial antagonisms and white fear without sympathizing with overt racial animus. It was a brilliant strategy. As his aide John Erlichman described it later, Nixon presented a series of positions on jobs, crime, education, and housing in such a way that a voter could embrace the Republicans and "avoid admitting to himself that he was attracted to a racist appeal."[1] The presidential election gave Nixon the additional chance to pull white ethnic Northerners toward the Republicans as Southern whites continued their headlong flight from the Democrats. The components of a stable Republican governing coalition were coming into focus.

Nixon's courtship of the Upper South, the white suburbs, urban ethnic workers, and lower-middle-class whites lay behind his appeal to the "Middle Americans," the "silent majority" of hardworking, industrious, tax-paying white men and their families. Having chosen to avoid Goldwater's overture to the Deep South, he never had to embrace Wallace's appeal to white racists, states' rights, or Southern pride. By avoiding the danger of alienating Northern whites who could not abide the South's explicitly racial regime, he could limit himself to the comfortable economic formulas that would appeal to moderate voters. He never attacked *Brown* or the 1964 Civil Rights Bill but felt free to criticize judges and bureaucrats who wanted to go beyond the formal statements of racial equality and address education, social isolation, and unemployment through busing and open housing. The landmark civil rights legislation of 1964 and 1965 carried an implicit promise of federal support for measures that went beyond threatening the foundations of Southern segregation. They menaced white privilege in labor and housing markets across the nation. The construction industry became a case in point. Affirmative action wouldn't become an important Republican wedge issue until after Nixon left office, but civil right organizations' insistence that Blacks be hired at construction sites provoked resistance from white workers across the country. As manufacturing jobs began to shrink with the economy's transition from manufacturing to finance, insurance, and real estate, urban white workers mobilized to protect their jobs and pressed for union protections against Black advances. Defending high-paying, secure construction jobs went hand in hand with defending home values as flash points for working-class white resistance. Demonstrations and brutal confrontations at construction sites around the country testified to the rapid reorientation of the civil rights movement's priorities. Perennial struggles over education and housing provided an additional source of tension. The four years of urban uprisings in the mid-Sixties and the affirmative policies they generated in court-ordered busing and pressure for open housing destabilized hundreds of neighborhoods across the country. Wallace had attracted a large Northern white working-class and petty-bourgeois constituency, and Nixon was able to build on his considerable successes. Historically segregated patterns in employment, schools, and housing were coming under sustained attack in Northern cities, and the civil war that broke out in the Democratic Party pitted civil rights organizations against an increasingly hostile white population. Nixon recognized what was happening and was quick to take advantage. Directing his attack against the lazy, the self-centered, and the disorderly made it easy to target people who demanded change but refused to serve in the military, work hard, or "play by the rules." As violence engulfed major cities from Newark, Detroit, Minneapolis, Chicago, and Harlem to smaller ones like Plainfield, New Jersey, millions of middle-class whites made it clear that they were no longer interested in paying taxes to support ungrateful Blacks. Further efforts to address racial injustice met a stone wall of white resistance.

In the middle of all this, a young Republican staffer named Kevin Phillips developed a powerful and convincing analysis of the "emerging Republican majority." American elections, Phillips said, are won by focusing on voters' resentments. They're not about abstract beliefs, hopes for the future, or gauzy invocations of a glorious past. They're about "who hates whom," and Phillips knew that Wallace was basically right about "the whole United States" – even if he had overstated his argument. As important as it was, Phillips's argument was very close to the position that Nixon had already developed. The candidate's new focus was on undeserving, demanding Blacks and the condescending liberals who catered to them. It led him directly to the white "silent majority."

The trick was to finish Wallace's work without being Wallace. Phillips supplied the analysis and Nixon deployed it. Phillips argued that racial, ethnic, and regional antagonisms had been the lynchpins of the country's political history from Jefferson to Nixon. Elections had been won and lost, and durable coalitions had arisen and decayed, on the basis of politicians' ability to place themselves on the side of the hardworking, mainstream middle against the moneyed and the arrogant. Understanding and focusing their resentments had made populism a democratic force at earlier moments in the nation's history. But now populism was becoming a defensive middle-class argument for stability instead of a plebeian call for redistributionist change. Its heroes were no longer exploited farmers or oppressed workers. Now they were tax-paying, property-owning "middle Americans." Its elitist enemies were no longer greedy bankers and industrialists. Now they were dangerous Blacks and condescending liberal elitists.[2]

The Democratic Party, Phillips argued, had committed a fatal error that had made the New Deal coalition vulnerable to attack. He identified its Achilles' heel in a classic passage that outlined an historic opportunity for Nixon and his successors during a period of political crisis and social breakdown:

> The principal force which broke up the Democratic (New Deal) coalition is the Negro socioeconomic revolution and liberal Democratic ideological

inability to cope with it. Democratic "Great Society" programs aligned that party with many Negro demands, but the party was unable to defuse the racial tension sundering the nation. The South, the West and the Catholic sidewalks of New York were the focal points of conservative opposition to the welfare liberalism of the federal government; however, the general opposition which deposed the Democratic Party came in large part from prospering Democrats who objected to Washington dissipating their tax dollars on programs which did them no good. The Democratic Party fell victim to the ideological impetus of a liberalism which had carried it beyond programs taxing the few for the benefit of the many (the New Deal) to programs taxing the many on behalf of the few (the Great Society).[3]

Wallace had recognized this, said Phillips, but Republicans were better positioned than him to take advantage of it. Aiming his campaign at the conservative white suburbs, Nixon understood that Democratic "social engineering" had targets beyond civil rights in the South and was now obnoxious to Northern whites. A new political alignment was possible based on changing population patterns. Northern cities were being flooded with Southern Blacks, and whites had moved out in response. "The Negro problem, having become a national rather than a local one, is the principal cause of the breakup of the New Deal coalition," Phillips continued. A new governing coalition would be based on white voters who had just become hostile to a liberalism that had strayed from its popular commitment to redistributive economics and instead had become an adjunct of Black political power. The Northern anchors of this developing coalition would be built on a foundation of urban ethnics and suburban moderates, and it would do what Democrats had been failing to do. Liberals had once supported farm, highway, education, health, and Social Security spending against conservative austerity, but they had moved away from their support of poor whites. The inevitable reaction had taken shape by 1968, triggered by the newfound openness of the white South to Nixon and the Republican Party. Goldwater had articulated an early version with his unspoken opposition to any further government assistance to Blacks and Wallace had siphoned off considerable Southern support from Nixon for the moment, but the future was clear. Now, said Phillips, a new governing movement was ready for a national audience. Centered in the urban "combat zone," the Anglo-Saxon "heartland," and its old bastion in the South, a powerful conservative coalition was taking shape. Goldwater's candidacy had started the process, but his opposition to federal spending on social welfare doomed his 1964 campaign and opened the door, first to Wallace and then to Nixon. A new sort of conservatism could be based on white racial resentment, particularly if it preserved important measures of economic welfare. Working-class and petty-bourgeois whites in the country's industrial heartland were being squeezed from above and below. It proved easy to convince them that the most important threat came from the Blackening neighborhoods in their cities. As long as white voters could be persuaded to look down, rather than up, they could be persuaded that threat came from the Black poor rather than from corporations and the rich.

The fault line was homeownership and residential segregation. The single-family home had become the sign of full participation in the "American way of life," the measure of citizenship in the postwar consumers' republic that was taking shape. It was a powerful identity as well as a financial investment. Tens of thousands of families in Detroit, Chicago, Brooklyn, and other northern cities understood that their whiteness had an important psychological benefit that complemented its economic one. At the same time, their homes and neighborhoods were much more than the material rewards for years of moral sobriety and healthy "values." They had become the material expression of years of hard work, savings, prudent living, and aspirations for upward mobility and a better life for their children. But the simultaneous occurrence of Black migration and deindustrialization set in motion profound political currents that would reconfigure national politics. As many white families' economic interests, communal identities, and membership in the middle class came under threat, they blamed Blacks for what was happening to their way of life. Egged on by politicians and the evening news, it was easy for them to ignore systemic matters and focus on what they believed was going on around the corner or in the local subway station. Abstract impulses like discrimination, deindustrialization, government policy, and the like took second place to the crime, slovenliness, disordered families, and welfare dependence that were visible every evening on the local news. When their "right" to live in segregated neighborhoods came under attack, they turned to the government to defend them. Since they were addressing the same government that had made their white neighborhoods possible in the first place, this was a perfectly understandable demand.

As whites began to name their identity, they came to defend it. Blacks became the sign of threatening changes, symbols of everything that was going wrong. And, because there was little incentive to think of the broad social, economic, and political factors that were at work, American history got boiled down to individual experience. Rather than talk about urban sanitation policy, housing segregation, inadequate schools, obstacles to homeownership and residential improvement, insufficient policing, or employment discrimination, millions of whites and the candidates who spoke for them concluded that the urban crisis was Blacks' fault. Everywhere they lived, it seemed, things fell apart. It was easy to assume that Blacks were imminent threats to safety and well-being. Many white people concluded, on the basis of their myopic individual observations and snippets on the television, that Blacks were unwilling to live by the rules that structured an orderly society. The notion that white people were aggrieved and persecuted focused on Black people as the aggressors and liberals as their enablers. A constant feeling of precariousness lay behind a growing conviction that white people were being abandoned – a pervasive sentiment that would set the conditions for Nixon's ability to pose as their defender. An insistent demand for "law and order" focused attention on the widely shared conviction that it was time to stop the disintegration, call a halt to socially destructive behavior, and insist that the elementary rules of social life be observed. Busing and open housing came to be synonymous with danger and threat, unearned rewards for bad behavior. The gauzy optimism of postwar liberalism seemed increasingly out of touch with the requirements of civilized interactions. A broader orientation might have reoriented matters, but race was the historic attractant that focused the gaze of millions of white voters. Local context and individual experience came to dominate the way people thought. Every Black neighborhood, millions of whites concluded, was dirty, chaotic, dilapidated, full of menacing young people, and physically dangerous. The mere presence of Black people threatened white wealth as Blacks became the symbols for everything that was going wrong and served as scapegoats for real and perceived grievances. Under the circumstances, whites focused on monopolizing valuable resources for themselves in employment, education, housing, and public services. Their hoarding came at the expense of the Black urban poor and was openly aided by politicians, corporations, local businesses, and their fellow white citizens.

Housing was the time bomb in the North. Blacks lived in overcrowded, substandard houses in segregated neighborhoods in cities from Chicago to Boston and St. Louis to Philadelphia. Many had come North with hopes of economic security, good schools, steady employment, and homeownership. Between their isolation in the poorest-paid jobs, their overcrowded neighborhoods, and their systematic exclusion from the housing market by banks and real estate brokers, they were largely unable to build the wealth that would have enabled them to improve where they lived. The visible deterioration was more proof to white people that Blacks would ruin whatever neighborhood they moved into and another indication to banks that they were bad credit risks.

Newly threatened white security seemed like the result of nature, the market, the bad habits of the poor, and an accumulation of individual choices by deserving and industrious citizens. The story was self-serving, even if it seemed to make sense. The social, economic, and political choices made by politicians and institutions have proven to be far more important than the fixation on family structure, aversion to work, hedonism, and rejection of the work ethic that have figured so prominently in conservative mythology since Nixon. For all his commitment to what remained of the welfare state, it was Nixon who effectively ended public housing in 1973 and diverted anti-poverty funds into revenue-sharing programs that were under the control of local authorities and designed to lower property taxes on white homeowners. Blaming the poor for their situation absolved the white middle and working class from any responsibility. Deindustrialization, capital flight, cutbacks in social protections, housing discrimination, unemployment, and government policy were the material roots of the racialized urban crisis but were consigned to the back burner.

None of this was preordained. There was nothing in the logic of white protest that required the racist tinge that it adopted. Historical, economic, and political choices framed the discussion in ways that prompted white people to conclude that Blacks were the problem. While racism and white nationalism have been latent in American history and have had a powerful mass base for many years, it was political leaders and institutions that channeled white peoples' anxieties in such destructive ways. Much of this was new and came to the surface during Nixon's administrations. As broad white support for desegregation and integration in the South began to wane with increased attention to segregation and discrimination in the North, increasing numbers of respondents began to tell pollsters that the civil rights movement and the federal government were moving "too fast." This became the bedrock position of the Nixon campaigns and administrations.

The early, pre-1968 history of the civil rights movement featured Blacks as the victims of Southern history, the injured party whose nonviolent struggle was aimed at restoring the dignity of labor, the possibilities of citizenship, and the promise of full participation in American society. But as the focus shifted from equality before the law and began to focus on the material resources necessary for full membership, whites bitterly resisted. Having come to economic prosperity and psychological dignity relatively recently, many began feeling that they were being victimized by forces they could not control. Their distress soon broadened from their desire to preserve their segregated neighborhoods. Welfare was a particularly volatile subject, representing an unjustified transfer of resources from those who worked to create wealth to those whose idleness signified that they didn't. It became identified with parasitism, and the increasingly popular notion of a "culture of dependency" became an accusation. It was during the conflicts over housing, welfare, and education that homeowners who had become accustomed to taking their privileges for granted began articulating what it meant to be "white." The New Deal coalition began to break apart because of an accumulation of racial wedge issues that precipitated white fears of losing dominance. Current fears of racial "extinction" have deeper roots than those of the Tea Party, the Proud Boys, and Donald Trump.

Wallace had broken loose much of the white South from the Democrats and started the broadest political realignment since the Great Depression. His historic role began with the prospect of increased Black voting following the Civil Rights Act of 1964 and the Voting Rights Act a year later. Kevin Phillips knew that this would incense whites in the Deep South, the region with the most acute "Negrophobe" politics. Many white voters would temporarily return to the Democrats in subsequent elections, but their overall motion was toward the Republicans. And they weren't alone. The reaction of white voters to Black gains was about to spread as the politics of race moved out from Dixie. By 1968, white defection from the Democrats had become as consequential as Black movement toward them.[4]

A real commitment to economic populism helped solidify the allegiance of poor Southern white voters. Goldwater had declared himself an enemy of the

New Deal, which had benefited the South and remained popular. Even with this burden, many Southern whites had voted for him because of his de facto defense of Jim Crow. But Wallace had defended most of FDR's economic measures from the beginning of his political career. The same was largely true of Nixon, who said that "we have learned at last to manage a modern economy to ensure its continual growth" at his 1969 inaugural speech and famously announced that "I am now a Keynesian" while president. He was never afraid of deficit financing, easy money, and government spending to stimulate the economy and was not interested in undermining Social Security, Medicare, collective bargaining, or other policies that were important to the Republicans' lower-middle- and working-class white base. He was happy to leave the basic institutions of the New Deal and the Great Society untouched and instead ran on a set of issues that would later comprise the "culture wars." By 1972, he was able to tie together drugs, demonstrators, pornography, welfare, abortion, riots, and crime – all with suggestions that the Democrats were beholden to Black voters and civil rights organizations. As a weakened Democratic Party became vulnerable to attack as a collector of taxes and an unprincipled dispenser of favors to its "special interests," white working- and middle-class voters became receptive to claims that their property values and childrens' education were being held hostage by civil rights organizations and the liberals who catered to them. Open housing and "forced busing" became the flash points of racial politics in the North as segregated neighborhoods and schools found themselves at the center of bitter political struggle. Phillips had demonstrated that the New Deal coalition could be split apart by race. Nixon's opposition to open housing and busing now and his decision to go slow on enforcing federal court orders in the South were the logical outgrowths of the "emerging Republican majority."

Nixon was an expert at retailing the politics of white grievance and was able to ride a growing wave of racial resentment and anxiety. His campaign and presidency served notice that white America had grown tired of the civil rights movement, the rise of Black power, the urban uprisings, and troubling new questions about race in the North. Nixon's invention of the "silent majority" was an attempt to describe the developing alliance of Northern Catholics and Southern Protestants that would cement the Republicans as the party of aggrieved white people. Since the Wallace phenomenon was not, and could not be, a national one, Nixon's strength came from white voters in the North and South who were deserting the Democrats over racial issues. A moderate racial conservatism, Phillips announced, would attract the white South that had begun drifting back to the Democrats and those Northern blue-collar ethnic voters who had flirted with Wallace but then moved toward Humphrey.

Nixon's appeal to white voters stemmed from a careful consideration of the main currents of American politics rather than from his own history. His flexibility on this matter stood in some contradiction to his earlier positions on issues concerning civil rights and racial justice. During the campaign of

1956, he had gone to Harlem to announce that "America can't afford the cost of discrimination," after which the Eisenhower–Nixon ticket was endorsed by Congressman Adam Clayton Powell, the nation's foremost Black political figure. Nixon had worked behind the scenes to get the Civil Rights Bill of 1957 passed, for which Martin Luther King had thanked him personally. When Jackie Robinson endorsed him over John F. Kennedy in 1960, he cited Nixon's superior record on civil rights. Indeed, Nixon got 40 percent of the Black vote in 1960; Goldwater would get 6 percent four years later. Even as he ran on a tough "law and order" platform, attacked antiwar protestors, and conjured up images of violent Blacks threatening peace and tranquility, he also spoke to suburban white audiences about the need to help the Black poor and marched in Martin Luther King's funeral procession. Still, for all his talk about moderation, Nixon knew how to position himself between Humphrey's racial liberalism on the left and Wallace's open appeal to bigotry on the right. He couldn't compete with Wallace for the Deep South, but he didn't need to since its white voters were coming toward the Republicans no matter what he did. This version of the "Southern strategy" focused on the Upper South and the northern suburbs, whose residents imagined themselves to be racially innocent but who had many of the same prejudices as voters in Tennessee or North Carolina. As it happened, questions about "forced busing" and court-ordered desegregation of white suburbs was finally settled in 1974, when the Supreme Court – with four Nixon appointees – ruled in *Milliken v. Bradley* that suburbs did not have to be included in metropolitan desegregation plans. The court's position that existing school districts should not be undermined left affluent suburbs white and solidified Nixon's appeal to parents who could avoid integrated schools by moving out of the cities. It contributed mightily to the crisis of urban liberalism, since the burden of court-ordered busing fell most heavily on white working-class urban residents who didn't have the resources to flee. The Democrats' foundational alliance of Southern whites, Northern workers, and Black voters was coming apart. The blue-collar, angry ethnic populism that emerged from the struggle over busing, most notably in South Boston, Detroit, and Chicago but in many other Northern cities as well, would generate claims that upper-middle-class suburban do-gooders made others pay for liberal "social engineering" while congratulating themselves for their decency and rectitude.

Nixon solved the problem by distinguishing between formal, explicit de jure segregation, a phenomenon of the Jim Crow South, and de facto segregation, which was prevalent in the rest of the country. The first was a product of law and explicit state policy, the second a result of segregated housing whose origin in government policy went unexamined. Nixon did encourage the desegregation of Southern public schools, although nothing prevented white parents from pulling their children out and sending them to private and Christian "academies" to avoid integration. But by refusing to oppose de facto segregation in the rest of the country, he consciously sided with Northern parents, almost all of them white, who opposed busing Black children to their segregated "neighborhood schools." This policy was followed by Gerald Ford after he succeeded Nixon – and so, paradoxically, was support for an expansion of the welfare state. The Employment Retirement Security Act (ERISA) regulated the pension funds established by employers, requiring that they live up to the promises made to employees. The Energy Policy and Conservation Act required every American car manufacturer to achieve an "average fuel economy" of 18 miles per gallon by the 1978 model year – a mandate that would cost the industry somewhere around $70 billion. But while he followed in Nixon's relatively progressive economic footsteps, Ford also moved to the right on race. As hundreds of school districts across the country confronted court demands that they desegregate, controversy erupted everywhere. Ford's history was not unlike Nixon's. He had supported *Brown*, voted for the Civil Rights and Voting Rights Acts – and opposed busing to achieve racial balance in Northern schools. Like Nixon, he tried to navigate the narrow line between the traditional Republican support for formal civil rights on one hand and widespread white opposition to quotas, open housing, and busing on the other. As whites resisted what they thought were attacks on their neighborhoods, schools, families, identities, jobs, and aspirations, Ford adjusted – just as Nixon had.

Home-owning white families' demand that Washington protect their investments were rooted in a long history of federal support for residential segregation. When Congress created the Federal Housing Administration (FHA) in 1934, it put federal policy squarely behind insurance for private mortgages, a drop in interest rates, and a decline in the down payment required to buy a house. But these benefits were limited to white families. The FHA had adopted a system of maps that rated neighborhoods according to their social and racial stability. Green areas were denoted on maps that described all-white neighborhoods. Black neighborhoods were usually considered ineligible for FHA backing because their residents were poor credit risks or their neighborhoods were too unstable. These neighborhoods were rated as "D" and their outlines were traced on official maps with red lines. Redlining rapidly spread to the entire real estate and banking industries by virtue of government policy. When white homeowners in the North claimed that Washington had an historic and moral obligation to protect their segregated neighborhoods, they had a lot of American history on their side. Their sense of abandonment, threat, and grievance was an ideological expression of their material interests.

Nixon's promise to go slow on racial matters and crack down on violence and crime resonated with a broad sector of the white electorate. The self-styled champion of the "silent majority," his 1968 victory against both Wallace and Humphrey signaled the effective end of the civil rights era, the slow-motion crackup of the New Deal coalition, and the beginning of Republican dominance in presidential elections. The two key domestic issues were the speed of Black advance and the scale of urban unrest, both of which imperiled the Democrats' base in the Northern white working class. Nixon's strategy to hold the line on Black legal progress, appoint racial conservatives to the judiciary, and go slow on school desegregation reflected his assessment of the domestic political environment. His combination of vague calls for peace in Vietnam and dog-whistled appeals to white backlash made for a brilliantly successful 1968 campaign. Race and the war delivered the *coup de grâce* to political liberalism. A few months after his victory, Nixon told an audience of college students that "we live in a deeply troubled and profoundly unsettled time. Drugs, crime, campus revolts, racial discord, draft resistance – on every hand we find old standards violated, old values discarded."[5] There was an important measure of truth in his warnings, and the fact that life had gotten meaner and more restricted was not lost on large swaths of white opinion that was steadily moving toward a bitter racial conservatism. As Nixon began to articulate the politics of restoration, an era came to an end and the Republican Party moved toward a "colorblind" strategy when it came to busing, affirmative action, quotas, set-asides, and other programs. They were able to contrast this with the Democrats' embrace of color-conscious policies that would guarantee that whites would always "lose." Nixon knew that things had changed. Equal voting rights and access to public accommodations still had broad national support, but they described the outer limits of what was acceptable. One of Nixon's most trusted advisors knew that his boss understood this. H.R. Haldeman's 1969 diary reported the president's words. "You have to face the fact that the whole problem is really the Blacks. The key is to devise a system that recognizes this while not appearing to."[6] The pretense of "colorblindedness" would be indispensable to building that system.

Much of Nixon's appeal would anticipate the Republican focus on welfare and other issues that congealed into the "culture wars" of the 1980s and 1990s. He articulated the resentments of "forgotten Americans" who were besieged by federal regulations and taxes while being asked to pay for the dysfunction of an urban underclass. Conservative cultural populism helped to construct a durable alliance between corporations and the rich, on the one hand, and the white lower-middle- and working-class, on the other. The basic contradiction between these two central pillars of the Republican coalition was visible during this period, but the alliance proved to be a durable one because of the enduring power of racial politics. Traditional business conservatives, who had no particular interest in attacking "drugs, sex, and rock and roll," were perfectly happy to enlist large numbers of white voters but were also aware that their allies were not disposed to do away with the New Deal's social protections. Their friends in the "radical center" were largely lower-middle-class, white, and male.[7] They liked Social Security, Medicare, and spending on education but hated taxes, were worried about cultural changes, wanted "law and order," and resented Black demands. They knew that their alliance with the wealthy and powerful might not work out as they hoped. It would take Ronald Reagan to mount a full-scale assault on FDR's legacy, but even he had to be careful. For the moment, Nixon would protect Medicare, Social Security, unemployment insurance, and other programs that were important to his white voting base. He turned out to be a "big Washington spender," just the sort of politician that his party would later attack with great effect. He nationalized the Food Stamp program, was friendly to organized labor, expanded Social Security, wanted a guaranteed family income, and flirted with a national health insurance system. In a move that would become impossible within a few years, he supported an affirmative action initiative and fought for it in Congress, giving official support to programs that had been developing under the radar for years. He supported income guarantees for elderly and disabled citizens and large increases in Social Security, Medicare, and Medicaid. He established a new alphabet-soup list of federal regulatory agencies, ranging from the Environmental Protection Agency (EPA) and the National Highway Traffic Safety Administration to the Occupational Safety and Health Administration (OSHA) and the Consumer Product Safety Commission. He did veto the 1972 Clean Water Act, complaining that its enormous cost would "wreck" the budget – but the veto was overridden by the Congress in a bipartisan repudiation that included many Republicans. Regulations were tightened up and strengthened. OSHA empowered federal agents to inspect individual businesses for health and safety violations without warrants and to levy fines with no avenue for appeal. An amendment to the Clean Air Act of 1963 included clear mandates for compliance and enjoined the EPA from considering cost in establishing clean air standards. None of this prevented Nixon from agreeing with domestic policy advisor Daniel Patrick Moynihan's suggestion that Blacks had made extraordinary progress and a period of "benign neglect" was in order. When it came to race, activism in one policy area didn't mean activism in another. Even as Nixon moved his party to the left on economics, he moved it to the right on race and culture. It wouldn't be long before Ronald Reagan would cement a more coherent right-wing ruling regime, but for the moment Nixon knew how important it was to court white voters by reassuring them about the New Deal and its social safety net. Plutocracy wouldn't find its open Washington champion for another few years.

Phillips's strategy pointed to Northern ethnics, Southern whites, and moderate suburbanites. If he was right and politics was about "who hates whom," then the assertiveness of Northern Black Democrats was driving whites into the Republican Party despite their lingering attachment to the Democratic Party of their parents. And in the South, the enfranchisement of Blacks and their migration toward the Democrats had triggered an outmigration of white racial conservatives toward the once-hated Republicans. A racially driven realignment was congealing, and raw numbers would guarantee that the GOP would be its beneficiary. The emerging coalition of Southern whites and future Reagan Democrats would become the foundation of Republican electoral success. As Nixon moved to capitalize on Northern disenchantment with Democratic liberalism, he promised to contain welfare costs, oppose busing, strengthen policing, and offer an alternative to a Democratic Party that had become "out of touch." By the time he ran for reelection in 1972, the Democratic coalition was in an advanced state of decomposition. Nixon's reelection campaign was organized around busing, crime, welfare, inflation, and peace and he won in a landslide. He took every Southern state and the Republicans continued building a coalition that was anchored in Dixie. Nixon's 1968 victory accelerated the process of demolition that came to a head four years later.

Kevin Phillips knew what had brought about the end of the New Deal coalition – the governing American political order for more than 40 years. Part of it was that the Republican Party was a different organization than it had been, largely due to its changing orientation toward racial matters.

> Secondly, the vastness of the tide (57 percent) which overwhelmed Democratic liberalism – George Wallace's support was clearly an even more vehement protest against the Democrats than was Nixon's vote – represented an epochal shifting of national gears from the 61 percent of the country's ballots garnered in 1964 by Lyndon Johnson. This repudiation visited upon the Democratic Party for its ambitious social programming, and inability to handle the urban and Negro revolutions, was comparable in scope to that given conservative Republicanism in 1932 for its failure to cope with the economic crisis of the Depression.[8]

The crisis of the Democratic Party was a sweeping one, ranging from military failure in Vietnam to social failure at home. Nixon combined a patriotic defense of "traditional values" with an appeal to racial resentment, and it earned him a loyal following among voters who could no longer abide continuous assaults on their most cherished ideals. And just as H.R. Haldeman had recorded the broad strokes of Nixon's racial strategy, so his other chief advisor, John Erlichman, noted it in more detail as he anticipated the future and its "war on drugs":

> The Nixon campaign in 1968, and the Nixon White House after that, had two enemies: the antiwar left and black people. You understand what I'm saying? We knew we couldn't make it illegal to be either against the war or blacks, but by getting the public to associate the hippies with marijuana and blacks with heroin, and then criminalizing both heavily, we could disrupt those communities. We could arrest their leaders, raid their homes, break up their meetings, and vilify them night after night on the evening news. Did we know we were lying about the drugs? Of course we did.[9]

Appearances to the contrary notwithstanding, Nixon's domestic policy was not just dog whistling and deception. One of the most astute American politicians of the twentieth century, he inaugurated an important moment in the Republican Party's embrace of white backlash. He was able to combine an appeal to white voters' prejudices and to their material interests. Even though he ran and governed as the president who broke the crucial alliances that lay at the heart of the Democratic coalition, he refused to attack the New Deal or the Great Society. He was never shy about appealing to white voters' racial fears and resentments but governed as a mainstream Republican Keynesian. He assured disenchanted white voters that he was on their side and then proved it by strengthening a welfare state that enjoyed wide support. These two foundations of Nixon's approach were perfectly in tune with the main currents of the time. By the time Ronald Reagan became president, the GOP had perfected the first and no longer bothered with the second.

Nixon represented a new phase in the Republican Party's use of race as both an electoral strategy and a rhetorical instrument of governance. He legitimized and adopted much of Wallace's appeal by successfully appealing to an increasingly resistant white population. An important stratum of middle- and working-class whites who felt personally put-upon and directly threatened by Black social and economic demands found their tribune in him. Their resentment was older than the many-headed crises of the mid-Sixties. The conservative counterrevolution that swept Nixon into the White House was centered in the same opposition to racial equality, open housing, and integrated schools that had been deeply rooted in the industrial North since at least the 1940s. That opposition had been an active and constitutive feature of the New Deal even before World War II had precipitated a massive Black migration out of the South.[10] Postwar racial politics followed a familiar pattern. Amplified by Wallace, white racial conservatism had prepared the ground for Nixon. His landslide victory in 1972 convinced much of the Republican Party that it could win elections by appealing to a sense of white grievance that was rapidly becoming a powerful national force. A history of explicit rules and implicit assumptions had institutionalized white power and provided millions of white families with structural advantages that had profound effects on their life chances and their children's possibilities. Those advantages had come under serious assault for years, and millions of white voters were ready to defend themselves. Nixon knew this and effectively neutralized the Wallace threat because he recognized and capitalized on the opportunity it posed. It was really Nixon who brought Wallace into the GOP, and institutionalizing appeals to racial resentment would prove an important step in the Republicans' willingness to throw caution to the winds and accept its role as the party of white people. But there was a limit to Nixon's use of racial politics, for it was always tied to the specific purpose of his electoral campaigns and building domestic support for some legislative initiatives. He was decidedly uninterested in what would later become the Holy Trinity of Republican Party conservatism. Regressive tax cuts, massive privatization, and broad deregulation held little interest for a president who remained a big-spending, big-government believer in New Deal economics until Watergate drove him from power. Gerald Ford would continue Nixon's approach until defeated by Jimmy Carter in 1976. The Republican Party had not yet been taken over by its most ideological and purposeful wing. That would soon change. When its 1980 nominating convention came to Detroit, Ronald Reagan was ready to start reinventing it as a white party bent on pulling up the New Deal and Great Society roots of Democratic Party liberalism. He would find that racial resentment was a potent tool as he set the GOP about its work of constructing a political base for plutocracy. In doing so, he broke with 30 years of state-building that had been led by Democrats, the party of government, with the GOP as willing junior partners. As the New Deal coalition lay in ruins, Reagan would begin consolidating a new set of alliances that would remake American politics and introduce historic levels of economic inequality as the goal and result of the government's economic and social policy. It wasn't long before he was able to refashion conservative politics around the related axes of antistatism, taxes, and welfare by framing the question around what was being taken from whites rather than what was being provided to everyone.

Notes

1 Dan T. Carter, *From Wallace to Newt Gingrich: Race in the Conservative Counterevolution, 1963–1994* (Baton Rouge: LSU Press, 1999), p. 30.
2 Michael Kazin, *The Populist Persuasion* (Ithaca, NY: Cornell University Press, 1995).
3 Kevin Phillips, *The Emerging Republican Majority* (New York: Crown, 1969), p. 37.
4 See Carol Anderson, *White Rage: The Unspoken Truth of Our Racial Divide* (London: Bloomsbury, 2017).
5 Jonathan Rieder, *Canarsie: The Jews and Italians of Brooklyn against Liberalism* (Cambridge, MA: Harvard University Press), pp. 154–155.
6 The Associated Press, "Haldeman Diary Shows Nixon Was Wary of Blacks and Jews," quoted in *The New York Times*, May 18, 1994.
7 Donald Warren, *The Radical Center: Middle Americans and the Politics of Alienation* (South Bend, IN: University of Notre Dame Press, 1976).
8 Phillips, *The Emerging Republican Majority*, p. 25.
9 Quoted in Dan Baum, "Legalize it All," *Harper's*, April 20, 2016.
10 Tom Sugrue, *The Origins of the Urban Crisis: Race and Inequality in Postwar Detroit* (Princeton, NJ: Princeton University Press, 2005).

3
WHISTLING FOR PLUTOCRACY

Richard Nixon had reoriented the Republican Party's racial politics by promising to go slow on civil rights enforcement and reassuring insecure white voters that he would protect them from the cultural, racial, and political challenges of the Sixties. Even as he strengthened the core provisions of the welfare state and introduced some important new programs to strengthen social protections, his promises to hold the line would become the GOP's basic position in the period of retrenchment and restoration that followed his presidency. That promise would become the bedrock position of all his successors, chief among them Ronald Reagan.

Nixon had left civil rights enforcement initiatives intact, even if he studiously ignored many of them. But Reagan had a different idea of what "holding the line" meant. Defending the racial status quo now required rolling back federal activity and neutering the agencies responsible for enforcing existing policy and legislation. He had been hostile to the civil rights movement for years before entering national politics, benefiting from a congealing racial conservatism that enabled him to take advantage of white pushback as support for civil rights began to fracture. He had opposed every piece of civil rights legislation – particularly the Civil Rights and Voting Rights Acts – but that didn't stop him from arguing that the disappearance of official discrimination meant that the work of the civil rights movement had come to an end. Any further governmental measures to rectify existing racial disparities would be an unjustified expansion of bureaucratic power, require unjustified government interventions on behalf of minorities, and erode freedom for everyone. A clear implication that social progress for Blacks would now come at the expense of freedom for whites always circulated in the background of assertions like this, but it usually went unsaid. Reagan insisted that enforcing existing law was the outer limit of Washington's legitimate activity, but even that limit existed more in rhetoric than in reality. Nixon had often declined to enforce civil rights legislation while president, but Reagan went further, building on his predecessor's legacy by energetically deploying federal power to stifle further progress. Both men understood the limits of white popular opinion, which still supported equality in voting rights and access to public accommodations but opposed more intrusive measures like busing and affirmative action. Having benefitted for decades from government assistance, millions of whites were unwilling to dispense with the fiction that they had earned what they had without substantial outside help. The Reagan invention of a "colorblind" racial policy translated that refusal into a wide-ranging assault on Washington's protection of the civil rights movement's accomplishments.

Reagan offered something new that would prove far more consequential than his party's willingness to stoke and benefit from racial animus. As soon as he was elected president, and just six years after Nixon's resignation, his administration set the conditions for the most dramatic upward distribution of wealth in modern American history – a process that has continued, with many advances and some retreats, for more than 40 years. It was made possible by two coordinated sets of policies that have decisively changed the structure of American society – both of which required aggressive government action, Reagan's rhetorical attack on Washington notwithstanding. A series of attacks on the welfare state accompanied the trifecta of regressive tax cuts, deregulation, and privatization that has constituted the basic Republican economic position for the past 40 years. Taken together, they have created a mass of insecure, threatened, and angry white voters whose station in life has not changed for almost two generations and whose material and psychological distress has come to play a pivotal role in national politics. Prompted by conservative politicians who blame racial minorities and immigrants for their plight, they have become steadily radicalized as inequality has intensified. They formed the mass base for Donald Trump's explicit white nationalism.

Reagan didn't invent the conditions that made possible his attack on the welfare state, but he was well positioned to take advantage of them. By the end of the 1970s, a widespread feeling of threat and dispossession had prompted millions of white families to withdraw support from a liberal regime that had lost much of its legitimacy. The moral and economic order to which they were deeply attached – and from which they had materially benefitted – was breaking down during the Carter presidency. The moderate Keynesianism that had organized a successful period of growth, stability, and prosperity was no longer able to deal with the twinned crisis of recession and inflation. As if "stagflation" weren't enough, a series of other shocks undermined the confidence of millions of voters in the basic understandings that had organized the country's politics for two generations. The Arab oil boycott, Iranian hostage crisis, hollowing out of the nation's industrial core, continuing racial unrest, relentless urban decay – a succession of crises battered the optimism of earlier years and convinced many disenchanted voters that they were being victimized by forces they could no longer control. Carter's embrace of austerity and deregulation marked the end of American capitalism's

Golden Age amid a series of crises that doomed his presidency and opened the door to a New Right that had been shut out of national power but which was, in the words of one of its leading activists, "ready to lead."[1]

After years of organizing, movement conservatives finally took over the Republican Party at its 1980 national convention. Their jubilant nomination of Reagan signaled the end of the long period of bipartisan agreement about how to manage a modern economy. Very few observers suspected that the former actor would be such a consequential president. After a forgettable movie career, he had broken into national politics with "The Speech" supporting Goldwater's presidential campaign and his successful run for governor of California two years later. Coming on the heels of the giant Watts Rebellion, his campaign was able to take advantage of the terror that the uprising brought to white families across the Golden State. Watts had exploded the fiction that the end of Jim Crow in the South was also the end of racial discrimination elsewhere. By the time the National Guard imposed order after five days of violence, 34 people were dead, more than a thousand were injured, and property damage totaled more than $200 million. In case anyone labored under the illusion that the country's racial issues were confined to the South, it was now clear that unrest could erupt into mass violence anywhere. Reagan was well positioned to take advantage of a potent mix of white fears that the uprising provoked. "Our city streets are jungle paths after dark," he proclaimed during his campaign for governor, clearly identifying the source of danger to anyone who was listening. Jumping on the opportunity presented by widespread alarm, he called for legislation that would "untie the hands of our law enforcement officers," even as police brutality was the immediate cause of the Watts Rebellion and of much urban unrest around the country. The target of his Nixonian call for "law and order" was not lost on California voters, particularly since he warned that "a jungle is closing in on this little patch that we've been civilizing for so long a time."[2] By the time he had launched his gubernatorial campaign in January 1966, white backlash against the civil right movement had begun to reshape national politics and posed a mortal threat to the prevailing liberal order. Running on promises to lower taxes, defend segregated residential housing, reimpose "law and order," and trim back government intervention in the economy and society, Reagan was elected governor by white voters in Southern California, many of whom had come from the South and the rural West. Like much of the industrial Midwest, these were two formerly Democratic areas whose loyalty to racial liberalism was being challenged as the civil rights movement broadened its activities and moved out from Dixie.

Watts had raised the explosive issue of "law and order" in a way that could no longer be swept under the rug, although much depended on the way in which public figures responded to it. For his part, Reagan charged ahead with an uncompromising defense of the existing racial order and never abandoned it for the rest of his time in public life. Urban unrest provided him with an effective issue with which to appeal to white voters, and it accompanied disputes about housing to create a potent mix of racially charged issues for a political entrepreneur who was willing to take advantage of white fear and resentment. The statewide anxiety provoked by Watts and the anger raised by efforts to address residential segregation were the immediate issues that made him governor. His break from his family's past mirrored that of millions of white voters.

Reagan's parents had been racial liberals, and he had followed in their footsteps early in his acting career. Active in anti-racist organizations for a time, he began turning to the right as he made his career in the movie industry. He began informing on Hollywood leftists to the FBI just after the end of World War II, was instrumental in breaking a strike after being elected president of the Screen Actors Guild, and probably informed on suspected communists during the blacklist that followed the war. By the early 1950s, he had become a firm anticommunist liberal and was moving steadily to the right. His conviction that the Democratic Party was little more than a stalking horse for Bolshevism echoed the views of a rapidly developing Republican right wing that would soon declare itself an enemy of both the New Deal and of civil rights. Much of his evolution denied his parents' rather progressive politics even as he paid rhetorical homage to the New Deal. His father had gotten a job with the Federal Emergency Relief Administration and had managed to protect his family from the worst of the Depression, and Reagan never attacked FDR even after becoming a conservative by assaulting the New Deal, excoriating welfare programs, and denigrating their recipients. Ever the entrepreneur, Reagan took advantage of an opportunity that coincided with his own political evolution. Race provided a launching pad for an ambitious would-be politician who was convinced that he had a more important role to play than a career in B movies.

Two developments came together to prepare the ground for Reagan's 1966 gubernatorial campaign. The statewide alarm that followed the Watts uprising was amplified by a local dispute that mirrored the fights about residential segregation that had shaken the New Deal coalition in Detroit, Chicago, and other Northern cities. The California legislature had passed the Rumford Fair Housing Act in 1963, prohibiting racial discrimination in the sale and rental of all residential units of over five units. Outraged property-owners, real estate interests, the construction industry, and newly energized conservatives adopted the same arguments about property rights and government overreach that had driven similar protests against open housing legislation in the Midwest. A potent coalition quickly took shape, and a year later, California voters approved Proposition 14 by a margin of two-to-one, repealing the Rumford Act and providing new material for Reagan as he toyed with the idea of running for governor. It was during his campaign two years later that he first deployed Goldwater's claim that open housing initiatives were a tyrannical governmental interference with property rights. No governmental entity, Reagan said, has any business mandating that property-owners treat all potential buyers equally. If a seller wants act like a bigot, that is a private choice that lies beyond the legitimate purposes of government. As Reagan put it during one of his many speeches attacking the Rumford Act, "If an individual wants to discriminate against Negroes or others in selling or renting his house, it is his right to do so." He often added that he wouldn't ever approve of blatant discrimination, of course, but the wink-wink wasn't lost on property-owners who felt under siege. The fiction that housing segregation was a matter of individual liberty and market freedom disguised decades of active governmental and institutional activity that produced segregated residential markets, but general ignorance of how public and private actors had acted made Reagan's dog whistle credible. In a shift from their demands that Sacramento stop supporting open housing, white people who opposed residential integration rallied to the "property rights" cause, insisting that the government had a moral and financial obligation to protect the value of their homes. It turned out that white residents of the Golden State were just as reluctant to live near Blacks as were white people who lived elsewhere. As resistance to the civil rights movement hardened, *Newsweek* reported that 70 percent of whites felt that it was pushing political equality "too fast," and a Harris poll found that 46 percent of white Americans would be opposed to a Black family moving next door.[3] Even after the California Supreme Court ruled Proposition 14 unconstitutional, Reagan made political hay by attacking unelected judges for overturning the will of four and a half million voters and continued to insist that the issue was property rights and not racial animus. His repeated attacks on open housing legislation served him well once he decided to run and fueled his primary victory against George Christopher, a comparative racial liberal.

Reagan became California governor because of his ability to capitalize on racial backlash without appearing to be a racist. White resentment about taxes, crime, residential integration, and the civil rights movement's turn toward the North had suddenly made millions of voters available to the Republicans just as Reagan moved to tap into a rich vein of middle-class racial anxiety. Reagan's appeal to disenchanted Californians turned out to be the tip of an iceberg. The themes he rode to Sacramento had national implications. He was starting to appeal to millions of whites around the country who were ready to move away from the Democratic Party and abandon much of the New Deal consensus that had organized national politics for a generation. Reagan always assured his listeners that he shared their pain.

> I've spent most of my life as a Democrat and I recall very well when the moment came to change and to reregister, when the leadership of the Democratic Party repudiated the constitutional concepts of individual freedom and local autonomy and states' rights and a little intellectual elite in the nation's capital had engaged in social tinkering, and I say to you, "you didn't leave your party, the leadership of that party left you."[4]

Circumstances had changed the tone of politicians' appeals to white voters even if the substance remained intact. By the time Reagan ran for governor, candidates could no longer use explicit racial appeals in asking for votes. So, they developed indirect ways of talking about race by "dog whistling" about issues that they knew would appeal to racial fear while allowing themselves a measure of deniability. Pretending that they weren't talking about race when they were left no doubt in the minds of aggrieved white voters who liked to believe that they were racially tolerant and looked for opportunities to say that they were worried about matters that had nothing to do with race. Conservative candidates from Goldwater on had figured out how to oppose integration and civil rights on the basis of principles that supposedly had nothing to do with either. The Arizona senator's "constitutional" objections to civil rights legislation in the name of protecting citizens from intrusive government had started the routine use of dog whistles, and Republican candidates proved themselves to be masters of this technique during the Nixon administration. Reagan was the best of them all.

Lee Atwater, a senior operative for the Reagan campaign in 1980 and its political director four years later, then manager of George H.W. Bush's presidential campaign of 1988, and finally Chairman of the Republican National Committee, explained the dog whistle to a political scientist in 1981. Fully aware of its explosive implications, he asked not to be directly quoted. Although some accounts of his famous description differ in minor details, its overall direction and meaning are clear. The trick was how to talk about race when you weren't talking about race, something Atwater had perfected when working to get South Carolina senator Strom Thurmond reelected in 1976. It was now a matter of

> how abstract you handle the race thing.... You start out in 1954 by saying, "Nigger, nigger, nigger." By 1968 you can't say "nigger" – that hurts you, backfires. So you say stuff like, uh, forced busing, states' rights, and all that stuff, and you're getting so abstract now, you're talking about cutting taxes, and all these things you're talking about are totally economic things and a byproduct of them is, blacks get hurt worse than whites.... And if it is getting that abstract and that coded, we're doing away with the racial problem one way or another. You follow me? Because obviously sitting around saying, "We want to cut taxes, we want to cut this," is so much more abstract than even the busing thing, uh, and a hell of a lot more abstract than "Nigger, nigger." So any way you look at it, race is coming on the back burner.[5]

Atwater knew what he was talking about. By 1980, the Republican Party had become the home of white voters who were hostile to the very idea of paying for any further racial progress, and cloaking that opposition in the "abstract" language of tax reduction was a perfect dog whistle. Reagan's repeated promise to lower taxes was an effective political trap for postwar racial liberalism. It allowed him to say that the Democratic Party had become little more than an unprincipled coalition of "special interests" jostling for the opportunity to take money from hardworking, deserving white taxpayers and, by implication, give it to lazy, undeserving Blacks and the meddling bureaucrats who liked to play with social experiments. Lumping civil rights organizations together with "union bosses," environmentalists, feminists, and other elements of the Democratic coalition made it possible to denounce all of them as self-interested grifters looking for a free handout. Taxes always takes from some and gives to others, and a helpful dog whistle or two would remind racially conservative white voters who was taking from whom.

Reagan wasn't entirely wrong when he said that the Democratic Party had lost its way. The slow-motion collapse of its New Deal coalition had eviscerated the overarching sense of purpose that had animated postwar liberalism. Its grand domestic project of modest reform, regulation, and redistribution had collapsed as its material basis dissolved. An overarching commitment to an important measure of economic justice and political democracy was being replaced by unprincipled quarreling over a shrinking set of resources. As long as the economic pie was getting larger, the Democrats had been able to organize a broad political regime that could deliver both "guns and butter." Although it grew increasingly difficult to manage the tensions between them, Johnson's Vietnam War could coexist with his Great Society and War on Poverty. But as the country fell into economic decline, it became harder to sustain an expensive anticommunism in foreign affairs and an expensive program of domestic reform at home. And, once the Civil Rights and Voting Rights Acts had cut out the foundations of Jim Crow in the South, further racial progress would mean higher taxes and fewer automatic privileges for white voters who had come to consider their place in the country's racial hierarchy to be their birthright.

Things had started unraveling during the late 1970s. Edward Kennedy did his best to resurrect the old governing coalition when he challenged Carter for the Democratic nomination in 1980, but it was too late. By the time Reagan ran for president, economic stress had produced a mass of sullen, unhappy, and disenchanted white voters who were no longer in a sharing mood. Carter's grim call for austerity and sacrifice gave voice to a national environment that had turned sour. Under these circumstances, opposition to taxation was an effective argument against social programs of all kinds, and Reagan proved to be a master of disguise. Crime, property rights, and welfare would serve him equally well as he became the expert dog whistler. Conservative antistatism derives much of its power from the Democratic Party's support of the civil rights movement and by the time he became the Republican candidate for president, Reagan had figured out how to harness it to a broad attack on the foundations of the New Deal and the welfare state. As he aggressively wielded governmental power to attack progressive taxation, economic regulation, and governmental intervention, he set the tone for a generation of conservatism. White racial anxiety was now the tip of a spear that could be used to assault the welfare state. Things had changed dramatically since Nixon.

The succession of crises that marked public life in the late 1970s had produced a genuine grassroots rebellion against the liberal state. It assumed the outward form of a drive to lower taxes, derided as an unjustified transfer from the productive many to the parasitical few. Conservative politicians and activists were able to amplify it into a generalized assault against further spending on social programs, government assistance to Blacks and the poor, support for abortion rights and the Equal Rights Amendment, and a host of other causes that had been the bedrock positions of a New Deal coalition that now lay in ruins. Reagan never tired of repeating that Washington had become the mortal enemy of prosperity and freedom, developing a wide-ranging rhetorical assault on the welfare state and marrying it to a defense of old-fashioned "family values." He was the perfect candidate for white voters who were determined to defend their social position and psychological identity. For the moment, he was content to pose as the defender of efficiency, liberty, and prosperity against the overweening power of an increasingly oppressive central state and the meddling bureaucrats who exemplified the inherent tendency of political power to overreach. His critique was aptly summed up in his crowd-pleasing observation that "the nine most terrifying words in the English language are 'I'm from the government, and I'm here to help.'" His audiences loved it, for it solidified their belief that they had what they had because of what they had accomplished. Left unsaid was the vast amount of indirect and direct help they had received from the very government against which the candidate was now positioning himself. Reagan's "magic of the market" replaced public regulation and democratic debate as the criterion of action. Government-led downward redistribution of wealth, he repeatedly assured his listeners, was tantamount to theft. He was a little quieter about his intention to use government to organize one of the most aggressive *upward* redistributions in the country's history.

His presidency stood in some contrast to his record as governor. An enlightened and bipartisan approach to state government had fueled California's growth during the Sixties. A vast spending program had built a network of freeways, aqueducts, bridges, canals, schools, colleges, universities, and other physical and social infrastructure that fueled the Golden State's astonishing progress. Reagan had to deal with a Democratic majority in Sacramento and switched to a relatively pragmatic approach during his first term, signing an expansion of voting rights, presiding over a huge tax increase to cover a budget shortfall, and leaving office with a larger state government than had been in place when he was first elected. But he made up for his political compromises with hardline stances on critical public issues. His frequent attacks on the Black Panthers as criminal revolutionaries, his public baiting of Angela Davis and Eldridge Cleaver, his insistence that college students "obey the rules," his orchestration of violent crackdowns on student unrest at Berkeley and San Francisco State, and his continuing opposition to welfare, busing, and open housing helped endear him to a Republican Party that was moving in the same direction. His insinuations that Blacks were not ready for full citizenship and that money spent on social welfare was wasted had found an institutional home.

Once he had secured the presidential nomination, candidate Reagan turned his attention to the South. A campaign based on fervent anticommunism abroad and hostility to the welfare state at home would require some deft campaigning. His tough law-and-order positions during the tumult of the Sixties made it easy for him to craft a message blaming liberals for coddling out-of-control youth and Blacks. His appeal rested on his skill in appealing to racial resentment while not appearing to be a racist, a stance that appealed to the remnants of the Goldwater wing in Dixie and resonated with millions of white voters around the country. His aides were sure he could make inroads into Carter's domination of the region four years earlier, and that the South would provide his path to the White House. After a scheduling problem prevented his opening address to the National Urban League in New York – an address that was intended to reassure suburban white voters that he wasn't a bigot – Reagan began his campaign at the Neshoba Country Fair in Philadelphia, Mississippi. It was here that he told his audience that

> I believe in states' rights. I believe in people doing as much as they can for themselves at the community level and at the private level. And I believe that we've distorted the balance of our government today by giving powers that were never intended in the Constitution to be given to the federal establishment. And if I do get the job I'm looking for, I'm going to devote myself to trying to reorder those priorities and to restore to the states and local communities those functions which properly belong there.[6]

The meaning of this particular dog whistle was not lost on anyone. Each and every one of the 10,000 eligible voters in Philadelphia who came to Reagan's speech on that day had been alive in 1964, when James Cheney, Michael Schwerner, and Andrew Goodman were killed in their town at the very beginning of Mississippi Freedom Summer. The Deep South was up for grabs in 1980, and Republican representative Trent Lott had suggested that Reagan say something to indicate his support for white Southerners who had resisted the civil rights movement and still resented Washington's interference. Philadelphia, Mississippi, ironically bearing the same name as Pennsylvania's "city of brotherly love," had become the poster child for murderous Southern white racism. Reagan's opening salvo represented the beginning of a concerted Republican campaign to make inroads into Carter's earlier domination of the region.

To do so, Reagan had to grapple with the South's historic attachment to the New Deal. From the Rural Electrification Administration to the Tennessee Valley Authority and many other federal initiatives, the South had been a major beneficiary of Democratic social and economic programs. George Wallace had established his reputation in Alabama politics by supporting the New Deal even as he appealed to the state's history of racism and violence. What was new about

Reagan was his clear intention to undo many of FDR's social protections and channel wealth upward. Always ready to exploit racial anxiety and a pervasive sense of vulnerability among white voters of modest means, he championed "traditional values," attacked abortion rights, defended the nuclear family, preached a starry-eyed patriotism, and embraced other social issues that would become dear to the emerging New Right. But when all was said and done, his core positions were remarkably stable throughout his public career: regressive tax cuts, deregulation, and privatization.

Reagan was able to take advantage of a broad and powerful shift to the right that had developed during the late 1970s. It had deep roots, had been germinating for some time, and was no longer limited to a few rich people and big corporations. Tax rebels, pro-life opponents of *Roe v. Wade*, critics of gay rights, opponents of unions, fundamentalist critics of public schools, enemies of the Equal Rights Amendment – they had been denied broad influence for years and were cut off from each other, but they had become increasingly coherent, unified, and influential during the crisis of the Carter presidency. Keynesianism's failure to solve the linked phenomena of inflation and recession had stimulated a sea change in the nature of American populism. The authentic language of American protest, populism had once been an ideology of the left. But times had changed. A commitment to taxing the rich, redistributing wealth downward, reining in Wall Street, and regulating the corporations had become resistance to meddling bureaucrats, defense of the status quo, and protection for middle class property-owners from the demands of the poor.[7] This evolution was accelerated by the inflation that ravaged the economy and battered families – an inflation that was not susceptible to standard Keynesian solutions, accompanied as it was by a crippling recession. Economists debated a number of possible culprits for this unprecedented storm of "stagflation": Johnson's refusal to raise taxes to finance the Vietnam War; Nixon's wage and price freeze and his move to end the convertibility of the dollar; the Arab oil embargo. But Reagan had a simpler explanation: the government was spending too much money, a claim he repeated throughout the 1980 campaign. Once the results were in, he used that argument as a battering ram to demolish the New Deal and the Great Society.

Paradoxically it seemed, Carter largely agreed with Reagan during the last period of his presidency, arguing for more regulatory "reform" in the communications sector after having deregulated much of the nation's railroad, trucking, airline, and financial industries. Uninterested in the Democrats' historic alliance with organized labor, he moved away from liberal orthodoxy as he embraced austerity and urged Americans to do with less. Edward Kennedy's 1980 challenge illustrated the cleavages in the party of the New Deal whose leader was now open to austerity, balanced budgets, regressive tax cuts, and deregulation. Threatened by its Republican enemies and abandoned by its Democratic "friends," the cause of social reform took a sharp rightward turn. The difference between Democrats and Republicans was becoming more a matter of style than of substance, but the

Republican candidate had a real program to offer. Reagan's confident claims that routing wealth upward would deliver more jobs and balance the budget at the same time illustrated the contrast between his sunny optimism and Carter's dark embrace of austerity.

There were real economic issues to worry about. Average economic growth had slowed, inflation was around 10 percent overall, and food prices had gone up by a staggering 16 percent after averaging 3 percent during the previous two decades. The "golden age" of postwar American capitalism came crashing to an end as a long period of steady growth, high employment, increasing productivity, generous contracts, and low inflation yielded to pessimism and fear that scarcity and austerity were becoming permanent features of a society in decline. There was a powerful groundswell from the grassroots that was amplified, publicized, and protected by a vast amount of money and energy coming from newly politicized corporations and the rich. After decades of bipartisan consensus about how to manage a modern economy, a great change was in the works. A discontented electorate was ready to jettison some of the basic assumptions of an entire period of American history.[8] Reagan's avuncular friendliness and genial good humor made it possible for him to pose an alternative to Carter's embrace of austerity and tell the country that everything would be better if the size of government was reduced, if its ability to distort the economy was paralyzed, and if it "got its hands out of your pockets."

After opening in Lowndes County, Reagan's campaign expanded its geographic range and targeted white voters who felt under attack by a federal government that seemed to have become their enemy. Appearances in racial hotspots like South Boston, Cicero, Illinois, and Milwaukee made it clear that he intended to go after the votes of the Northern whites who had rallied to George Wallace. He repeatedly claimed that the country's racial problems were over, solved by decent individuals who had acted out of their inherent American kindness rather than because of laws passed by Congress or regulations imposed by government agencies. When asked why he had opposed the 1965 Voting Rights Act, he protested that it had been "humiliating to the South" and explained his opposition to the Civil Rights Act of a year before as a Goldwaterite defense of constitutional principles against an overreaching federal government. His illustrated his claim that individual action was the only path to progress by saying – falsely, it turned out – that he had agitated for integrating Major League Baseball while working as a sports announcer. Like Nixon and Wallace, he targeted aggrieved white voters who felt they were being unjustly taxed, blamed, and regulated for the benefit of minorities. Many of these voters in Midwestern industrial cities were already disposed to blame minorities for their economic difficulties because broader economic trends just seemed too powerful to contain. By 1980, the percentage of all manufactured goods sold in the United States that were imported rose to 40 percent; just ten years earlier, the figure had stood at 14 percent. The collapse was especially dramatic for American cars, which were markedly inferior to their Japanese competitors. The resultant decline in cities like Detroit, Flint,

Dayton, Akron, Pittsburgh, Milwaukee, and Chicago that had been centers of the American auto and steel industries prompted many white workers in steel, aluminum, glass, and rubber factories to blame minorities for their difficulties. Their distress had prompted many of them to support Wallace and vote for Nixon. The relentless evisceration of the country's industrial core, most pronounced in the Midwest, prompted their continuing migration to the GOP in 1980.

The genuine economic and psychological difficulties experienced by many whites created fertile ground for Reagan's dog whistles. His infamous warnings about the Chicago "welfare queen" was perfect fodder for those who felt they were shouldering an unfair burden for the country's past racial sins and present economic woes. He had tried it out during his unsuccessful presidential bid in 1976, talking about an unnamed, presumably Black, grifter in Chicago who "used 80 names, 30 addresses, 15 telephone numbers to collect food stamps, Social Security, veterans' benefits for four nonexistent, deceased veteran husbands, as well as welfare. Her tax-free cash income alone has been running $150,000 a year."[9] Four years hadn't done anything to interfere with Reagan's ability to whistle. Dusting off the story, he now claimed that she had had "eighty names, thirty addresses, [and] twelve Social Security cards [who] is collecting veteran's benefits on four non-existing deceased husbands. She's got Medicaid, getting food stamps, and is collecting welfare under each of her names. Her tax-free cash income is over $150,000."[10] As if that weren't bad enough, Reagan's thieving "welfare queen" went tooling around the Windy City in a Cadillac. The whole story was a fiction, but the dog whistle appealed to an aggrieved section of the hardworking white electorate that was tired of being ripped off by indolent Black women, parasitical Black men, and their enablers in a corrupt welfare system that had become an enemy of hard work and self-reliance. As if his 1976 tale wasn't enough, Reagan drove the point home by telling his white audiences a similar fiction about a "strapping young buck" who liked to buy T-Bone steaks with public money "while you were waiting in line to buy hamburger." He became an expert at infuriating people about the misuse of their tax dollars and frightening them with warnings about crime and violence. His winning combination of friendly optimism and racial resentment seemed appropriate for a time when racist dog whistles were useful tools to remind white voters of what was important.

A deep, visceral hostility to the state, and an accompanying confidence in the "magic of the market," served as his rhetorical and programmatic battering ram as he sought to cripple the New Deal and its commitment to the idea that a modern government was responsible for a measure of social protection. He blamed Washington for everything from the Depression to crime, welfare, out-of-wedlock births, and almost all the very real problems the country faced in 1980. In a rhetorical tour de force delivered during an interview with a skeptical journalist, Reagan linked race, welfare, and Medicaid and blamed all three for encouraging abortion:

Sheer asked Reagan whether his opposition to abortion didn't contradict his objection to government intrusion into family life. Reagan replied that the *problem* with abortion was the government intruding into family life: "In some of our inner cities, there are actually cases, many more of them than you would believe, that young girls, under age, who deliberately go out to have a baby so that they can get what they call 'a pad of their own' because getting the baby, unmarried, they can become put on the Aid to Dependent Children program.... Being on the welfare program makes her eligible for Medicaid. So she then goes and gets rid of the baby, and the government pays for it with tax dollars and the government is bound by law to protect her privacy and not let her own parents know."[11]

Reagan's 1980 campaign prefigured the themes that would mark the eight years of his presidency and reflected the positions he had articulated during his run for California governor 14 years earlier: rein in government spending and regulation, decrease taxes, cut back public bureaucracy and government "planners," privatize Social Security, and turn around the "spreading philosophy that the criminal must be protected from society and not the other way around." Much of this was taken directly from George Wallace, and all of it would come to mark conservative politics for the next 40 years. Nixon had solidified a good deal of Wallace's appeal during his "law and order" campaigns, and Kevin Phillips's "Southern Strategy" had rested at the heart of Republican presidential politics since 1968. To hear Republicans tell it, the swing votes in national elections came from white voters whose jobs and security were threatened and quality of life jeopardized by a government that coddled street criminals, welfare chiselers, and the lazy unemployed. As they turned toward the GOP, Reagan brought their economic insecurities and racial resentments together and constructed a conservative populism that transformed American politics for a generation. From the concerns of the Christian Right about feminism, school prayer, Armageddon, and evolution to the antistatism of traditional populist conservatism and a studied indifference to issues of race, he articulated a plain-talking Americanism that looked back to homogeneous small towns stocked with friendly white people of middling incomes who were devoted to family, church, neighbors, and nation. His great achievement was to expel the overt resentment and bitterness from conservative populism and infuse it with optimism, consensus, common sense, and ordinariness. He was certainly indifferent to minorities and hostile to labor, but he never appeared to be mean-spirited. The key to his rhetorical success was his ability to update the traditional opposition between "the people" and the "special interests," redefined now as liberal insiders, union leaders, and minority organizations who wielded their power to benefit their narrow constituencies and thwart the public will. Under these circumstances, it was very hard to label him as the instrument of the corporations and the wealthy – the old Achilles' heel of the right. His campaign's slogan – "Make America Great Again" – promised a rebound after the "malaise" of the Carter years. There were many issues on the table during the campaign, ranging from Iranian hostages in Tehran to stagflation in Washington and paralysis in Detroit. But Reagan's dog whistles made it clear to white voters that he was their candidate. They heard the message; Reagan won 64 percent of their ballots in the presidential election.

His constant evocations of ordinary people and his reassuring optimism notwithstanding, the Reagan presidency was a regime of business and the rich. Following the Heritage Foundation's influential "Mandate for Leadership" that accompanied his inauguration, his administration made slashing taxes on corporations and the rich one of its first priorities. The candidate's dog-whistled attacks on welfare smoothed the way for the president's program of reducing taxes, but their impact was sharply regressive and would help concentrate wealth at the very top of American society. The rugged, white individual of Reagan's mythical America had started out defending his autonomy and modest property from tyrannical governmental intrusion. Hostile to governmental regulation of the market, his sturdy independence was married to resentment of government efforts to force unwanted social experiments and racial integration. Reagan's tax cuts were touted as the way to shrink government, defend hardworking white Americans from the greed of the undeserving poor, restore liberty to the land, and liberate the economy from the clutches of meddling bureaucrats and the special interests to whom they were beholden. The cuts that were enacted in 1981 alone showered $164 billion on the corporate sector alone, one of the most generous business tax reductions in American history. The largest retrenchment in nonmilitary spending in American history, his first budget imposed $35.2 billion in cuts to discretionary programs created during the Great Society to help the poor. Food stamp programs, housing support, Head Start, school lunch programs, the Job Corps, the Office of Economic Opportunity, the Legal Services Corporation – hardly any government program that addressed poverty and economic inequality was spared. He followed that up with a continuing program of breathtaking generosity toward the rich. Over the eight years of his presidency, his administration lowered the top marginal tax rate on individual incomes from 70 percent to 28 percent, with the promise that these cuts would result in more investment, an expanding economy, more jobs, and higher incomes for all. It didn't work out that way, of course. Only corporations and the rich really benefitted. Tax cuts for the wealthiest 1 percent of the population came to roughly $1 trillion during the 1980s and another $1 trillion every decade after that. The richest Americans, the big winners from Reagan's generosity, tripled their net worth from 1978 to 1990 – almost all of that gain coming at the expense of the poor and the middle class. It was the biggest upward transfer of wealth in the country's history, all of it made possible by the very government whose interventions in the economy had been the object of Reagan's rhetorical scorn. It wasn't the idea of government intervention that truly bothered Reagan, his words notwithstanding. The target of his rhetorical antistatism was government intervention on behalf of social justice and economic democracy. Reagan's ability to whistle made possible one of the great "bait and switch" turns in recent American political history. His attacks on state regulation had propelled him to the White House, where he promptly initiated a politically driven, government-enabled set of policies that made possible the development of an American plutocracy and, years later, would fuel the appearance of a distinctly American white nationalism.

The president was an expert as using populist slogans to mask the fusion of economic and political power, a skill he took with him into politics from Hollywood.[12] He was no enemy of immigration and was not inclined to go further than conventional racial politics in exploiting the anxiety that had prompted the exodus of millions of white voters from the Democrats. Content with dog whistling, Reagan seemed to be little more than a standard Republican political entrepreneur who was willing to use coded appeals to white people for electoral advantage but who ruled as a relatively conventional racial conservative. But times had changed, the moderate Keynesianism that had brought postwar America its "Golden Age" no longer worked, and the economic transition that he helped set in motion would transform American racial politics and turn it into a far more dangerous tendency than it had been. His contribution to the contemporary development of white nationalism consists in the breathtaking accumulation of wealth and power that has characterized the past 40 years of American history. When combined with broad demographic changes, the economic distress of millions of families has established the conditions for the growth of a tendency that now affects public life on a national scale.

There was nothing automatic or inevitable about the development of American plutocracy. It resulted from a set of specific policy decisions from several administrations that followed Reagan. As the GOP ended a long period of Democratic political domination, it brought an entirely new set of economic priorities to Washington. "Reaganomics" provided a name for the party's transition from the junior partner of official Keynesianism to the enabler of the "magic of the market" as it began a long attack on the New Deal, the Great Society, and assorted programs of social welfare. The president's rhetorical attacks and gestures toward privatization notwithstanding, Reagan generally left Medicare and Social Security alone because they were important to the millions of white voters who benefitted from them. But programs like Aid to Families with Dependent Children, Medicaid, public housing, mass transit, school lunches, voting rights, affirmative action, and others were far more vulnerable because they could be easily racialized.[13] Richard Nixon had called himself a Keynesian and refused calls from the Republican right to undermine the New Deal, but he had simultaneously declined to enforce existing civil rights legislation except in particularly egregious cases. This was particularly true of open housing, a sensitive flash point for millions of white families. Nixon had long said that residential discrimination was wrong, but simultaneously insisted that it was equally wrong to impose integration over local resistance by "bureaucratic fiat." This tactic of rhetorically affirming support for integration in the abstract while refusing to undertake the concrete steps to make it reality became the default position of white politicians who discovered that their reluctance made them enormously popular among white voters. Reagan simply continued the strategy of accepting redlining and denial of mortgages, refusing to enforce existing legislation, and making judicial and bureaucratic appointments that responded to the continued refusal of millions of white families to live near Black ones. His administration went further than Nixon, routinely failing even to affirm rhetorical support for residential integration and insisting on the right of homeowners to sell to whomever they wanted. Ignoring existing legislation and policies and refusing to gather the data that would have been necessary to support federal intervention in local housing markets, the administration's indifference meant that the country made virtually no progress on a problem that had become intractable. Adding insult to injury, Washington slashed federal spending for subsidized housing from $26.1 billion in 1981 to $2.1 billion just four years later.[14]

The Reagan administration's approach to school segregation was the same: ignore it by invoking colorblind principles as a justification for doing nothing. The persistent claim of colorblindness, which was made a centerpiece of the federal government's approach to racial matters during the Reagan presidency, has been a useful rhetorical device to claim that the country had moved beyond the antagonisms of the civil rights period and simply has to wait for people of good will to gradually reorganize their attitudes and behavior. It was during the Reagan presidency that it became the conservative response to demands for federal intervention in racial matters. The position was first articulated as a matter of national policy by John Roberts, now Chief Justice of the Supreme Court. Roberts played a crucial role in Reagan's Justice Department, opposed the Voting Rights Act of 1965, and developed the notion that the federal government should adopt racial neutrality as a governing principle to civil rights legislation and enforcement – a position that guaranteed nonintervention in pervasive, systematic, historically driven discrimination. His immediate boss was Reagan's Assistant Attorney General for Civil Rights William Bradford Reynolds, who built on wide hostility to affirmative action and other race-conscious standards and developed the position that "government-imposed discrimination" had created "a kind of racial spoils system in America" that now favored historically disadvantaged minorities as a matter of policy. Reynolds had focused his attention on affirmative action, presenting many arguments to the Supreme Court that race-conscious remedies to prior employment discrimination were directed against whites and were therefore impermissible. His public position was that he wasn't attacking minority participation in American society but was defending the simple proposition that the government should not tolerate discrimination against anyone – despite the history of systematic political support for the very discrimination that affirmative action was designed to address. The notion that innocent whites were being victimized for offenses they had not personally committed became explicit government policy. No head of the Civil Rights Division had ever made that argument before. Reynolds and Roberts reoriented federal policy so that ending busing became more of a priority than desegregating schools and dismantling quotas became more important than integrating workplaces or academia. Support for civil rights had suddenly become anti-white, a central claim of a white nationalism that would be explicitly articulated by Donald Trump.

The key innovation that Roberts, Reynolds, and other conservatives in Reagan's Justice Department brought to the politics of race was the requirement that *intentional* racial discrimination now had to be proven. When they developed the administration's opposition to the House-passed extension of the Voting Rights Act (VRA), they argued that discriminatory *effect* was too weak a standard and would imply that racial and linguistic minorities now had a right to elect representation proportional to their population in the community. This standard, they said, would require a complicated quota system to evaluate compliance with the VRA and would mean a massive federal intrusion into matters that both the Constitution and historical precedent reserved to the states. Reynolds and Roberts developed the argument that the federal government should intervene only when voting rules and procedures *intentionally* discriminated against minorities, a standard that is extremely difficult to prove. This "colorblind" standard has carried over to the contemporary Supreme Court, which has increasingly held that, just as *Brown* made the use of race in finding segregation unconstitutional, so is the use of race in organizing integration.

The same logic determined the court's opinion in a 1986 case that broadened the standard of conscious intent and applied it to affirmative action. In *Wygant v. Jackson Board of Education,* the majority sharply limited the grounds for affirmative action programs by eliminating de facto societal discrimination or integrating the professions as legitimate rationales for granting racial preferences to underrepresented minorities. Breaking from its Warren-era role as defender of minorities, the court now announced that white people needed protection from government programs that were intended to address racial discrimination against historically disadvantaged groups. Broad sections of the job market continued to be segregated because a conscious intent to discriminate had migrated from a consideration of the Voting Rights Act to the job market. Under George H.W. Bush, the court extended *Wygant*'s notion of liberty to include white peoples' right to be free from racial preference when competing for government contracts.[15] Taken together, these two decisions redefined "strict scrutiny" over the use of racial classifications by government institutions and rewrote its own precedents to protect white people, saying there was no difference in the eyes of the Constitution and the law whether the person injured was white or a person of color.

The myth of colorblindedness had led directly to Supreme Court decisions that eviscerated government programs aiming at redressing the effects of conscious discrimination. The court's new standard made it very difficult to win voting rights and civil rights cases, since proving a conscious intent to discriminate is nearly impossible. The court was also troubled by how difficult it would be to redress earlier patterns of discrimination in voting and employment, arguing that measurement would always be arbitrary, that redress would necessarily be disorderly and chaotic, and that it would be almost impossible to organize a different system fairly. But *Brown* had gone far beyond a mechanical application of some sort of equity principle. Its animating core was that education is a requirement of effective citizenship. *Croson* and *Wygant* struck down government efforts to ensure full participation in economic life. Reagan's dog whistles had done their job. The superficial neutrality of "colorblindedness" put official Washington, including the Supreme Court, in the position of defending the benefits that had flowed to white families from past discrimination and continued to do so in the present. Such a position makes it almost impossible to deal with past and present discrimination. The alternative to accepting the results of a deforming and distorted history is to be as conscious of race in attacking discrimination as its organizers were in establishing it. To insist that we stop taking race into account is to insist that we stop trying to integrate. This is the hidden meaning behind Chief Justice Roberts's "colorblind" formulation in 2007 that "the way to stop discrimination on the basis of race is to stop discriminating on the basis of race."[16] Justice Harry Blackmun, appointed to the court by Richard Nixon, had phrased matters in the exact opposite way when he concurred in the Bakke case. "To get beyond racism, we must first take account of race. And in order to treat some persons equally, we must treat them differently," he wrote.[17] The distance between these two formulations illustrates how much things have changed.

The official position of the Republican Party on matters of race remains true to the principle of "colorblindness" that was developed during Reagan's presidency. That position doesn't deny the possibility of informal, unofficial racism but now defines it as a private matter that lies beyond the government's legitimate reach. It provides the bedrock excuse for nonintervention once the explicit, formal structures of Jim Crow have been eliminated. It has the soothing effect of reassuring white people that they deserve what they have and that political intervention in housing, education, and other areas are unnatural distortions of a system that operates fairly. Under the circumstances, it has been relatively easy to portray programs like affirmative action as hostile to whites, illustrating the old adage that equality can feel like oppression to those who have benefitted from favoritism. A powerful sense of white victimization had been germinating since the Nixon administration and now received official backing from Reagan. His frequent reminders that Martin Luther King hoped that someday people would be judged by the content of their character instead of by the color of their skin was particularly ironic. Now white claims of victimization and resentment could be safely articulated in an era of rightwing populism that functioned behind the façade of racial neutrality. The Reagan administration's central claim was that the end of official racial supremacy meant that group-based approaches could no longer play a privileged role in American jurisprudence. For the most part, civil rights remedies could be applied only to remedy consciously racist actions by individuals. Once the ally of racial progress, Washington now declared that equality before the law had reduced the race question to free markets, personal responsibility, individual decency, and official nonintervention.

The early stages of the crack epidemic are a case in point. As powdered cocaine began flooding into American streets, workplaces, and homes during Reagan's first term, its price dropped dramatically. Understanding that there was a huge market for the drug outside the offices of Wall Street stockbrokers, high-priced lawyers, and glitzy nightclubs, dealers began converting powder to a portable, cheap, purified, smokeable variety that could be sold in smaller quantities at lower prices to a larger clientele. Crack became enormously popular and widely available almost overnight as it generated enormous profits and generated an unlimited demand for more. By 1987, it was available all over the United States and had led to spikes in overdoses, hospital admissions, violent turf wars, homelessness, street crime, burglary, domestic abuse, and almost every imaginable marker of social collapse and disorder. Initially concentrated in the nation's cities, the drug was most devastating to a Black population that was isolated from housing and labor markets by historic patterns of discrimination. As the press generated a nationwide moral panic with endless stories of violence and mayhem, Congress responded in 1986 with laws that established a 100-to-1 disparity when it came to sentencing guidelines for crack as opposed to powdered cocaine. A raft of other laws and policies focused on crack and targeted young Black men for special attention. The era of mass incarceration began as the nation's jails filled up and a new version of Nixon's heralded, and unsuccessful, "War on Drugs" signaled the militarization of the nation's drug policy. Portraying Black Americans as particularly disposed to use and sell crack made it possible to criminalize a particular segment of the population and focus on it as a source of violence, addiction, and danger. The enormous damage inflicted on Black communities was mostly ignored, buried by an implicit assumption that it was all their fault and buttressed by a conviction that middle-class whites had to be protected from contagion. A full-court press of repressive policing, surveillance, and imprisonment sent hundreds of thousands of young Black men to prison with the resultant lost opportunities for housing, voting, and working.[18] While Black communities got the mailed fist of repression, First Lady Nancy Reagan spearheaded a campaign to make sure that people understood that crack was ultimately a moral and individual issue. "Just Say No," she advised.

Disguising social problems as individual pathologies made it possible to hide racial matters behind a pretense of colorblindedness. George Wallace and Richard Nixon had been happy to use both explicit and coded racist appeals to win elections, but both accepted the basic premises of Keynesian economic policy. Reagan carried his dog whistle with him to the White House and crafted a far more restrictive racial policy than either of his predecessors. It served as a useful cudgel to begin attacking the New Deal and Great Society at their core assumptions. Building on the claim that government colorblindedness was the appropriate policy now official racism had ended, his administration appealed to many whites' sense of victimization and seconded their conviction that Black progress had come at their expense. Just as government policy facilitated the concentration of wealth at the top, so government policy facilitated the continuing racial divide.

These two processes began to come together during Reagan's presidency, but the third piece of contemporary Republican politics would come later. When hostility to immigration began to accelerate after Reagan left office, a crucial ingredient was added to the racial animus that had powered the transition of the Republican Party from the responsible junior partner of the ascendant Democrats to the country's dominant political formation. For his part, Reagan demonstrated none of the hostility to immigration that would later characterize his party. In a 1990 speech commemorating the end of the Cold War, he asked

> I wonder yet if you've appreciated how unusual – terribly unusual – this country of ours is? I received a letter just before I left office from a man. I don't know why he chose to write it, but I'm glad he did. He wrote that you can go to live in France, but you can't become a Frenchman. You can go to live in Germany or Italy, but you can't become a German, an Italian. He went through Turkey, Greece, Japan, and other countries. But he said anyone, from any corner of the world, can come to live in the United States and become an American.[19]

Like many other rhetorical devices he used to great effect, Reagan probably never got this particular letter, but it didn't matter. It would soon become impossible for any Republican politician to articulate this classic understanding of civic nationalism. Reagan's view was a comfortable one for the corporate elite to which he was friendly, but it would soon be eclipsed by the suffocating inequality that he had set in motion. When it became the backdrop to accelerating immigration, long-term economic decline, geopolitical challenges, growing secularization, rapid urbanization, and a series of important cultural changes, the sense of victimization that had been germinating for years among millions of white families would explode into a conscious political movement. The process had been developing for years as conservative politicians blamed minorities for demanding too much, and it would prove easy for later political entrepreneurs to broaden that tendency to include immigrants. The Republican Party's ability to cast itself as the defender of besieged white people had been a crucial ingredient in its rise to dominance. There is very little evidence that Ronald Reagan would have looked kindly on the decidedly extreme positions taken by some of his successors, but Hegel was right in his observation that history often operates "behind the back" of its participants. The post-Reagan period would set the stage for the rise of an explicit current that would try to explicitly and formally define the United States as a country of, by, and for white people. Forty years of economic distress and economic concentration, opportunistic Republican race-baiting and defense of white people, and a broad sense of deprivation and threat would give rise to a distinct current of white nationalism soon enough.

Notes

1 Richard Viguerie, *The New Right: We're Ready to Lead* (Viguerie Company, 1981).
2 Melanie McFarland, "'The Reagans' Shows How the Gipper Paved the Way for Political Actors Pretending They Aren't Racist," *Salon*, November 16, 2020.
3 Daniel S. Lucks, *Reconsidering Reagan: Racism, Republicans, and the Road to Trump* (New York: Beacon Press, 2020), pp. 72–73.
4 Rick Perlstein, *Reaganland: America's Right Turn 1976–1980* (New York: Simon & Schuster, 2020), p. 420.
5 Perlstein, *Reaganland*, p. 747. See also Carol Anderson, *White Rage: The Unspoken Truth of Our Racial Divide* (London: Bloomsbury, 2017), p. 119 for a slightly different account.
6 Ben Fountain, *Beautiful Country Burn Again: Democracy, Rebellion, and Revolution* (New York: Ecco, 2018), p. 199. See also Perlstein, *Reaganland*, pp. 828–835.
7 Michael Kazin, *The Populist Persuasion* (Ithaca, NY: Cornell University Press, 1995) is the authoritative account of this evolution.
8 Steve Fraser and Gary Gerstle, eds. *The Rise and Fall of the New Deal Order* (Princeton, NJ: Princeton University Press, 1990).
9 "The Truth Behind the Lies of the Original 'Welfare Queen,'" December 20, 2013, at www.npr.org/transcripts/255819681?storyId=255819681.
10 Ian Haney Lopez, *Dog Whistle Politics: How Coded Racial Appeals Have Reinvented Racism and Wrecked the Middle Class* (New York: Oxford University Press, 2015), p. 58. See also Perlstein, *Reaganland*, p. 724, who refers to a *Chicago Tribune* story mentioning 127 names.
11 Perlstein, *Reaganland*, p, 749.
12 John Ehrenberg, *Servants of Wealth: The Right's Assault on Economic Justice* (Lanham, MD: Rowman & Littlefield, 2006).
13 See Jonathan M. Metzl, *Dying of Whiteness: How the Politics of Racial Resentment is Killing America's Heartland* (New York: Basic Books), 2019.
14 George Lipsitz, *The Possessive Investment in Whiteness: How White People Profit from Identity Politics* (Philadelphia, PA: Temple University Press, 2018), p. 32.
15 See *City of Richmond v. J. A. Croson Company*, 1989.
16 *Parents Involved in Community Schools v. Seattle School Dist. No. 1* at www.law.cornell.edu/supremecourt/text/05-908.
17 Lucks, *Reconsidering Reagan*, p. 138.
18 Michelle Alexander, *The New Jim Crow: Mass Incarceration in the Age of Colorblindedness* (New York: The New Press, 2012).
19 "The Brotherhood of Man," Public Broadcasting System (PBS), November 19, 2000.

4
THE WRECKER AND THE WARRIOR THROW A PARTY

It took some time to organize the Reaganite fiction that an upward redistribution of income and wealth would benefit everyone, but by the end of his presidency, the foundations of a new American plutocracy were in place. The extreme radicalization of conservative politics that followed flowed from the economic distress of a large segment of the country's white population that had come under even more pressure than before and was beginning to face new demographic challenges. For decades, white working- and middle-class men and their families had received substantial material, social, psychological, and political advantages from living in neighborhoods kept white by restrictive covenants, financial redlining, informal agreements, and – when all else failed – organized violence. They had benefited from their participation in labor markets kept white by employers and unions and in similarly segregated white-collar occupations like finance, real estate, higher education, and retail sales. Their children had benefited by attending schools kept white by their reliance on residential segregation and local property taxes. The civil rights movement's challenges to these institutions and practices had been intensifying for years and had elicited determined grassroots resistance. Republican political entrepreneurs and aspirants had been more than willing to take advantage of the opportunity, helping to shape successive conservative administrations and setting the conditions for Newt Gingrich's destructive partisanship, Pat Buchanan's call to culture war, and the Tea Party's bitter nihilism. The Republican Party's transformation into an apparatus of white minority rule was driven by sustained racial conflict, widespread economic changes, and the acceleration of inequality in all areas of American life. Earlier suggestions that Blacks were demanding too much took a far more vicious turn, now suggesting that racial minorities and immigrants were unfit for full membership in the polity and posed a mortal threat to "the American way of life." The intensification of white racial

DOI: 10.4324/9781003182962-5

animus on the Right immediately following the Reagan presidency marked an environment where the stakes were significantly higher than earlier and the tone exponentially angrier and more apocalyptic.

Three important actors help situate the fragmentary attempts to organize permanent minority rule that have now come to characterize much of conservative politics. Gingrich's ferocious partisanship, Buchanan's early presentation of the basis for white nationalism, and the Tea Party's conviction that it was speaking for the white victims of organized persecution presented disconnected versions of the accumulating racial grievance that had been developing since the late Sixties. Donald Trump would combine all the elements and tell a story of racial betrayal that he would take to a national audience in 2016, but the sense of threat and loss had been germinating for decades. Trump didn't have to invent anything. The ground had been prepared by the broad, undeniable shift to the right that had brought Reagan to the presidency and lingered for years after his second term had ended. As the Republicans focused on the "social issues" of abortion, guns, crime, sex, and evolution for electoral purposes, many middle-class white families found that their fears of losing social supremacy were magnified by similar fears about their eroding economic position. Millions of voters were no longer motivated solely by the economic interests that had moved their parents toward the Democratic Party. Once their faith in social liberalism had been broken and they had become afraid of losing their place in society, they were suddenly available to the Republicans. The GOP learned to change in response to this new opportunity. Barry Goldwater had been unable to shake his image of country-club wealth, George Wallace had remained a pariah because of his racial and regional history, and Richard Nixon had suffered from a general perception of nastiness and corruption. But Reagan was different. He provided an amiable and optimistic face to a movement that was no longer limited to a few corporations, some unrepentant white Southerners, and a handful of rich people. In his hands, the progressive economic program of American populism had been replaced by antipathy to regulation, hostility to social engineering, rejection of redistribution, and fierce attachment to the racial status quo. A potent new conservatism took shape as the defender of the beleaguered white middle class.

But Reagan's policies were marked by a deep paradox. Like his predecessors from both parties, he understood that the foundation of Northern working-class prosperity and security rested on a broad "possessive investment in whiteness."[1] What was different about his presidency was his administration's intention to translate a particular set of ideas into a coherent policy that would last. His historic importance lay in his willingness to use a broad feeling of insecurity and dispossession in a concerted campaign to funnel wealth upward and undermine middle- and working-class incomes in the process. His successful campaign to yoke white racial animus and anxiety to the politics of plutocracy would betray his supporters' material interests even as it reinforced their imagined position in American society. It shaped the country's public life for a generation.

Reagan set the stage for every national political actor who succeeded him. As the Democrats abandoned the field and moved away from posing any real alternative strategy, they took up a position as conservatism's junior partners – a reversal of the role the Republicans had played during Keynesianism's earlier hegemony. Since their broad appeals to economic equity and social justice were no longer attractive despite accelerating inequality, the Democrats gradually abandoned much of their earlier commitment to the New Deal. Convinced that the politics of class no longer made electoral sense, they responded to the New Right's success with the "social issues" by preaching more of the same. As the Republicans became more excited and politicized during Reagan's presidency, Democratic leaders convinced themselves that the population was no longer interested in big ideas and that it was time to move past ideology. They had a choice, and they made it. Polling data indicated the electorate liked Reagan the man but disagreed with most of his policies and had little use for his vice president. But Massachusetts governor Michael Dukakis was unwilling to pose a credible alternative to Reaganomics, and he organized his 1988 presidential campaign against George H.W. Bush around claims of "competence" and administrative expertise. Under the circumstances, it proved easy for Lee Atwater to pull Willie Horton out a hat, remind white voters whom they could trust to keep them safe from predatory Black rapists, and help Bush ride whites' visceral fear of violent crime to the White House. The most effective political advertisement in a generation successfully marked Dukakis as a weak-kneed liberal who coddled vicious Black criminals and was unwilling to deal with an existential threat to white people everywhere. Everywhere one looked, the Republicans were preparing for battle and the Democrats were looking for a way out. It wouldn't take long before their propensity to organize against themselves would find a spokesman.

Long before Bush made the "L-word" a curse, the Democrats had decided that it was suicidal to present an alternative to a new age of post-material consumerism and self-indulgence. Coming in the middle of Reagan's success, centrists like Arkansas governor Bill Clinton organized the Democratic Leadership Conference (DLC) in 1985. The new organization took it for granted that expanding the welfare state was neither desirable nor feasible. Its leaders assumed that the white industrial working class was no longer a reliable ally and looked toward the moderate white suburbs instead. This meant talking less about economics, labor, minorities, cities, and big ideas and talking more about family, "values," volunteerism, work, and community. The presumption was that Americans were better educated and more prosperous, less interested in the divisiveness of politics and more self-absorbed, less inclined to support grand schemes of social reorganization and state activity, and more focused on "lifestyle," toleration, personal autonomy, and individual choice. Just when the Republican Party was busily engineering the largest upward transfer of wealth and power in American history, the DLC took the position that the most important questions that people were facing did not originate in economics, had little to do with the distribution of wealth, were no longer of general interest, and could not be addressed with the instruments of an earlier period. As a new plutocracy took shape, the Democrats convinced themselves that broad swaths of the population had developed a material stake in the status quo. Those who hadn't were no longer of interest.

The "new Democrats" suggested that the party's historic commitment to a measure of economic equality had become politically dangerous. It might have made sense during an earlier "Fordist" period of mass industrial production and the organization of a large, concentrated working class, but those days were gone forever. A post-industrial economy now meant that questions of economic redistribution were obsolete. Spokespeople for the "third way" insisted that an economically secure, socially tolerant, morally upstanding suburban white middle class was the party's future. The resources that made it possible to pursue the "American dream" of happiness, security, respect, and self-actualization were now a set of "post-material" values that would make it possible for the nice Democrats to compete in the suburbs against the mean Republicans. At a time when the Right was using state power to engineer the largest upward transfer of wealth in the country's history, the Democrats were retreating to a moralizing pseudo-sociology of personal fulfillment and benign neighborliness. Convinced that their future lay in their embrace of an apolitical and safe appeal to moderate white suburban voters, they went out of their way to avoid controversy. The approach worked, for the moment at least. Bill Clinton, arguably his party's most successful politician in a generation, was able to defeat George H.W. Bush's bid for reelection by moving away from core Democratic constituencies and seconding Republican insistence that neighborhood, tolerance, and volunteering could replace grand plans for economic redistribution. His renunciation of the state's role in social reform was the mirror image of Reagan's claim that the civil rights movement had come to an end, its work completed with the passing of government-sanctioned racial discrimination. "A thousand points of light" would replace comprehensive political programs for social welfare. Voluntary organizations, self-help initiatives, and the local focus of "civil society" would take over many of the functions that an earlier period had reserved for state agencies.[2]

Just as an earlier period had been dominated by the Keynesian New Deal Democrats, so the years after 1980 were dominated by the GOP. The politics of plutocracy served as both parties' center of gravity during a period in which only Bill Clinton was not a Republican. He spearheaded the formation of a "new Democratic" friendliness to markets, weakening of its former alliance with organized labor, openness to deregulation, commitment to low taxes, and its foundational claim that "the era of big government is over." A new coalition of minorities, feminists, and younger, college-educated whites meant that the regulatory, interventionist, and redistributionist impulses of an earlier period were shelved. Claiming to be the "party of FDR" would serve the same nostalgic, empty function for the Democrats as similar claims about being the "party of Lincoln" had been doing for the Republicans. Clinton led the Democrats into the promised land of a "post-material" future, one in which vulgar matters like wages and working conditions yielded to equity, tolerance, and acceptance. The market now replaced representative government as the arbiter of policy, organizer of distribution, and guarantor of the public good. A "neoliberal consensus" committed both parties to a reduced safety net, lower taxes, less regulation, smaller government, and a new friendliness to banks, corporations, markets, and monopolies.

In 1998, Toni Morrison said that Clinton "displays almost every trope of blackness: single-parent household, born poor, working-class, saxophone-playing, McDonald's-and-junk-food loving boy from Arkansas."[3] It's certainly true that Clinton was notably friendlier to Black organizations than his Republican predecessors. But he wasn't above using dog whistles to signal his political independence. His attacks on Sister Souljah, his gratuitous insults directed at Jesse Jackson, his ostentatious role in executing Rickey Ray Rector, and his "law and order" speech at Georgia's Stone Mountain monument to the Confederacy would have been unthinkable for a Democratic candidate in an earlier period. Now it was as uncontroversial as his campaign pledge to put 100,000 more police on the streets of the country's cities, remove welfare as a campaign issue by gutting it, and begin a ruinous policy of mass incarceration. Even though he and Bush generally avoided the sort of dog whistles that characterized earlier contests and he was known to be a relative racial liberal, Clinton was guided by the view that the Democratic Party had to move away from its identification with Black demands. He knew that the Republicans had prospered with wedge issues like crime, welfare, and taxes and was determined to avoid the traps that had ensnared earlier Democratic presidential candidates. His efforts to keep working-class whites loyal led him to emphasize that "it's the economy, stupid" and avoid the difficult "social issues" that had proved so dangerous for earlier Democratic candidates.

Always vulnerable to Republican charges that they were "soft on crime," Democrats had followed the GOP and embraced a punitive approach to intractable big-city violence. Clinton's vow to increase federal support for policing reflected his strategy of "triangulation" – adopting a pale version of Republican policies so he could neuter them as political weapons. In a similar vein, his campaign promise to "end welfare as we know it" was precipitated by a desire to remove an issue that Republicans had used to great effect. The same was true of his response to the crack epidemic, which led to a sharp increase in violent urban crime across the country as rival organizations sought to profit from the vast market for illicit drugs. Just as criminal groupings had organized the market for illicit alcohol during Prohibition, so the evening news featured endless stories of violence and mayhem from the middle of Reagan's presidency to the middle of Clinton's. Mass incarceration and increasingly repressive policing tactics failed to halt the chaos. Howard Cosell, the famed sportscaster, had informed the country that "the Bronx is burning" during the 1976 World Series. As the Goodyear blimp broadcast images of entire neighborhoods going up in flames, the Bronx became an international symbol of urban devastation. Violent drug dealing, rampant arson, hopeless young people, and countless indices of social disorder carried images of danger and devastation to millions of American homes. The nation's poorest county became the poster child for the failure of urban liberalism.[4]

More was involved than scenes of social collapse from the country's inner cities. The trick was to keep the chaos away from peaceful white neighborhoods, neat American suburbs, and bucolic small towns. Endless reminders that the nation's great cities were being strangled by an "urban crisis" was a useful way of reassuring millions of Americans that the federal government stood ready to protect them from the contagion. Just as the Central Park Five had been a warning of the dangers posed by violent Black and brown young men, so the South Bronx was a useful reminder that it was better to be safe than sorry. Safety required more policing, mass incarceration, physical isolation, and moral condemnation for a society that no longer had answers beyond programs that were politically unpopular and socially ineffective.

Drug addiction, street crime, broken families, rampant unemployment, and growing homelessness came to indicate the utter collapse of Black neighborhoods and institutions. As long as they could be physically restricted to minority populations, the moral contagion and physical danger they represented could be kept away from the larger society. But matters weren't so simple. As social disorder threatened to spill out of minority neighborhoods and engulf white areas, a dramatic escalation of moral panic served notice that white Americans demanded protection. Washington stood ready to help.

Most of the harsh and punitive legislation that was adopted by both parties during the 1990s was justified by the myth of the "superpredator," an updated version of the "wilding" epithet that had accompanied the persecution of the Central Park Five. John J. Dilulio Jr., then a conservative political scientist at Princeton, coined the term in 1995 to explain why a small percentage of minority boys and young men accounted for a large percentage of serious offenses. Using an amplified "culture of poverty" explanation that had proved to be so popular on the right, he blamed soaring rates of violent crime on the absence of fathers and other measures of domestic failure. Family breakdown explained why young Black men could not distinguish right from wrong and duty from pleasure. With no internal moral checks on their behavior, it was no wonder that they were attracted to easy money, quick revenge, mindless violence, and empty hedonism. Although he has come to regret his role in the tragedy that unfolded, Diliulio popularized a notion that would inflict enormous harm on the nation's Black and brown youth even as it assured anxious whites that condemnation, isolation, and repression would limit the damage. Claiming that a coming wave of 30,000 young "murderers, rapists, and muggers" would be roaming the country's streets by the year 2000, he warned that "superpredators" would terrorize peaceful citizens and pose an existential threat to public order. It never happened. Indeed, by the time his incendiary essay was published, crime rates were already beginning to fall. Two reporters observed that "by 2000, when tens of thousands more children were supposed to be out there mugging and killing, juvenile murder arrests had fallen by two-thirds."[5]

Despite its inaccuracy, the phrase caught on because it served a useful polemical purpose. Yesterday's wilders were today's superpredators, but the different terminology described the same dystopian fantasy. The notion that hordes of savage, lawless minority youth would be spilling out of their ghettos to wreak havoc and revenge on civilized white neighborhoods was an amped-up version of the Central Park Five story that had propelled Donald Trump to a measure of notoriety. The picture of criminal minority teens served to remind upstanding white Americans that the urban crisis was a moral one first and foremost. Scholars and pundits agreed that dozens of years and billions of dollars had not solved the problem because pathology had become endemic to urban Black "culture." The time had come to stop coddling populations whose behavior would not improve. Inner-city America was so dysfunctional that there was little hope that its inhabitants could become productive, contributing members of society. They had become permanent problems instead. The "superpredator" described a slice of the population that had become an active menace to those around them. The reminder was driven home by newspaper columnists, talk-show hosts, political candidates, local newscasters, and millions of law-abiding families seated around the dinner table. Presidential candidate Bob Dole used the term during his 1996 campaign as he tried to tar his opponent with the "soft on crime" label. Not to be outdone, First Lady Hillary Clinton demonstrated her triangulation skills by showing that she could be just as harsh as any Republican. By the end of the century, the phrase had fallen out of favor because the phenomenon it purported to describe was so demonstrably false. Nevertheless, it had been enormously useful in sowing the seeds of the moral panic that would contribute so importantly to the self-serving picture of a white America under siege.

It was one thing to talk about the threat that conscienceless young Blacks posed to the wider society of law-abiding, tax-paying citizens. It was quite another to describe the threat they posed to children. The enormous spike in violence that accompanied the crack epidemic devastated inner-city neighborhoods, upended social relationships, and destroyed local organizations in cities across the country. More policing and mass incarceration failed to halt the mayhem. As long as it was possible to pretend that it was only urban youth who were affected, the larger society could intensify the repression and insist on isolating the sources of danger. But it was not enough. By the middle of Clinton's presidency, a wildly popular and influential music genre had spread out from the South Bronx and begun to penetrate white neighborhoods everywhere.

Hip-hop had begun to take root as early as the 1970s. As it broadened its appeal, developed a mass following, and displaced other forms of popular music, its development paralleled that of the neighborhoods from which it drew strength. Just as the Vietnam War had transformed rock 'n roll a generation earlier, the crack epidemic introduced elements into hip-hop that had been absent from the music's early phases. The tone grew more bitter as rappers began routinely referring to women with contempt, glorified violence, proclaimed consumerism as the highest virtue, and preached a mindless hedonism that swamped the earlier, more innocent messages of brotherhood and young love. Gun battles between rival drug crews, turf disputes that ended hundreds of young lives, local dealers living ostentatious lives of vulgar consumption and routinized misogyny, death from overdose, and swamped hospital emergency rooms testified to the speed with which crack overwhelmed local communities and devastated countless families. All of this was registered by hip-hop, which one rapper described as the "CNN of the streets." Young Black men adorned with tattoos and "bling," accompanied by menacing bodyguards in sunglasses, driving fancy BMWs, and swaggering into nightclubs personified the nihilism and desperation of urban America. Even more than during the tumultuous Sixties, inner-city Black neighborhoods became associated with a moral contagion and physical danger that could bring down the entire society if it weren't quarantined and contained.

Then the music and its associated affectations began to spread out of the cities into the white suburbs and small towns. Young people everywhere started sampling it, imitating the dress and manners of their favorite rappers, organizing mass dance parties, and legitimizing "gangsta rap," a much more pointed music filled with rage and defiance that provided a firsthand window into the country's devastated neighborhoods even as it became increasingly associated with white kids from the suburbs. The ironies of the situation were not lost on astute observers. "The Wire," HBO's pathbreaking series about American social collapse set in Baltimore, features an iconic scene between Herc, a white cop surveilling a Black drug crew, and Carver, one of the kids he's watching. "Hey, yo" Herc calls out as Carver saunters past his car.

> Lemme ask you a question. Where do you guys get those hats with the bills over the ears like that? I go into all the shitty stores, and the only ones I can find are the ones with the bills in the front.

Carver's ready to help. "Yeah, that's the one," he says. "Just turn it sideways on the head."

Herc is an ignorant oaf, but he represented millions of young whites who found hip-hop, rap, and almost all forms of inner-city music enormously attractive. Gone were the days when it was only music. A popular observation suggested that if you wanted to know what suburban white kids would be wearing in two years, all you had to do was look at what inner-city Black kids were wearing now. The War on Drugs had been lost for years, and the popularity of a culture transformed by crack soon became an international phenomenon as hip-hop became the favorite music of young people from Johannesburg to Stockholm and Taipei to Casablanca.

Teenagers always have to deal with parents who don't understand their lives. Just as white family members were left dumbstruck when Elvis Presley and Fats

Domino began to supplant Frank Sinatra, Perry Como, Lawrence Welk, and Guy Lombardo, so contemporary parents were left aghast when their kids started imitating inner-city gangsters. But historic parallels tell only so much. The early years of rock 'n roll featured sweet, innocent music of young love and teenage angst. Even as Black music had broken through to white audiences for the first time since the advent of jazz, it was subversive of outmoded racial mores that were being undermined across the entire society. Hip-hop and gangsta rap were different because they seemed to be so much more pointedly destructive. Their nihilistic hedonism, glorification of violence, mindless consumerism – and, importantly, their protest of police misconduct, social isolation, and racial discrimination – were married to a level of alienation that seemed much more threatening than anything associated with rock 'n roll. Frankie Lyman's whining question about why teenagers fall in love was a pale, innocent precursor of NWA's *Straight Outta Compton*. It was all too much to ignore. Both parties announced their readiness to defend white America. As Republican presidents Reagan and Bush repeatedly invoked "family values" to provide cover for plutocracy, so Tipper Gore proposed to censor rap lyrics. Denunciations of superpredators came from both sides of the aisle. So did attacks on the populations whose rapping was increasingly unacceptable.

Rudy Giuliani came to be the white face of the mailed fist. As he mounted a racially tinged campaign against David Dinkins, New York's first Black mayor, the man who had made his reputation going against mafia bosses repositioned himself as a tough-guy enforcer and disciplinarian. His political base was white civil servants, police officers, firemen, and employees of the Sanitation Department who were living in the shrinking white enclaves of the outer boroughs. Ceaseless attacks on Dinkins for being weak and cowardly in the face of provocation and crime allowed Giuliani to pose as the defender of social order against Black criminals and extortionists. His family had taken him out of Brooklyn when he was young and he grew up in a leafy suburb, but he was always able to pose as the street-smart mayor who would get tough on crime, clean up Times Square, and tame an unruly metropolis. He repeatedly insisted that New York had to become just like any other city by pushing a "broken windows" approach to policing that appealed to distressed whites and stood in sharp contrast to Clinton's pandering to traditional Democratic "special interests."

President Clinton had his work cut out for him. As he began to move the Democratic Party away from the New Deal and recast liberalism as toleration and lifestyle in a post-industrial society that had moved past issues of economic distribution, he ran straight into a newly invigorated Right. As soon as he was elected to the House of Representatives, Newt Gingrich had become convinced that intensifying the level of partisan acrimony was key to what would become the successful Republican effort to seize majority control of the House of Representatives for the first time in 42 years. When he engineered the 1994 Republican takeover of the chamber, Gingrich initiated a struggle with Clinton that would define American politics for most of the 1990s. It would establish a tradition of Republican polarization that, when added to Buchanan's culture war and the Tea Party's grievances, would set the conditions for the GOP's turn toward white nationalism and Donald Trump.

Elected in 1979 from what had been a reliably Democratic district, Gingrich was an early beneficiary of the broad shift to the right that would bring Ronald Reagan to the White House. As a loyal Republican backbencher, he quickly grew tired of the prevalent view that his party was destined to be a permanent minority grouping. The House had been run by a Democratic majority with two brief interruptions since 1933, but Gingrich knew that an historic opportunity had presented itself. He also knew that it would require a makeover of the congressional Republican Party to take advantage of it.

Ever since Goldwater, the GOP had carried with it the image of a staid, polite, suburban, country-club apparatus of business-friendly legislators who were content to respect the existing rules of political combat and reach out to the Democrats when it served the interests of conservative policy. Gingrich knew that the old way of doing things would no longer work if the Republicans were to upend the Washington status quo and cement a permanent right-wing governing coalition in place. Armed with reams of data and relentlessly badgering his colleagues, he tirelessly worked to transform the House Republicans into a fighting organization animated by a hyper-partisan approach to political combat and permanent polarization. The radicalization of the Republicans' approach to political warfare was his major contribution to what became the GOP's turn toward white nationalism. Seen in retrospect, it was all the more striking because he had begun his career as a relative racial moderate.

Situating himself as a Rockefeller Republican, Gingrich was convinced that the GOP had to reach out to Black voters if it were to play a role in national affairs. After moving to Georgia in 1970 to teach history at West Georgia College, he began preparing for a career in elective office and established an identity as a conventional anti-tax, small-government, pro-business Republican. His stance was in marked contrast to the overt racism of the area's Jim Crow Democrats, and Gingrich combined a relatively progressive position on racial issues with an early commitment to environmental protection. But he was also a foreign-policy hawk, opposed any move toward national health insurance, fought against the Humphrey–Hawkins full employment bill, supported Georgia's "right to work" legislation, and thought that abortion should be left to the states. By the time of his successful third run for Congress in 1978, he had embraced supply-side economics, thought the regulatory state was stifling growth and innovation, opposed the Equal Rights Amendment, and made welfare "reform" a central element of his appeal. His main calling card, though, was a campaign against corruption – a position that he would take to a national audience and provide him with a path to individual power and his party with a path toward institutional majority status. He took his seat in the House just two years before Reagan's first inaugural and immediately started agitating for the endless partisan warfare that would characterize his career as he began to create a durable conservative majority in the House.

Gingrich's role in paving the way for Trump does not lie in his explicit use of racism for political advantage. It consists in his permanent campaign against real and perceived enemies in which he cast himself and the Republican Party as holy warriors dedicated to saving American politics from entrenched corruption that had become so pervasive that the majority Democrats had become handmaidens of institutionalized evil. The only way to rid the body politic of the rot was to end the Democrats' long reign as the House majority. An environment of permanent campaign and righteous crusade became Gingrich's calling card and went a long way to transforming the Republican Party into a militant organization single-mindedly focused on defeating its enemies. From the Contract with America to the rise of the Tea Party, he presided over an era of division and combat. Gingrich's single-minded ruthlessness was never a strategy for governing. It was always a path to power, nothing more.

Or less. It was his instinct for endless partisan warfare that would set Gingrich apart from his Republican colleagues in the House. Driven apart by issues of race and civil rights, the Democrats and Republicans were beginning the sorting process that Gingrich worked tirelessly to accelerate. Conservative Democrats and liberal Republicans had become much fewer in number, and the chances for cooperation across boundaries of party and ideology were narrowing as well. It was Gingrich who understood what was happening, retailing the tactics that capitalized on the same widespread distrust of Washington that had brought Reagan to the White House. And it was his skill at mobilizing a media-driven campaign of confrontation that played an important part in moving national politics to the right and seizing power from the Democrats. Politics was warfare, and Gingrich proved to be an expert general. The cause was never this or that piece of legislation or policy initiative. It was the conquest of power first and foremost, and then its retention. Alliances of convenience, hyperbolic claims to the media, coddling of racial backlash, intimations of nativism, and reactionary populism – all were on the table as Gingrich transformed the Republican Party into a wrecking machine that he turned loose on the very government that had facilitated his prominence. The key to his strategy was to paralyze Congress's ability to legislate, then use the resulting gridlock to ask voters to throw the do-nothing Democrats out of Washington. Militarizing the Republicans' traditional antistatism would have serious and long-term consequences.

The GOP had developed a set of policy issues that provided a veneer of unity between different party factions. Reaganite supply-side tax cuts, deregulation, balanced budgets, higher military spending, cuts in welfare, and opposition to the Equal Rights Amendment had become central Republican campaign positions. They were never particularly important to Gingrich, though. Generally uninterested in policy matters, he was convinced that permanent conflict could create the conditions for party unity and a durable Republican House majority. This required conquering the institutional levers of power. And that required tarnishing the Democrats as the party of Washington corruption, self-interest, and dysfunction. His long, tenacious campaign to unseat House Speaker Jim Wright allowed him to define the Democrats as "the establishment" at a moment of widespread popular disenchantment with Washington – and particularly with Congress. Under the circumstances, the Republicans didn't have to try to do much legislating. All they had to do was undermine the public standing of the Democratic majority. Gingrich found that there was a lot to work with.

Even after the Watergate reforms had promised to clean up the way Washington conducted itself, the old system was pretty much intact. The campaign-finance system was left standing, the revolving door between lobbyists and legislators continued to turn, private money still sloshed around congressional offices, and pork-barrel spending was alive and well. Since the Democrats were in the majority after their win in the off-year election of 1982, they were particularly vulnerable to charges of institutional corruption. Gingrich didn't let up for a second. His campaign against Jim Wright stirred up a deep well of nihilistic rage on the right that would come to a head with the Tea Party rebellion. He had important allies. Antiestablishment Republicans, eager to tear down the status quo no matter what the cost, were prepared to turn their party into a monolithic enemy of legislative liberalism. Gingrich offered them a link to movement right-wingers outside Congress and to an increasingly agitated right-wing media presence that saturated the airwaves with tales of malfeasance and corruption. This is the moment the Republican Party became a wrecking crew, intent on delegitimizing the very government of which they were a part, paralyzing the federal government's ability to do much of anything, and then making Washington the synonym of dysfunctional villainy as part of a long-range plan to take it over. Attacking the Democrats, traditionally the party of government, was the agency through which this process unfolded. As Gingrich's Republican allies relentlessly hounded Wright for transgressions that were not particularly serious and certainly not particularly rare, it became clear that the purification that Gingrich was demanding of Democrats was entirely one-sided. Indeed, the debate about corruption was never about the conditions of good government. And even as Wright resigned before the House could take action on the charges against him, Gingrich had proven that partisan campaigns worked and could carry the day against the needs of governance. Even his "Contract with America," touted as the positive face of the incessantly combative Republican strategy of demolition, proved to be more a campaign document than a serious plan for legislating.

Following Gingrich's lead, Republicans systematically sabotaged any legislative initiatives in Congress and turned the 1994 midterm election into a national referendum on the suitability of the Democrats to hold power. When the GOP achieved an historic victory by picking up 54 seats in the House and becoming the majority party in both houses for the first time in 40 years, it proved that Gingrich's strategy of creating gridlock and paralysis could work. Gingrich himself became Speaker in 1995, five years after driving Wright from Washington. The Republicans immediately launched a protracted war against President Clinton, imposing a shutdown of the federal government in a manufactured budget dispute with the White House, launching investigation after investigation, impeaching the president for transgressions that never resonated in the population, and doing everything they could to attack the Democrats and paralyze the entire administration. Instability and gridlock became the rule as permanent partisan warfare became normalized and a nihilistic search for power became the modus operandi. The chickens eventually came home to roost, but that didn't stop the headlong rush to dysfunction. Even after he had been reprimanded by his colleagues in 1997 for his own financial improprieties, Gingrich remained Speaker until he resigned altogether from the House in January 1999. He left behind a poisoned, bitter, and long-lasting legacy. The hyperpartisanship and permanent conflict that he organized accounted for a good deal of the institutional paralysis and dysfunction that has elicited broad popular contempt. The legislative process broke down amid the Republicans' insatiable appetite for combat, attack, and scandal. Gingrich's conviction that anything is permissible in the pursuit of power really began the process that has cemented the Republican Party's unique standing among most of the world's conservative political formations. Two of the most insightful and nonpartisan observers of contemporary American politics write that "The GOP has become an insurgent outlier – ideologically extreme; contemptuous of the inherited social and economic policy regime; scornful of compromise; unpersuaded by conventional understanding of fact, evidence, and science; and dismissive of the legitimacy of its political opposition."[6] It was Gingrich who greased the skids for its obstructionism and partisanship by showing that they could work.

If Gingrich was the post-Reagan arsonist and wrecker, Pat Buchanan was the period's leading culture warrior. A special assistant to Republican presidents Nixon, Ford, and Reagan, he was a consummate Washington insider in everything but his ideological extremism. But it wouldn't be long before his marginalized positions would migrate to the center of the Republican Party. Labeled a "paleoconservative" for lack of a better term, Buchanan combined American nationalism, Catholic ethics, nativistic anti-imperialism, and cultural traditionalism in a mixture that anticipated many of the themes that would animate Donald Trump's campaign and administration. His role was to develop themes of emergency, siege, and crisis that would resonate with broad swaths of the GOP's beleaguered white base, solidify his position at the center of conservative politics during the 1990s, and legitimize some of the visceral hostility to immigration that would appeal to millions of Republican voters. His ability to articulate a broad discontent with Clinton on the Republican right would accelerate the period's "culture wars" and give shape to the deep sense of vulnerability and loss that would come together in the Tea Party and pave the way for Trump's embrace of white nationalism.

The Democrats had been moving away from the broad politics of redistribution and regulation for years before the Clinton administration. Its willingness to adopt the "third way" was predicated on the claim that capitalism was working for the majority of the population and that the Democrats' core constituency was no longer an industrial working class that was economically liberal and culturally conservative. Rather, the party's new focus was on a suburban "middle class" in a situation where economic scarcity was no longer a driving issue and voters could be mobilized around themes of inclusion and fairness. A "post-material" Democratic Party had to embrace tolerance of different lifestyles, consumption, and good behavior. But Clinton's confidence was misplaced. The claim that old cultural taboos were obsolete was deeply offensive to many social conservatives and as inequality began to accelerate, a populist right began talking about cultural threat and the power of elites, a new front in the marginalization of "the people." The trifecta of "guns, God, and gays" became the slogan driving the Republican Party's call to culture war.

This was Buchanan's moment. His 1992 campaign against George H.W. Bush's drive for renomination seemed quixotic at first, but he wanted to establish a firm position on the Republican right and articulate a platform of immigration reduction, social conservatism, semi-isolationism, and American nationalism. These positions stood in direct opposition to the acceptance of immigration and relative social moderation that had characterized establishment Republican Party politics from Nixon to Reagan. When he won 38 percent of the New Hampshire primary and collected three million primary votes across the country, Buchanan served notice that a substantial minority of the Republican electorate was ready to embrace a crusade that would pivot on issues of "culture" and focus on the threat from immigration and social liberalism. The famous speech he delivered at the 1992 Republican National Convention announced his belated support of the Bush ticket and called on the party to wage a war for the "soul of America." There is a "religious war going on in our country," he announced as he called out the troops to defend civilization from the new infidels.

> The agenda Clinton & Clinton would impose on America – abortion on demand, a litmus test for the Supreme Court, homosexual rights, discrimination against religious schools, women in combat units – that's change, all right. But it is not the kind of change America needs. It is not the kind of change America wants. And it is not the kind of change we can abide in a nation we still call God's country.[7]

Buchanan's announcement that public morality was now a defining political issue cut to the heart of his claim that a clear definition of right and wrong was essential to the nation's moral health and political viability. His position was widely derided by pundits and editorial writers when the speech was delivered, but it appealed to a substantial group of culturally conservative Republican voters. As the Christian Right began to congeal and exert an outsized influence on conservative politics, it began to rely on many of Buchanan's arguments about cultural "extinction" and would adopt his hostility to immigration to forge a key link to many of the grassroots activists who would later organize the Tea Party. The anti-immigration trumpet he would wield and the semi-isolationism he would articulate were relatively new positions for Republicans, who had embraced immigration for years as part of their drive to weaken unions and keep wages low and who had embraced international trade and treaty arrangements as central to the rules-based international order that they believed would work in the country's interests.

Buchanan pioneered the break with this establishment Republican consensus by announcing that "the crisis of Western civilization consists of three invasions and mortal perils: dying populations, disintegrating cultures, and invasions unresisted."[8] A series of books and speeches appeared after his presidential campaign, complete with endless warnings about terminal crisis and "the death of the West." His hyperbolic warning about a "state of emergency" focused on immigration from Mexico, presumed to be a conquering horde more loyal to their homeland than to the United States. This moment, he announced, is different from earlier tides of migrants from Europe.

> This is not immigration as America knew it, when men and women made a conscious choice to turn their backs on their native lands and cross the ocean to become Americans. This is an invasion, the greatest invasion in history. Nothing of this magnitude has ever happened in so short a span of time.[9]

And the stakes are enormous, reaching to the very survival of the country and the survival of civilization itself:

> Against the will of a vast majority of Americans, America is being transformed. As our elites nervously turn their gaze or welcome the invasion, we are witness to one of the great tragedies in human history. From Gibbon and Spengler to Toynbee and the Durants, the symptoms of a dying civilization are well known: the death of faith, the degeneration of morals, contempt for the old values, collapse of the culture, paralysis of the will. But the two certain signs that a civilization has begun to die are a declining population and foreign invasions no longer resisted.[10]

Much of Buchanan's language of invasion, subversion, and cowardice was borrowed from earlier racist and nativist political figures. And lest there be any doubt about what was at stake, he spelled it out. "America faces an existential crisis," he announced. "If we do not get control of our borders, by 2050 Americans of European descent will be a minority in the nation their ancestors created and built. No nation has ever undergone so radical a demographic transformation and survived."[11] Terrorists, criminals, drug dealers, kidnappers, and rapists – the migrants coming to the United States were demonstrably different, and much more dangerous, than earlier waves of European immigrants who had "created and built" the country. Unlike the earlier Irish, Italian, and Jewish immigrants of earlier periods, contemporary Black and brown immigrants cannot be assimilated. Part of the reason is that they don't want to be, and part of the reason is that their home governments are happy to use them as fifth columns to accomplish long-stated national goals. Millions of immigrants now owe their allegiance to their countries of origin rather than of adoption, and the danger is intensified because American immigration policy no longer even attempt to civilize them and turn them into Americans. Anticipating Trump's incendiary claims about immigrants 20 years later, Buchanan charged that they bring "an assembly line of diseases" and impose the costs of combating them on American taxpayers. Cholera, diphtheria, malaria, polio, bedbugs, hepatitis, syphilis, measles, gonorrhea, tuberculosis – all are brought in by illegal immigrants, who are actively undermining public health when they're not contributing to crime and overwhelming the nation's schools, pushing native-born workers out of jobs, dragging wages down, intensifying poverty, and turning the country's great cities into crime-infested slums.

Buchanan was clear about where the threat came from. The root of the problem lies with the threat posed by immigrants from Mexico, the Caribbean, and Central America. The danger they present is an existential one, made all the worse by the Democrats' current infatuation with toleration, acceptance, and multiculturalism. The United States is on the road to becoming a multilingual, multiethnic, multicultural conglomeration split into warring ethnic tribes who coexist uneasily without a clear national identity to hold them together. Because the new immigrants are so resistant to assimilation, they insist on retaining precisely the habits and lifestyles that place them in direct opposition to the success stories of earlier immigrants. Things will get worse as they demand that the larger society protect them from the consequences of their own behavior. The country will be overrun by uneducated, dependent, uninsured, idle, poverty-stricken migrant populations who consume far more in public services than native-born whites and who already constitute an insupportable burden on public welfare and personal safety. It is imperative to "halt the invasion now" in a country where white Europeans are fast becoming a minority, he announced.[12] Earlier periods of economic abundance might have made it possible to integrate immigrants into the general white population without paying too high a price, but that was no longer the case.

Buchanan was the first important Republican figure in recent years to start warning about the demographic bomb that was threatening to blow up American politics. He was far more prescient than most observers thought, and he became something of a godfather to the more explicit white nationalism that has migrated to the center of the Republican Party. For years, he has been warning that the unraveling of what used to be a unified and coherent civilization is accelerating. He hasn't exactly been a voice crying in the wilderness. George W. Bush and his chief advisor Karl Rove knew that the Republicans faced a demographic problem and had decided to address it by going after the Latino vote. Bush spoke a bit of Spanish, tried to appeal to the social conservatism of Texan Latinos when he ran for governor, and won 44 percent of the Latino vote in his reelection campaign of 2004. Even so, the initiative proved to be of limited use for a GOP that remained the party of limited government and a reduced safety net. Buchanan thought this was a political dead-end and he has been insisting that the party had to change its basic orientation if it were to survive. Only the Republicans, he has endlessly repeated, can make a credible case against massive immigration, since the Democrats were increasingly dependent on minority votes. Directing his considerable polemical skill against Bush and then the Republican leadership, he has been arguing for a policy that would prioritize border security and punish companies that prospered by hiring undocumented workers. But he thought that the GOP was paralyzed by fear, cowardice, political correctness, and election-year opportunism. Beholden to the industries that profited from low-wage immigrant labor, it was incapable of pivoting to the "America First" strategy that Trump would enthusiastically develop. Buchanan's repeated calls for a change in the Republican Party's embrace of globalization was mirrored by his claim that it had to reorient itself around tradition, culture, patriotism, soil, and sovereignty. He insistently called for a new Republican Party, populist in form and nativist in content. A radical break with its recent past was an indispensable first step.

> Corporate America and its K Street arm, on which the GOP depends to keep the party machinery greased and its candidates flush with cash, demands a constant resupply of cheap labor to hold wages down. For the corporate elite, immigration means low-wage workers to replace high-wage Americans, while taxpayers assume the social costs – welfare, Medicaid, rent supplements, food stamps, clinics, cops, courts, prisons, and legal services for the immigrants. The Business Roundtable believes in socializing costs, while privatizing profits. To Corporate America, mass immigration is the gift that keeps on giving.[13]

Paranoid warnings about an "Aztlan Strategy," a nefarious plot to recover the lands lost during the Mexican War, sharpened Buchanan's focus on globalization's threats to national boundaries and popular traditions. The "Hispanicization" of the American Southwest is the logical consequence of unrestricted immigration and poses a direct danger to national sovereignty and identity. Large parts of the country are populated by a fifth column. "Stated bluntly," Buchanan warns, "the Atzlan Strategy entails the end of the United States as a sovereign, self-sufficient, independent republic, the passing away of the American nation. They are coming to conquer us."[14]

The "they" for the moment were the dark-skinned, Spanish-speaking migrants from the South. But Buchanan's nativistic warnings imply that something far more sinister is at work, and he was not shy about trotting out a grand theory to explain the importance of the debate. At the end of the day, he warned, nations are constituted by ethnicity, blood, soil, memory, race, and tribalism. "Creedal" foundations and abstract ideas about membership, constitutions, citizenship, and rights are not strong enough to organize a viable polity. Americans had become a "people" long before the Declaration of Independence, the Revolutionary War, or the Constitution. Their history demonstrates that the cement that binds a people together is not provided by ideas but by "language, customs, and habits."[15] There's a more general rule at work here: nations are formed by history, race, culture, tradition, language, faith, ethnicity, and attachment. A commitment to justice and democracy is not a sufficient glue to hold together a civilization as dynamic and restless as the American. Samuel Johnson was wrong. Patriotism is not the "last resort of scoundrels." It's the foundation that organizes attachments and membership in a national community. This is why it is naïve to expect immigrants from the South to become Americans, he claimed. First of all, they don't want to. Second of all, they can't.

This rejection of civic nationalism and early flirtation with white nationalism led Buchanan to the general conclusion that "Language, faith, culture, and history – and, yes, birth, blood, and soil – produce a people, not an ideology."[16] He thought he had discerned the logic of contemporary history, since states founded on cosmopolitan notions of civic nationalism were dying from Yugoslavia to Africa and the Soviet Union. Polyglot, cosmopolitan states were starting to look more like Towers of Babel than durable political frameworks for human civilization. Everywhere one looked, they were splintering along fault lines of blood, culture, religion, and race. Old unities were being pulled apart, and the United States was no exception. Particularism and division were becoming the fundamental rules of the international order. The world was changing fast, and the stakes were very high:

> The crisis of the West is of a collapsing culture and vanishing peoples, as a Third World that grows by 100 million people – the equivalent of a new Mexico – every eighteen months mounts the greatest invasion in the history of the world. If we do not shake off our paralysis, the West comes to an end.
>
> By 2050, a depopulated Europe will have been overrun by African and Arab peoples and resemble the Bosnia and Beirut of today more than the Europe of Churchill and de Gaulle. By 2050, America will have become a multiracial, multiethnic, multilingual, multicultural conglomerate – a Balkanized Brazil of 420 million, a Tower of Babel, a replica of the Roman Empire after the Goths and Vandals had passed over.[17]

The immediate future, Buchanan warned, is one of division and disintegration, powered by endless immigration and the breakdown of internal control.

A conglomeration of people with almost nothing in common is taking shape, aided by a feckless establishment hobbled by a counterculture that mindlessly celebrates "diversity" and refuses to enforce the elementary rules of civilized life. Echoing earlier attacks on Blacks, Buchanan warned that threats to national identity and social peace were creating an intolerable situation. "Millions have begun to feel like strangers in their own land," he warned.[18] Their sense of dispossession is raw and visceral.

> The chasm in our country is not one of income, ideology, or faith, but of ethnicity and loyalty. Suddenly, we awoke to the realization that among our millions of foreign-born, a third here illegally, tens of thousands are loyal to regimes with which we could be at war, and some are trained terrorists sent here to murder Americans. For the first time since Andrew Jackson drove the British out of Louisiana in 1815, a foreign enemy is inside the gates, and the American people are at risk in their own country.[19]

The threat from abroad is one thing. The threat from within is quite another. A new elite of cultural traitors is working hard to undermine the greatest civilization in human history, Buchanan warned. Amid the devastation of eviscerated manufacturing communities and the loss of jobs everywhere, neither party is capable of rallying Americans to the defense of their country. From multicultural tolerance to international trade and mindless military adventurism, Democrats and Republicans alike have become thoroughly corrupted and preside over a "rigged" system that works only for their benefit. This means that the terrain of political conflict is now located in culture and habits. Attacking religious faith, celebrating women's choice to forego motherhood, valuing diversity and individualism over solidarity and patriotism – it all means falling birthrates for white Americans, de-Christianizing the West, and weakening the ties that sustain societies and provide protection for individuals. The Democrats are the primary handmaidens of this assault as it takes shape in the New World, and it's up to the Republicans to save the country. But they have to change before they can fulfill their historic destiny. They must make the case for controlling immigration, defending religious faith, combating cultural relativism, rejecting international institutions, strengthening American sovereignty, restoring the country's manufacturing economy, and embracing conservativism's obligation to defend beleaguered white people. Buchanan's belief that morality, faith, and culture are at risk led him to call on the GOP to wage a war on abortion, gay marriage, pornography, the Confederate flag, and other areas of cultural conflict. Old-fashioned patriotic values should emphasize American greatness, white women should be encouraged to have children, and the necessities of the whole should take precedence over the preferences of the few. Cultural erosion, multicultural pandering to disloyal minorities, and tired nostrums about toleration and respect for others will not get the United States out of its death spiral. Only by waging a determined war can the Republicans save the beleaguered victims of contemporary culture, restore American greatness, and rescue the country from the extortionate schemes of race racketeers:

> White males are the victims of quotas, affirmative action, set-asides, and reverse discrimination. They are the preferred targets of abuse by academics, journalists, and feminists, as well as the Jacksons, Sharptons, and Bonds. Yet, none of their attackers are beloved of Middle America. If the GOP would come out for an end to racial preferences and a moratorium on immigration, and appeal to the great silent majority, as Democrats appeal to minorities, the party's chances in national elections could not but improve.[20]

Here is Trump in embryo, a decade and a half before that famous ride down the gilded escalator. Fusing racial animus and hostility to immigration, Buchanan began to develop a diagnosis and a cure for the disease that he claimed was undermining an entire civilization. The fit isn't an exact one of course, but several strands of what would later become an "America First" political program were dangling in the air long before Trump declared his candidacy. The dark Buchanan vision of foreign threat and domestic betrayal looked increasingly attractive as relentless economic distress and unending job loss were compounded by the election of a Black man as president. All that was left was a grassroots movement to demonstrate that Buchanan's early version of white nationalism could develop some political strength.

His hostility to foreign wars, international treaty obligations, and the welfare state notwithstanding, Buchanan was prepared to accept an important role for the central government. He had served several Republican presidents in important capacities and was not afraid to call upon Washington to enforce traditional moral codes, crack down on immigration, and impose order on the country's cities. He knew that Ronald Reagan had not been shy about using governmental power to engineer his massive upward distribution of wealth and income despite his rhetorical hostility to Washington. Buchanan understood the power of words; his important service in Washington had been as a consultant and speechwriter for Nixon, Ford, and Reagan. He was like many budding white nationalists in saying that the problem in American politics was not that the country had developed a large central government. His "paleo" designation and generally reactionary ideology did not mean that he was some sort of political dinosaur. He was smart enough to understand that a modern society with a modern economy needs a modern government. For him, the state was pursuing obnoxious and dangerous policies because it was in the wrong hands. His solution was simple: take it back.

The ruinous speculation that had brought on the Great Recession and "forever wars" combined at the end of the Bush presidency to make it possible for millions of white voters to support Barack Obama's candidacy. But the wave of good feeling and joyous hope that racism was on the run soon yielded to a wave of popular anger at a Washington establishment that was unable or unwilling to resolve these issues in ways that were palatable to broad sections of working- and middle-class whites. "You never want a serious crisis to go to waste. And what I mean by that is an opportunity to do things that you think you could not do before," Obama advisor Rahm Emanuel said. But grand hopes for a broad reorganization of the economy, or even for punishment to be meted out to the villains of the piece, were soon disappointed. Obama decided early on to rely on the same institutions and individuals who had brought on the crisis in the first place. Millions of people lost their jobs to recession and their homes to bankruptcy and foreclosure. Thousands more lost their sons and daughters in pointless, unwinnable wars in Afghanistan and Iraq. The financial institutions that had caused the economic meltdown received billions of dollars in government loans and guarantees, dwarfing programs that would assist the human victims of their greed and corruption. The bankers got huge bonuses, their banks got mammoth bailouts, and Wall Street got even bigger. One midlevel banker went to jail.

The lesson was not lost on millions of disenchanted voters. A festering sense that the system was rigged and that guilty powers could not be punished because of their proximity to power contributed to a right-wing populist explosion that would focus many of the disparate impulses that had been animating Republican politics for years. Primarily composed of the classic white petty bourgeoisie, the Tea Party expressed many of the themes of dispossession, threat, and loss that had animated Republican voters since Goldwater. Distinguished from ordinary conservatives mainly by the extremism of their views and the passion with which they were held, they were fanatically hostile to Barack Obama and the entire federal government. Convinced that they were the victims of an unholy alliance of foreign and domestic enemies, they claimed the mantle of traditional conservative hostility to federal spending – particularly on environmental protection, health care, and education. In a grim reflection of their conviction that they were under attack, they were hostile to any and all government attempts to redistribute income and wealth. This was a major reason for their fanatical hatred of Obamacare, one of the most powerful federal redistributionist initiatives in decades. Typical Tea Partiers were not hit particularly hard by the Great Recession but had very high levels of anxiety about taxation, cultural change, and national decline. They agreed with the classic conservative goals of lower taxation, deregulation, and privatization but supported Medicare and Social Security because they tended to be older and directly benefited from both programs. Their most venomous hatred was reserved for the higher taxes that would support social spending on the undeserving. A tyrannical federal government in the hands of America's sworn enemies is aiming to tax them to death and regulate everything. Since the system is fair and open and the market is just and efficient, it follows that minorities are held back by their own failings. Tea Party notions of "deservingness" was heavily racialized and developed from earlier conservative arguments about a culture of poverty. Their frenzied activity against Obamacare would push the Republican Party hard to the right and pave the way for the bitterness of Trump's destructive nihilism.

Five major themes powered Tea Party activists around the country. A decentralized movement that was not nearly as spontaneous as its spokespeople claimed, it was driven by a visceral hatred of welfare, of undocumented immigrants, of Arab Muslims, of the Affordable Care Act, and of Barack Obama. Their most powerful impulses stood in some conflict with their public claims. Their self-invented myth made it sound as if they were concerned about budget deficits, taxes, and the power of the central government. But their storied antagonism to Washington was not really that of small-government conservatives. It mostly organized around hostility to federal assistance to those deemed the "undeserving poor." It was concerns about race, national identity, and other social issues that really drove most of their activity. Their abiding obsession with Obama's birth certificate was a stand-in for the more profound claim that the first Black president could not possibly be a "real American." Arrogating for themselves the right to decide who belonged to the American polity and, more importantly, who didn't, many Tea Partiers gave voice to a more explicit white nationalism than Buchanan had raised. Their claim that Obama was an illegitimate president encouraged many of them to claim that he was a secret Muslim. And if he was a secret Muslim, then it followed that he was a terrorist working to undermine the United States from within. The twin claims of the birthers, that Obama had been born in Kenya and that he was in league with terrorists, became core positions of many Tea Partiers and became more central to the Republican Party as it began to absorb the movement's energy. By 2011, about half of Republican voters believed that Obama had been born abroad, a position that Trump would articulate. Obama's Hawaiian birth certificate did nothing to dissuade them. Their challenge to the provision for birthright citizenship that is guaranteed by the Fourteenth Amendment was a natural consequence of their conviction that Obama was not a "real American."

A relatively inchoate movement primarily comprised of enraged, disenchanted, and mobilized elements of the white middle class, the Tea Party was never a grouping of the poor or the unemployed. Angry conservatives believed deeply that their country had been stolen from them. They wanted it back. The oft-repeated Tea Party call to "Take it Back, Take Your Country Back" was an explicitly white nationalist slogan and was sometimes coupled with the claim that Obama was driving the country into a socialist ditch. Their eighteenth-century costumes, "Don't Tread on Me" flags, and ostentatious worship of the Founding Fathers could not disguise the fact that the core of the Tea Partiers' nationalism was a distinctly white variety. It excluded those deemed not to be "real Americans," including the sitting president of the United States and the native-born children of undocumented immigrants. Socialists and Muslims were often deemed not to fit within a newly defined understanding of a country by, of, and for white people. Appearing at the conjunction of nativism and the fear of a new majority that was taking shape, the racism that was a permanent feature of the Tea Party would occasionally burst into the light. Their claim that American cities were hotbeds of Black crime was seconded by their endless accusations of voter fraud committed by non-white citizens, their identification of Islam with terrorism, and their Buchananite fearmongering about an "invasion" of non-whites across the Southern border. Handouts to the poor and coddling of the lawless were fused in the Tea Party's reaction to Obama's election. Conspiratorial thinking was endemic to the Tea Party, dedicated to reversing recent demographic changes and convinced that a Democratic president represented an existential threat to everything its members believed in.

The basic issue driving the Tea Party and accounting for its frenzied level of activity was Obama's election. It was the specter of a Black president that fueled their obsessive hostility to the Affordable Care Act, not traditional Republican Party commitment to a small government. Their antagonism to an expansion of medical coverage to uninsured elements of the population was part of a larger attempt to restore what they thought were the conditions for American identity and greatness. The Tea Party was a reactionary attempt to turn the clock back to a white, middle-class, heterosexual, Christian male society. Seen in this light, it's simply the latest in a string of right-wing movements that have popped up when American society was being confronted by broad social changes. The combination of deindustrialization, losing wars, demographic changes, and urbanization have thrust conservative, rural white men into the difficult situation of a once-dominant group facing a challenge to its privileged position. The danger tends to be translated into a vast, sinister conspiracy that is undermining the foundations of civilization and ruining the country. Faced with what it sees as existential threat, Tea Partiers made an important contribution to the Republican Party's turn toward white nationalism. Whether it was an explicitly racist reaction to Obama's election or just the latest in a long string of reactionary political movements – or both – the Tea Party's base was relatively advantaged white Protestant males. The main forces of conservative politics through most of the country's history, this is exactly the section of the population whose status is most directly threatened by the sweeping demographic, economic, and social changes that are reorganizing American society. Their fear that they are losing control of "their" country has a real material basis and a strong dose of racial animus. Donald Trump disagreed with many of their positions, but the process that made the GOP into such a radical, uncompromising, abnormal political formation was accelerated by the Tea Party's fanatical response to Obama's election and Trump's subsequent ability to take advantage.[21]

Although the movement ranged itself against Washington and claimed to be in the tradition of conventional small-government conservativism, the Tea Party was a distinctly political phenomenon from the very beginning. Led by experienced conservative activists, the movement was determined to seize control of the Republican Party and use it to reorganize national politics. Convinced that the central government had fallen into the hands of America's enemies, they organized for political battle and proved to be tenacious fighters for a deeply reactionary vision of American society, economy, and politics. Their hysterical, energetic, and effective mobilization against the Affordable Care Act during the first years of Obama's presidency announced their intense focus on conquering the Republican Party. When they swept Congress in 2010's off-year election, their Freedom Caucus became a powerful voice in the House of Representatives and came close to acting as the voice of the entire Republican delegation. Their Buchanan-like desire to restore the country to its mythical past combined with their Gingrich-like obstructionism and willingness to paralyze Washington set the stage for Donald Trump.

This vision was not the only one available to the Republicans. In the aftermath of Obama's 2012 win over Mitt Romney, the Republican National Committee (RNC) commissioned a 100-page "autopsy report" that tried to chart a path forward for a party that had begun to sound "increasingly out of touch." The electorate was getting younger, Blacker, and browner, the "Growth and Opportunity Project" acknowledged, and the party had to adjust to this new reality if it hoped to survive. Its base of older white male rural voters was demanding a set of policy positions that were unacceptable to large majorities of new and minority voters, and there was only one way to deal with demographic realities.

> If we believe our policies are the best ones to improve the lives of the American people, all the American people, our candidates and office holders need to do a better job talking in normal, people-oriented terms and we need to go to communities where Republicans do not normally go to listen and make our case. We need to campaign among Hispanic, black, Asian, and gay Americans and demonstrate we care about them, too. We must recruit more candidates who come from minority communities.[22]

Casting the GOP as the white man's party was a recipe for disaster, the Project warned. The country was changing, and the party had to change with it. Failure to do so would doom it to permanent minority status.

The report's urgent recommendation that the Republican Party reach out to Black and brown voters carried with it a set of recommended policy changes. It also elicited a powerful pushback from important party officials, pundits, and grassroots organizers who argued that the GOP should amplify the politics of white grievance that had served it so well for years. Prominent among the Project's critics were Tea Party leaders, but they were certainly not alone. Maximizing white voter turnout rather than pouring resources into an ill-conceived outreach to minority communities would require continued fearmongering about Black criminals terrorizing white families and brown immigrants stealing white jobs. Such an argument caught on quickly in white nationalist circles within the Republican Party and rapidly buried the autopsy report. The RNC's "Growth and Opportunity Project" never had a chance. Voter suppression, border walls, open hostility to expansion of social welfare measures, and continued obstructionism triumphed. The rise of the Tea Party and its related Freedom Caucus signified that the GOP was being transformed from a real political apparatus into a sectarian grouping of right-wing wreckers. Its aging, rural, religious white male base harbored a deep contempt for what remained of its vacillating leadership, a deep hatred of "politically correct" globalist liberals, a visceral fear of immigration and a continuing racial animus that would set the conditions for a new type of political leader. Its resentment would be turned into a desperate rallying cry that would threaten the very foundations of constitutional democracy in the United States. Newt Gingrich's partisan extremism, Pat Buchanan's call to white nationalist culture war, and the Tea Party's bitter nihilism would combine into an explosive orange bomb that would roll down the gilded escalator of Trump Tower and blow American politics to smithereens.

Notes

1 George Lipsitz, *The Possessive Investment in Whiteness: How White People Profit from Identity Politics* (Philadelphia, PA: Temple University Press, 2018).
2 John Ehrenberg, *Civil Society: The Critical History of an Idea* (New York: New York University Press, 2017).
3 *The New Yorker*, October 1998.
4 William Julius Wilson, *The Truly Disadvantaged: The Inner City, the Underclass, and Public Policy* (Chicago: University of Chicago Press, 1993) and Jonathan Rieder, *Canarsie: The Jews and Italians of Brooklyn Against Liberalism* (Cambridge, MA: Harvard University Press, 1985).
5 Carroll Bogert and Lynnell Hancock, "Superpredator: The Media Myth that Demonized a Generation of Black Youth," The Marshall Project November 20, 2020.
6 Thomas Mann and Norman Ornstein, *It's Even Worse than it Looks: How the American Constitutional System Collided with the New Politics of Extremism* (New York: Basic Books, 2016), p. xxiv.
7 Address to the 1992 Republican National Convention, August 17, 1992, at https://voicesofdemocracy.umd.edu/buchanan-culture-war-speech-speech-text/.
8 Patrick Buchanan, *State of Emergency: The Third World Invasion and Conquest of America* (New York: St. Martin's Press, 2006), p. 2.
9 Ibid., p. 5.
10 Ibid.
11 Ibid., pp. 11–12.
12 Ibid., p. 46.
13 Ibid., p. 79.
14 Ibid., p. 128.
15 Ibid., p. 153.
16 Ibid., p. 162.
17 Ibid., pp. 245–246.
18 Patrick Buchanan, *The Death of the West: How Dying Populations and Immigrant Invasions Imperil Our Country and Civilization* (New York: St. Martin's, 2002), p. 3.
19 Ibid., p. 2.
20 Ibid., p. 222.

21 See Christopher S. Parker and Matt A. Barreto, *Change They Can't Believe In: The Tea Party and Reactionary Politics in America* (Princeton, NJ: Princeton University Press, 2013) and Richard Hofstadter, "The Paranoid Style in American Politics," *Harper's Magazine*, November 1964.
22 Republican National Committee, "Growth and Opportunity Project," https://online.wsj.com/public/resources/documents/RNCreport03182013.pdf.

5
THE TRIBUNE RIDES FORTH

Unwilling to accept the legitimacy of Barack Obama's election, Donald Trump would lead much of the Republican Party from half a century of conventional racial conservatism to a serious flirtation with white nationalism. By the time he announced his candidacy for president in an infamous appearance laced with attacks on immigrants and brimming with promises to restore the traditional social order, the GOP's range of electoral alternatives had narrowed considerably. Having decided to stick with the racial animus that had served it so well for so long, the party's activist rank and file had refused to seriously consider broadening its outreach to a more diverse constituency. The party's reaction to Obama's reelection had presented its leadership with a fateful choice, and that choice had begun its slide toward the abyss. It took only a shove to push it close to the edge.

Part of its dilemma was due to forces that continued to undermine the foundations of the country's political economy and stretch its politics to the breaking point. Unrelenting economic polarization, intensifying geopolitical competition, more "forever wars" in Iraq and Afghanistan, the misery of the Great Recession, rapidly changing demographics, and a host of intractable social conflicts were still upending many of the settled assumptions on which American domestic prosperity and foreign policy had been based. Having long used its appeals to localism, states' rights, and hostility to the federal government as a rhetorical device, the GOP had perfected the art of paralyzing Washington's ability to act and then had won elections by attacking Washington's inability to act. Even where the federal government was able to do something, the GOP was quick to criticize it for undermining the foundations of a safe and secure social order. The net effects of Newt Gingrich's unprincipled obstructionism, Pat Buchanan's alarmist call to culture war, and the Tea Party's bitter nihilism had come together

DOI: 10.4324/9781003182962-6

to produce a moment where Trump could intensify the GOP's traditional appeal to racial grievance. Now he could pose as the instrument of white revenge for half a century of persecution, contempt, and loss. Ever the quick-moving entrepreneur, he would stand apart from all other Republican presidential candidates in his willingness to take advantage of the elements of white nationalist sentiment that had been germinating for decades. This strategy required mobilizing already-resentful voters rather than spending much effort trying to convince the undecided to change their minds. Many white Americans had responded to the Republican Party's cultivation racial and ethnic hostility for years, and they would turn out to be Trump's "base" during his candidacy and presidency.[1] Trump's 2016 victory was the result of a back-and-forth between a skilled opportunist and a slice of the white electorate that was ready to cast its lot with its self-proclaimed savior.

Much of the Republican electorate had changed – and it was a change that Trump recognized, articulated, and encouraged. The old GOP reliance on Reagan's "colorblindedness" had summarized the party's racial conservatism from Goldwater's candidacy through the 1980s. It was not overtly hostile to the accomplishments of the civil rights movement and did not seek to turn the clock back to Jim Crow. Even as most Republican candidates and officeholders declined to enforce much civil rights legislation and ignored repeated calls to strengthen legal protection for minorities, they recognized that the population remained broadly supportive of equality before the law and equality of opportunity.

But something had happened to the Republican base between the end of Reagan's presidency and 2016, and Trump knew it – perhaps because it had happened to him as well. Masses of conservative white voters had become much more radical, alienated, insecure, and embittered. Continuing economic polarization and the effects of the Great Recession had combined with Obama's election and the grievances of the Tea Party to produce a Republican core that was convinced it was being persecuted and was facing extinction as the country went to the dogs. The trifecta of Gingrich, Buchanan, and the self-appointed patriots of the Tea Party came together to create the opportunity that Trump was insightful enough to recognize. Now he stepped forward as the Tribune of Whiteness, telling angry voters that he was prepared to deploy the federal government to protect their material interests, their psychological well-being, and their accustomed place in society. From voting rights to crime, immigration, deindustrialization, international competition, and everything in between, Trump ramped up the rhetoric of white grievance and focused it squarely on the Black and the brown. Nostalgia for a vanished past was manifested in endless complaints that whites were being persecuted for being white. The massive flow of wealth to the already-wealthy fueled the conviction that the political and economic systems were "rigged" from top to bottom and opened the door to Trump's populist claims that he would rescue the victims of theft, incompetence, and malfeasance. It soon became clear that he had never intended to do anything of the kind, but that hardly mattered. The campaign and presidency were all about the symbolism that led millions of white voters to cast their lot with a huckster who loudly proclaimed that "only I can fix it."

Powerful forces were at work. Obama's election had accelerated the politics of racial backlash as it crystallized an intensification of whites' sense of racial threat. Deeply influenced by a grim sense of danger and a visceral fear of losing something precious that they had come to expect as their birthright, millions of white voters had suddenly awakened to the peril of becoming a minority in "their" country.[2] A deep sense of victimization, carefully nurtured for years by Republican politicians and pundits, had warned that "reverse racism," quotas, affirmative action, and almost all government programs aimed at reducing poverty and discrimination would necessarily come at white peoples' expense. This sense of threat was particularly pronounced in conservative rural areas, where Republican politicians, newspapers, talk show hosts, and religious figures had been reminding white voters that Washington had been coddling Black criminals and rewarding welfare cheats. For decades, they had been told that sophisticated, educated urban elites looked down on them, had no respect for their "culture," were prepared to take away their guns and Bibles, and were willing to sacrifice them on the altar of multiculturalism and political correctness. Rage against globalization, diversity, secularization, and an assortment of other grievances would also spur the movement of relatively well-off whites toward Trump and cement in place a bloc of furious voters who became convinced that they had a spokesman at last. Racial resentment and economic anxiety would come together to produce a startling new moment in American public life.[3] Trump knew it and was prepared to transform white fear, white fragility, and white failure into a powerful new force.

His ethno-nationalist program was built on an astute recognition that equality feels like persecution to those who have become accustomed to privilege. Pat Buchanan had paved the way for Trump by linking white demographic anxiety, entrenched racial tensions, and increasing immigration to an assortment of problems.[4] Just a few years later, Obama's election came to symbolize a loss of status and power to many racially conservative white voters, fueling their conviction that non-whites were going to use their ally in the White House to rob them blind, cast them out of power, and reduce them to servitude. Their distress and rage broadened out into a generalized rejection of the postwar consensus that had solidified American political and economic policies. Intensified racial animus and mistrust turned out to be strongly correlated with millions of white voters' opposition to international trade accords, geopolitical treaty obligations, established immigration policies, and Chinese economic competition. As racial resentment and anxiety mushroomed after Obama's 2008 victory – and especially after his 2012 reelection – Trump stepped forward in the latest actor in the back-and-forth of American race relations. As extraordinary as his appeals were, they fit into an established historical pattern, personifying the inevitable pushback that has followed every advance toward racial democracy. Emancipation had given rise to "redemption" and Jim Crow, the civil rights movement was met by white backlash, and Obama's election led to the Tea Party and Trump.[5] It wasn't long before he would go even further and begin to lead his party to a rejection of civic nationalism and political democracy.

Fear of violent Black crime has long served as one of the useful tipping points in the politics of backlash, and no one was better able to take advantage of it than Donald Trump. The Willie Horton episode had convinced many Republican candidates and officeholders that inflaming the danger posed by Black criminals would always yield results at election time. On May 1, 1989, Trump moved past George H.W. Bush and Lee Atwater in the pantheon of race-baiting politicians riding to the rescue of innocent white victims of wanton violence.

The case of the Central Park Five provided a perfect moment for him, and the story line was a familiar one. As was often the case, the press had a field day with it. Patricia Meili, a young white woman, was jogging in Central Park during the evening of April 19 when the press breathlessly reported that she was set upon by a pack of Black and brown young men who were out "wilding," attacking and harassing innocent people just because they wanted to have some fun. The media frenzy that this horrific event set off was magnified by the tale of violent young hoodlums who had burst out of their neighborhoods and were hunting down white people in some grotesque parody of racial revenge. Trisha Meili, viciously raped and beaten to within an inch of her life, became the quintessential symbol of vulnerable white womanhood, singled out because of her gender and her race.

The case of the "Central Park Five" immediately became an allegory of the country's tortured race relations. Five Black and brown young men, all of whom were between 14 and 16 years old – Kevin Richardson, Raymond Santana, Antron McCray, Yusef Salaam, and Korey Wise – were arrested and charged with a variety of crimes ranging from assault to rape and attempted murder after confessing under intense and coercive police questioning. Two weeks after the attack, Donald Trump – known to the New York tabloid press as The Donald, a loudmouthed, smug, self-serving celebrity child of privilege whom nobody took particularly seriously – took out advertisements in four city newspapers fanning the flames of white hatred and terror and braying for revenge. "Bring back the death penalty. Bring back our police!" Trump's ad blared. "I want to hate these muggers and murderers," he continued. "They should be forced to suffer and, when they kill, they should be executed for their crimes." New York City was consumed by a tidal wave of white anger, fear, and desire for revenge.

Maintaining their innocence and documenting how the police had pressured them into false confessions, the Five were convicted and sentenced to the maximum for their charges and their ages. There the matter rested until Matias Reyes, a convicted rapist and murderer, met Korey Wise in prison. His confession to the authorities, corroborated by DNA evidence, began a long process that ended with the complete exoneration of the Five. In 2002, their convictions were vacated and 12 years later the young men were awarded a $41 million settlement by New York City – roughly a million dollars for every year of wrongful imprisonment.[6]

Almost every actor in this sordid tale has acknowledged that the entire legal system was guilty of a serious miscarriage of justice. Not Trump. To this day, he has continued to insist that he was right and has refused to apologize for his role in sending five innocent young men to prison. "They did it. They confessed," he has repeatedly said, denying that their confessions were coerced and claiming that they were playing the city for a sucker. He has attacked the financial settlement as "the heist of the century" and has seized every possible opportunity to call city and court officials weak and cowardly. As late as June 2019, he was calling the settlement a "disgrace." It didn't matter to him that Matias Reyes confessed, or that DNA evidence confirmed his guilt, or that the City of New York acknowledged that the Five had been unjustly imprisoned. Trump sees no reason why he should apologize for his inflammatory role or recant his falsehoods, and he has refused to do so. Why should he? His intervention in the case launched his public career.

Trump has been obsessed with race for the entire time he has been a public figure, and he has often strayed over the line that separates ordinary race-baiting from white nationalism. Claiming that "laziness is a trait in blacks" and opening his run for the presidency by disparaging Mexican immigrants as criminals and rapists sounded like perfectly ordinary racist dog whistles, even if they were characteristically vulgar and intemperate. So did saying that Obama's protection of the Dreamers – law-abiding immigrants who were brought to the United States as children – contributed to the power of Latino street gangs who made a living by terrorizing innocent whites. Calling for "a total and complete shutdown of Muslims entering the United States" and demanding that the federal government refuse to readmit Muslim citizens who were outside the country began to imply that Muslims could not be full members of the American polity. So did his complaint that a federal judge hearing a case about his fraudulent "Trump University" was biased because of his Mexican heritage and that 15,000 Haitian immigrants "all have AIDS" while expressing a preference for immigrants from Norway and complaining about immigrants from African "shithole countries." Calling some undocumented immigrants "animals" who would "pour into and infest our country" continued his nods toward a more overt white nationalism. Ordinary gestures toward old-fashioned racial animus easily mingled with more pointed suggestions about who could – and, more importantly, who could not – be full members of American public life.[7]

All caution was thrown to the winds when it came to Obama, and it was when he expressed his visceral hatred of the country's first Black president that Trump began to move toward a more explicit white nationalism. Endlessly repeated "birther" claim that Obama was born in Kenya and was thus ineligible for the office mingled with false suggestions that he had forged his birth certificate and "issued a statement for Kwanzaa but failed to issue one for Christmas." Further allegations that *Dreams of My Father* was ghostwritten by Bill Ayers were mingled with an offer of $5 million if Obama would produce his college transcript, since Trump repeatedly proclaimed that the president was clearly not smart enough to have gotten into Harvard Law School on his own.[8] When paired with his birtherist charge that Obama had won the election unfairly and was sitting in the White House illegitimately, the issues that Trump raised never concerned this or that fact about Obama's biography. They were always about what it meant to be an American citizen. Resuscitating Reagan's old slogan and promising to "Make America Great Again" harkened back to an idyllic period when political power was undeniably white, privilege was unqualifiedly male, and religious authority was unquestionably Christian. Trump's whole campaign was about putting the Black, brown, and female in their accustomed places and healing the psychic wound that Obama's election had inflicted on already-resentful white people.

Repeatedly reminding his listeners that minorities are dangerous and threatening was an important part of this strategy. Trump didn't need Willie Horton or even the Central Park Five to do so. It was enough to falsely claim, during one of his debates with Hillary Clinton, that "our inner cities, African Americans, Hispanics are living in hell because it's so dangerous. You walk down the street, you get shot." It was enough to remind white Americans that prominent Black leaders are often unpatriotic, ungrateful, and disrespectful. It was more than enough to tell four Democratic congresswomen, all of whom were American citizens and three of whom were born in the United States, to "go back" to "the totally broken and crime-infested places from which they came."

Mocking and denigrating minorities was one thing. As appalling as it sounded coming from a candidate and then president, it paled in comparison with praising overt white nationalists, fascists, Proud Boys, Klansmen, and assorted defenders of the "white race." The scattering of ordinary racism mixed in with nods toward white nationalism characterized Trump's entire campaign and presidency. From his refusal to disavow David Duke's endorsement to his unapologetic and enthusiastic claim that the some of the white supremacists and nationalists who marched in Charlottesville, Virginia, were "very fine people," Trump opened the door to the most virulent elements of the American racist, fascist, and white nationalist Right. His own personal history of racism and intolerance, which has been documented for years, never distinguished him from many other American political leaders from both parties. It was his willingness to cement in place some elements of an overtly nativist and white nationalist program that set him apart – all the way from suggesting to Laura Ingraham that Obama "doesn't have a birth certificate, or if he does, there's something on that certificate that's very bad for him" to proposing a ban on all Muslims who wanted to enter the country and repeating his false claims that he saw Muslims dancing for joy after the destruction of the World Trade Center. Building on the powerful base of white racial animus that the Republican Party had exploited for decades, he broadened his attacks to include Latino immigrants and Muslims as imminent threats to white prosperity, security, and safety. *The Apprentice* had started in January 2004, and from then on Trump had gleefully used his television persona to say things that conventional public personalities would avoid. He continued to do so while sitting in the Oval Office, smugly suggesting that this made him more believable than conventional politicians. The events in Charlottesville featured fascists, Nazis, white nationalists, and others chanting "Jews Will Not Replace Us" and echoing the Nazi slogan of "Blood and Soil." Trump's reaction prompted two of his "very fine people," white nationalist leaders Richard Spencer and David Duke, to recognize that he was their champion. "There is no question that Charlottesville wouldn't have occurred without Trump," said Spencer.

> It really was because of his campaign and this new potential for a nationalist candidate who was resonating with the public in a very intense way. The alt-right found something in Trump. He changed the paradigm and made this kind of public presence of the alt-right possible.

For ex-Klansman David Duke, the Charlottesville rally was a "turning point" for his own movement, which seeks to "fulfill the promises of Donald Trump."[9]

Quantity often goes over to quality, and the sheer volume of Trump's appeals to white people who imagined that they were threatened with permanent loss set him apart from all other modern Republican political figures. Richard Nixon and Ronald Reagan were famously willing to engage in racist banter and traffic in racist stereotypes, but they made some effort to keep these excursions private. His willingness to deploy Willie Horton did not prevent George H. W. Bush from appealing for tolerance whatever his personal views. His son launched a foreign war under false pretenses but made every effort to invoke the principles of civic nationalism, tried to broker a compromise on immigration policy, and repeatedly called for tolerance of Muslim Americans after 9/11. Rhetorical Republican fidelity to elementary principles of fairness and inclusion certainly helped disguise policies designed to reassure anxious whites that they had a defender in the GOP, but the illusion meant something and seemed to be a firewall against more explicit invocations of racial privilege and white grievance.

Trump demolished that firewall. His political slogan might just as well have been a promise to "keep America white." His racial attitudes did not stand alone of course and accompanied a rejection of bipartisan international commitments, a new economic nationalism, a denial of human responsibility for global warming, an attack on the natural world, regressive fiscal and budgetary policies, and an explicit embrace of the most parochial and intolerant elements of the Christian Right. He articulated a very broad, if incoherent, political program that rejected many of the basic understandings of American politics. Most of his innovations had little or nothing to do with race. Promises to defend the material and psychological interests of white people were nothing new, after all. But taken as a whole and stretching over his entire administration, his public embrace of important elements of white nationalism constituted a sea change in American politics. Much too chaotic in his public and private life to present an organized program, he nevertheless legitimized some of the most destructive impulses of a Republican base that had been molded by appeals to racial animus for decades and had become inflamed by the election of the country's first Black president.

Trump's rhetorical attacks on people of color had specific themes that harkened back to decades of Republican electoral strategy and drew on a deep well of racial animus. Blacks were identified with crime, welfare, and violence; Latino immigrants with murder, drugs, and slovenliness; Muslims with terrorism and sharia law. All were denigrated as imminent dangers to white Christian Americans. A consistent electoral strategy successfully mobilized disaffected white voters who had been attracted to the GOP before Trump ran for president. Charging into areas where his Republican predecessors had not dared, Trump succeeded in appealing to racial conservatives and extremists by being explicit about his self-appointed role as the defender of white people against violent, grasping, and undeserving minorities. His own racism, the racism of his supporters, and more than half a century of Republican pandering made it possible for him to assemble a broad white coalition that ranged across the economic spectrum. Numbers tell the story. The median income of Trump voters in 2016 was $70,000 a year. A third of them had yearly incomes between $50,000 and $100,000, another third earned over $100,000, and another third had yearly incomes below $50,000.[10] Economic distress, continuing deindustrialization, and the aftereffects of the Great Recession certainly played a role in his campaign's success, but the decisive variable explaining 2016 was race. It's doubtless true that many Trump voters were not conscious racists or white nationalists. But it's equally true that they were willing to elect a candidate who embraced both as matters of personal preference and state policy.

The debate about whether it was economic anxiety or racial animus that accounted for Trump's astonishing victory begs the question. It was both, and they reinforced each other. He made a direct appeal to a broad sector of the white population who felt aggrieved and threatened by changing economic trends and demographics. The confluence of these two factors explains why he was able to marshal white fear and rage while disavowing accusations of personal racism. His promise to "Make America Great Again" meant restoring Washington to its default position of serving the interests of white people. The combination of economic insecurity and racial animus reinforced his repeated claims that whites are "losing" and are the innocent victims of nefarious interest groups and cowardly politicians through no fault of their own but because of the color of their skin. Trump's themes of economic malaise and demographic crisis yielded only to his linked promise to restore the racial order.

Trump avoided targeting Blacks in his campaign, focusing instead on Latino immigrants and Muslims. But he did so on the basis of an anti-Black racial history that was so entrenched in the Republican Party that he never had to invoke it. While the Democrats campaigned on economic issues and the principles of civic nationalism, Trump based his 2016 campaign on identity politics and racial anxiety. It was relatively easy for him to do so, since the Republican leadership had long decided to organize itself as the white party. Class and race worked together to create a narrow Trump victory. His voters made more money than Clinton or Sanders supporters, and their personal economic situation was only part of what shaped their voting preferences. Indeed, repeated public opinion surveys have demonstrated that whites who express a higher level of resentment about Blacks have been more likely to identify as Republicans for decades. Since the 1990s, a similar correlation has emerged between resentment toward Latinos and Muslims and Republican partisanship. Trump's successful campaign was powered by the mutually reinforcing nature of racial animus, economic dislocation, cultural anxiety, and demographic changes. He repeatedly insisted that American society as a whole was under attack, a set of claims that helped drive white voters toward him. Given the country's history and present circumstances, it was relatively easy for him to racialize economic grievance. He insistently reminded white voters that he was prepared to reverse their sense of fear and loss by making the federal government their ally once again. Conservatives had been shocked and outraged by Obama's presidency, lending credence to Trump's suggestions that minority gains could only come at their expense. John McCain and Mitt Romney, two conventional Republican presidential candidates who ran against Obama, had avoided race-baiting during their campaigns, but Trump went all in. He knew that Obama's election had channeled and focused white notions of identity and interest under siege.[11] Economic distress and racial animus came together to make his candidacy and subsequent victory possible.[12] As Jacob Hacker and Paul Pierson observed,

> If the question is whether many Trump voters were motivated by racial resentment, the answer is yes. If the question is whether the rise of plutocracy contributed to the party strategies and voter mindsets that allowed Trump to tap that resentment, the answer is an equally emphatic yes.
>
> Extreme inequality drove the Republican Party toward strategies of division and demonization to rally their white voting base. Extreme inequality was also a powerful contributor to the alienation of that base. The voters who swung to Republican between 2012 and 2016 generally came from areas where the increasing riches of the plutocracy had coincided with long-term economic decline. Trump did well in areas where unemployment was higher, job growth slower, earnings lower, and overall health poorer. (One of the strongest county-level predictors of Trump's vote was the rate of premature death among white Americans). Backlash against immigrants and racial minorities certainly does not require America's extreme inequality. But right-wing populism is most potent where, and among those who feel, opportunities for economic security and advancement have been lost.[13]

Material and psychological rewards flow to privileged groups. Higher wages, longer life, increased wealth, and better health care are matched by heightened prestige, access to public space, social deference, and greater levels of formal and informal authority. Both sorts of payoffs are important, and perceived threats to either can trigger powerful responses of fear, anxiety, and resentment. They can also set in motion powerful political currents that aim at preserving or restoring threatened or lost rewards. White people have enjoyed both types for so long that they have come to regard them as something of a birthright. Perceived threats to their privileges have taken different forms in different historical periods, but they have elicited similarly hostile responses. Accelerating inequality had made these responses even more visceral and desperate than usual, intensifying the pressure on insecure families and individuals while offering them fewer means of alleviating perceived threat. When Trump promised to "Make America Great Again," he knew that declines in wealth, security, and mobility for millions of white families were matched by similar declines in social standing, dignity, and psychic well-being. This was particularly true in rural areas and in the Midwestern states that had been hammered by deindustrialization and disinvestment for decades. Frustration and anger were powerful components of Trump's appeal, and his ability to focus blame on Black and brown people intensified his attractiveness to a broad swath of the white population who thought that they had found their champion at last. The development of an American plutocracy meant that income and wealth had been stagnant for non-college households since the Reagan presidency, more and more people were feeling besieged by powerful economic forces, and fear of threat and loss were widespread. Under the circumstances, Trump's campaign was able to fuse material and psychological appeals to a white population that was ready to blame shadowy elites, domestic minorities, and new immigrants for their troubles.

Presidential candidate Ronald Reagan had made a successful play for the Southern white vote in 1980 by reminding whites in Philadelphia, Mississippi, that they could count on him to defend states' rights. No one had any illusions about what that meant, nor did they have any illusions 37 years later, when President Donald Trump stood in neighboring Alabama to attack Black football players for taking a knee during the national anthem. "That's a total disrespect of our heritage," said the New York resident now running for president.

> That's a total disrespect of everything that we stand for. Wouldn't you love to see one of these NFL owners, when somebody disrespects our flag, you'd say "Get that son of a bitch off the field right now. Out! He's fired."[14]

Reagan's sunny optimism was matched by Trump's snarling imitation of his role on *The Apprentice*. Reagan had whistled. Trump roared. Reagan had nodded toward white prejudice and lynching. Trump openly embraced and politicized them. When this New Yorker referred to "our" heritage and what "we" stand for when talking to a crowd of white Alabamans, few could have doubted whom he meant by "our" and "we."

He didn't hesitate to adapt the murders of Michael Schwerner, Andy Goodman, and James Cheney to the requirements of a new period. Alabama Senate candidate

Roy Moore's statement that America had been great in the days of slavery because "families were strong, our country had direction" did not prevent Trump from endorsing him. Nor did an Arizona guilty verdict for criminal contempt delivered against Maricopa County sheriff Joe Arpaio for racially profiling people he claimed were illegal immigrants. Trump's explicit nods toward white nationalism served to reinforce his slogan's reminder that America was great in the good old days when it was governed by white Christian men. Now it was threatened by hordes of dangerous immigrants, foreign religions, domestic minorities, and unpatriotic elites. Having won the presidency on a narrative of victimization, Trump used his time in office to milk it for all it was worth. An intensifying anxiety among white voters that their material interests and social standing were under threat in a country that was rapidly diversifying met a politician more than willing to stoke those worries and willing to benefit by deploying them as partisan weapons. That sense of loss had been germinating among white voters for years. The deep belief among millions of whites that they are getting less than they deserve and are being discriminated against because minorities are getting more than *they* deserve had lurked under the surface for years. It took an arsonist to help it burst into flames and begin to burn the house down.

The Tea Party had remade much of the Republican Party by organizing its members' obsessive hatred of President Obama. As determined as they were to erase the country's first Black president from history, Trump's election and subsequent administration were driven by much more than his personal enmity for his predecessor. The backlash against the Democrats for daring to nominate and elect a Black man was part of a larger pattern. Donald Trump was the first president in modern American history to make explicit appeals to white racial anxieties and calls for white solidarity the central focus of his campaign and administration. As millions of racially conservative white voters began to see politics through a more intense racialized lens after Obama's election, so they had turned to Trump when he started warning them about just what a Black president might mean for them. The Republican Party that had started talking seriously about courting Black and Latino voters after losing to Obama in 2012 was intensifying its identification as a white party just four years later.[15]

From stoking the racial tribalism of the base to embracing the leadership's refusal to broaden the GOP's appeal, Trump positioned the Republican Party as the protector of white people. It had ridden that role to electoral success, but Trump's view of racial matters is the single most important feature of how he has remade the party. His great accomplishment was recognizing the role that white grievance and racial animus was playing in the Republican base and then embarking on a strategy to intensify and focus those hostilities. His zero-sum vision that minority gains can only come at the expense of white people led him to reject the view that the only way the Republican Party could grow was by making overtures to non-white voters. Given how popular the GOP remains among white voters in the Deep South, Appalachia, and areas of the northern Midwest, Trump concluded that the only viable path forward was to encourage further racial polarization. He shared this strategic decision with Jeff Sessions, Steve Bannon, and Stephen Miller and used it to organize his presidency. Trump's intervention in the case of the Central Park Five, his embrace of birtherism, the attempted Muslim ban, and his nod toward the "very fine people" of Charlottesville were not the careless remarks of an undisciplined public figure. As he became the candidate of the Republican Party's white nationalist element, he consciously made racial polarization the central strategic impulse of his campaign. And, more importantly, it became the blueprint for governance. Half a century of Republican racial politics was coming full circle.

Donald Trump ran for office and governed as a racial reactionary, speaking for a white, older, Christian, rural, undereducated America that is under grave threat from a multitude of causes that lie beyond its control. His claims that whites are being persecuted by political liberalism and that his self-appointed task was to protect the "real America" were desperate attempts to stem the tide of demographic changes that are relentlessly hostile to his constituency. An essential element of this orientation was to move the Republican Party's racial politics away from its Reaganite claim of colorblindedness toward a more explicit embrace of political power as an ally and protector of white people. This development was a qualitative change that he brought to both the Republican Party and American politics and can help explain his policies of unconstrained policing, weakened civil rights enforcement, restrictions on minority voting, attacks on immigration, and endless rhetorical celebrations of what it meant to be white. This reorientation has moved past declining to enforce civil rights legislation and policies while paying lip service to the principles of civic nationalism, tolerance, and inclusion. A far more proactive approach has replaced earlier passivity. Trump did not come by this orientation all by himself. His amplification of the policies of racial grievance and threat were a direct response to the radicalization of the Republican base. He recognized what had happened to that base in the years separating Reagan's candidacy from his own. His effort to erase the Obama presidency from history carried the GOP beyond its traditional racial politics.

Trump has been able to bend the Republican leadership to his will, but it doesn't mean that he has successfully addressed the party's core dilemma. One of its elements is programmatic and is shaped by its fealty to wealth. More than any other politician since Reagan, Trump's policies were heavily skewed toward plutocracy. He shepherded more huge tax cuts for the rich through Congress, jettisoned thousands of environmental and other regulations, transformed the federal judiciary, eviscerated much of the central bureaucracy, and developed a broad cadre of followers at the local and state levels. The plutocracy had its greatest supporter in the White House. But the other half of the Republican dilemma remains in place, for it was essential to the party's electoral prospects to appeal to a wide swath of voters whose material interests would be gravely damaged by its economic policies. Trump did his best to disguise regressive tax cuts, deregulation, and business-friendly judicial appointments with relentless attacks on immigration, pieces of the promised border wall, hostility to abortion, charades of religious faith, assaults on minority voting, and rhetorical support for white nationalists. These two elements of conservative politics had been a staple of Republican electoral strategy for decades. But the demographics are beginning to catch up with it, and the shape of a new strategy has not yet appeared. After all, the Republican Party must win elections if it were to continue to strengthen plutocracy. The GOP has profited from America's racial tensions for decades by identifying itself with the grievances and antagonisms of its white population. It will continue to do so, but that will not solve its existential problem.

Taking advantage of racial resentment and cultural backlash worked well for Richard Nixon, but the United States has changed substantially in the past 50 years. It is much more diverse, better educated, less overtly Christian, more urbanized, and more tolerant than ever. Trump voters represent a steadily shrinking slice of the electorate. But the party is trapped by its past and its leadership demonstrates no desire to break with positions that served it well in an earlier period. It has chosen to legitimize notions of racial superiority, stoke fear of immigrants and minorities for political ends, and paint a picture of an embattled white population that has to defend its power by any means necessary. These notions, once the preserve of fringe white nationalist groups, have migrated into the mainstream of American politics.

The GOP has been suggesting for years that Blacks cannot be fully trusted to responsibly discharge the obligations of citizenship. Such implications have a long history. Republican presidential candidates have repeatedly benefited from claims about Black Americans' disorganized domestic life, rejection of the elementary rules governing social behavior, abstention from the basic understandings regarding work, and willingness to live as a nonproductive parasitical element. Trump gleefully built on that legacy and extended it to immigrants, echoing Buchanan's claim that they cannot become full members of the American polity because they will not fully accept republican ideas. This is a classic *herrenvolk* conception of membership and citizenship, fully reflected in the "blood and soil" mantra of his "very fine people." His open hostility to all non-Nordic immigrants, the stereotyping of Latino immigrants that began with the announcement of his candidacy, his open contempt for Blacks, the immigration restrictions and caging of children, his barriers against imports, the repeated attacks on "cosmopolitans," and vilification of big cities are all of a piece. The boundaries of Trump's understanding of citizenship are the boundaries of skin color. Forged in the country's largest and most cosmopolitan city of his youth, they are reinforced by the perspectives of the small towns and rural areas that now house his most fervent supporters. Their desperate sense of moral decline is their rebellion against a country that is becoming more diverse and cosmopolitan. It is a direct cause of the white nationalism that now characterizes much of the Republican Party's approach.[16] This tendency is the fusion between a sense of white vulnerability, long-standing racial resentment, deep economic distress, and wide anger about cultural and demographic change.

This is not a particularly new idea. The country's founding generation firmly believed that whiteness was one of the prerequisites for virtuous, independent republican citizenship. Antebellum colonization ideas were predicated on the understanding that Black people could not live next to white people as full members of the polity. The same was true of the country's many restrictive immigration policies and laws. As the popular nineteenth-century phrase had it, the United States was a "white man's country." The country's poisonous racial history made it relatively easy for Trump to repurpose a sentiment that was initially focused on Black people and generalize it to include many others. Its continuing historical strength is manifested in the back-and-forth between the economic distress and racial animus that worked together to elect him. When 66 percent of his voters said that the 2016 election represented "the last chance to stop America's decline," the accumulated weight of history surfaced in contemporary politics.[17] Trump was its unwitting spokesman, organizing his campaign around the core claim that changing demographics, economic woes, and cultural challenges have presented an existential threat to white Christian America – a threat that only he could defeat. Claims about illegal immigrant voting, Muslims celebrating terrorist attacks, and dark warnings about Black criminality came together to paint a picture of a threatened white civilization facing overthrow. When Trump delivered his dystopian inaugural address, he warned of a society in the midst of decline, called for swift action to reverse decades of crisis, and repeated most of the incendiary attacks on those he thought responsible for the mess. His base loved the speech. Trump had ridden the wave of their sense of grievance and rage to the White House because he recognized the wave for what it was.

It certainly wasn't the Republican leadership that had elected him. They stood indicted of cooperating with Obama, not being "strong" enough, of selling the country out to domestic and foreign enemies. Despite the obvious reservations of the party's dignitaries, Trump had responded to the fear, resentment, anxiety, and anger of the base and had intensified it in response. His takeover of the GOP reflected the fact that the issues that were now animating the party's voters went far deeper than the old Reaganite mantra of low taxes, deregulation, and privatization. Now they were also cultural: race, immigration, abortion, and religion played important parts in Trump's campaign and were the core of his inaugural address. What used to be a party of fiscal restraint, free markets, and limited government had become a party of nationalism, xenophobia, immigration restriction, overt racism, misogyny, and existential resentment. A very high level of white anxiety had been coupled with the inability of congressional Republicans to articulate a credible alternative to Obama that went beyond wall-to-wall opposition. The rise of the Tea Party, the war with Obama, and the fevered hostility to Washington that gripped the GOP after its 2010 sweep had described a party that was paralyzed. When Trump called its leaders "weak," he knew what he was talking about. Someone had to break the logjam, and he was the perfect candidate for the job. No one, he said, was listening to the grievances of the party's white base. No one was able to channel their indignation and their rage. No one was willing to fight for their "way of life." Hostility to immigration, promises to bring back American industrial jobs, legitimation of white grievance, railing against the bank bailouts, combating globalization, turning the tables on white victimization, ignoring science, experience, and expertise – that was Trump's campaign, and it would be his presidency. No wonder he outflanked the traditional Republican leadership so easily. An astonished former president listened to Trump's inaugural speech and was struck by its dark pessimism and its grim promises. "That was some weird shit," said George Bush as he left the podium. Indeed, it was. And there was more to come.

Notes

1 Thomas Edsall, "Trump's Cult of Animosity Shows No Sign of Letting Up," *New York Times*, July 21, 2021.
2 Richard C. Fording and Sanford F. Schram. *Hard White: The Mainstreaming of Racism in American Politics* (New York: Oxford University Press, 2020).
3 Pippa Norris and Ronald Inglehart, *Cultural Backlash: Trump, Brexit and Authoritarian Populism* (New York: Cambridge University Press, 2019).
4 See Chris Cillizza, "Pat Buchanan Says Donald Trump Is the Future of the Republican Party," *Washington Post*, January 12, 2016; Clarence Page, "The Ethnic Card: Donald Trump's Mouth, Pat Buchanan's Ideas," *Chicago Tribune*, May 6, 2016; Adele M. Stan, "White Supremacy and Trump's Battle for the 'Soul of America,'" *American Prospect*, May 6, 2016; Leonard Greene, "Pat Buchanan Calls Donald Trump 'The Great White Hope' in Latest Racist Rant," *New York Daily News*, May 29, 2016; Sam Roudman, "Pat Buchanan Is 'Delighted to Be Proven Right' by 2016 Election," *New York Magazine*, November 1, 2016; Tim Alberta, "'The Ideas Made It, But I Didn't,'" *Politico*, May–June 2017; Aaron Rupar, "Trump Promotes Pat Buchanan Column That Makes White Nationalist Case for His Border Wall," *Vox* January 14, 2019; Hunter, "Maryland Public Television is Giving White Nationalist Pat Buchanan a New Television Gig," *Daily* Kos August 15, 2019; Jennifer Senior, "Let the Culture Wars Begin. Again," *New York Times*, August 24, 2020.
5 Carol Anderson, *White Rage: The Unspoken Truth of Our Racial Divide* (London: Bloomsbury, 2017).
6 *The Central Park Five*, a documentary by Ken Burns, and *When They See Us*, a Netflix miniseries by Ava DuVernay, present the case and its resolution.
7 See David Leonhardt and Ian Prasad Philbrick, "Donald Trump's Racism: The Definitive List, Updated," *New York Times*, January 15, 2018.
8 Reuters staff, "Trump to Give $5 Million to Charity if Obama Releases Records," *Reuters*, October 24, 2012.
9 David A. Graham, Adrienne Green, Cullen Murphy, and Parker Richards, "An Oral History of Trump's Bigotry," *The Atlantic*, June 2019.
10 George Lipsitz, *The Possessive Investment in Whiteness: How White People Profit from Identity Politics* (Philadelphia, PA: Temple University Press, 2018), p. 283.
11 Ashley Jardina, *White Identity Politics* (New York: Cambridge University Press, 2019).

12 There's an extensive popular and scholarly literature on the mutually reinforcing themes of racial animus and economic distress in the 2016 election. See, inter alia, Sean McElwee and Jason McDaniel, "Anatomy of a Donald Trump Supporter: What Really Motivates This Terrifying Political Movement," *Salon*, May 16, 2016; Sean McElwee and Jason McDaniel, "Economic Anxiety Didn't Make People Vote for Trump. Racism Did," *The Nation*, May 8, 2017; Greg Gilbert, "UW Professor Got it Right on Trump. So Why Is He Being Ignored?" *Seattle Times*, June 14, 2017; Emma Green, "It was Cultural Anxiety that Drove White, Working-Class Voters to Trump," *The Atlantic*, May 9, 2017; Thomas Edsall, "Donald Trump's Identity Politics," *New York Times*, August 24, 2017; Ashley Jardina, Sean McElwee, and Spencer Piston, "How Do Trump Voters See Black People?" *Slate*, November 7, 2016; William Saletan, "What Trump Supporters Really Believe," *Slate*, August 29, 2017; Thomas Wood, "Racism Motivated Trump Voters More than Authoritarianism," *Washington Post*, April 17, 2017; Ronald F. Inglehart and Pippa Norris, "Trump, Brexit, and the Rise of Populism: Economic Have-Nots and Cultural Backlash," *Harvard Kennedy School*, August 2016; Antoine Banks, "Anger Makes Ethnocentrism among Whites a Stronger Predictor of Racial and Immigration Policy Opinions," *London School of Economics* at http://bit.ly/2uhO8yk; Zach Beauchamp, "Donald Trump's Victory Is Part of a Global White Backlash," *Vox*, November 9, 2016; Thomas Edsall, "The Peculiar Populism of Donald Trump," *New York Times*, February 2, 2017; Michael A. McCarthy, "The Revenge of Joe the Plumber," *Jacobin*, October 26, 2019; Steven Shepard, "Study: Views on Immigration, Muslims Drove White Voters to Trump," *Politico*, June 13, 2017.

13 Jacob Hacker and Paul Pierson, *Let Them Eat Tweets: How the Right Rules in an Age of Extreme Inequality* (New York: Liveright, 2020), p. 139.

14 Sophie Tatum, "Trump: NFL Owners Should Fire Players Who Protest the National Anthem," CNN, September 13, 2017.

15 Emily Badger and Nate Cohn, "White Anxiety, and a President Ready to Address It," *New York Times*, July 20, 2019.

16 Sean Illing, "A Princeton Sociologist Spent 8 Years Asking Rural Americans Why They're So Pissed Off," *Vox*, March 13, 2018.

17 Robert P. Jones, "Trump Can't Reverse the Decline of White America," *The Atlantic*, July 4, 2017.

6
TOWARD WHITE MINORITY RULE

By the time Donald Trump decided he should be president, Republicans had accumulated half a century's experience in using racial resentment and prejudice to win elections. The legacy was a mixed one. Even as they had pandered to white fear, animosity, and anxiety to get elected, successful GOP candidates had governed as conventional racial conservatives and preserved most of the civil rights movement's formal gains. But as the party gradually repositioned itself into a Southern-based white organization, it became the agent of post-Nixon attacks on the welfare state and the social movements that sought to extend its benefits. Economic developments worked to shape political history as a painful period of economic restructuring scrambled old political allegiances and gave rise to new ones. By the end of Barack Obama's presidency, a substantial portion of the American electorate was ready for Trump and his turn toward white nationalism.

The turn had deep roots and had been developing for a long time. Trump's candidacy served to bring many of its different streams together and begin to organize the Republican Party's embryonic commitment to minority rule. As the civil rights movement gathered momentum and forced a reshuffling of national allegiances, Southern commitment to white supremacy and Jim Crow had anchored Republican power in Dixie.[1] Northern support for George Wallace had been largely based on an economic defense of what it meant to be white. Working-class and petty-bourgeois voters who gravitated to the Alabama governor were defending their access to protected and well-paid union jobs, segregated housing, and white schools for their kids. These developments had helped anchor the broad prosperity enjoyed by millions of white families in the North. Deindustrialization and globalization had provided the material background to the civil rights movement's challenge to the privileged access to income, wealth, and security that many white families had come to regard as their birthright and were determined

DOI: 10.4324/9781003182962-7

to protect. Later developments reflected continuing resistance to extending racial justice beyond formal statements of equality. When the continuous hollowing out of the country's industrial base combined with the Great Recession to threaten the security of millions of families, it didn't take much to broaden hostility from Black to brown. The election of the country's first non-white president added fuel to the fire as intensifying white resistance to immigration developed on a foundation of heightened racial animus. The different target should not obscure the historical similarities. Trump was able to link perceived threats from people of color to the secure jobs, safe neighborhoods, privileged access to education, and other elements of white middle-class life. Recent hostility to immigration and long-established resentment of Blacks came together to reinforce his dark warnings of crisis and threat.

Trump was not particularly innovative in his willingness to take advantage of established patterns of racial prejudice. The Republican Party and its most loyal constituents had become acutely aware of the demographic cliff they were facing before he was elected, and Trump took note of a very different set of political and ideological requirements than those faced by his predecessors. His frequent denunciations of the Republican establishment for being weak and failing to defend its supporters was merged with his rejection of some of the basic tenets of traditional civic nationalism and his increasingly explicit embrace of white minority rule. As a simple will to power came to characterize the GOP, a broad and increasingly explicit insistence that the national government step forward as the defender of white power carried Donald Trump, and the Republican Party he continues to lead, far beyond the dog whistles of an earlier period. Important elements of the Republican Party's nascent vision of a racialized political order began to fall into place. One of the country's two major political parties was on the verge of becoming an instrument of white nationalism.

Elements of the pushback had been germinating for years, but they assumed a new meaning during the Trump candidacy and presidency. Determined, violent, and continuous white resistance to Black advancement had been a hallmark of the country's history for generations. Every step forward had been met with countermeasures. As newly freed ex-slaves began to farm the land, establish schools, and organize families, they encountered the Black Codes, sharecropping, Hayes–Tilden, and a series of Supreme Court decisions that eviscerated the Civil War constitutional amendments and brought an end to Reconstruction. The Great Migration was greeted with segregated Northern slums, dysfunctional schools, police and vigilante violence, and isolation in the most demeaning jobs. The *Brown* decision was met with massive resistance, the Declaration of Southern Principles, private segregated "academies," opposition to busing, and a renewed defense of residential segregation. The civil rights movement came to an end with white flight, mass incarceration, resistance to reform that went beyond formal equality before the law, and a continuing pattern of de facto white supremacy. The election of a Black president was greeted by the Tea Party, intransigent Republican obstruction and destructiveness, obsessive hatred of Obamacare, accelerated incarceration, voter suppression, and birtherism. The GOP led the pushback and benefited from it, but the Democrats had often joined in. For every Nixonian claim to represent the "silent majority," there were Clintonian attacks on Sister Souljah and attacks on welfare programs. For every Reaganite reminder that "young bucks" were ripping off hardworking, tax-paying whites, there was the pledge to "end welfare as we know it." Seen in this light, Donald Trump's time in public life seems like the continuation of established trends.[2]

It is, but his dalliance with racial antagonism was qualitatively different from that of his Republican predecessors. The situation had changed dramatically, and country's racial issues had hardened. If intensified racial animus was the way whites reacted to the civil rights movement and the social disorder of the Sixties, then it should have declined in the face of the recent drop in violent crime and relative social peace. If intensified racial animus was the way whites reacted to Black unemployment and welfare dependence, then it should have declined as employment grew and welfare rolls declined. If intensified racial animus reflected increases in Black out-of-wedlock births, drug addiction, and other measures of social disorder, then it should have declined as crime, family breakdown, and the opioid crisis spread to hundreds of white neighborhoods and towns. But it didn't. The extraordinary thing about the spike in racially tinged politics is that *it happened in the absence of dramatic changes in objective conditions*. The heightened racial resentment that prepared the ground for Trump's immigrant-bashing campaign was not the same sort of direct white response to social crisis that had characterized earlier periods. In many ways, racial animus is permanent and functions autonomously. Trump recognized this, deployed it in a broad attack on immigration and communities of color, and rode it to the White House.

American racial history was the backdrop to his campaign and subsequent time in office, but economic distress has influenced the development of a distinctly right-wing populism in many countries that had a different past. Globalization, its attendant "China shocks," heightened economic competition, deindustrialization, disinvestment, and restructuring have hollowed out industrial areas from eastern Germany and France to northern England and the American Midwest. A strong correlation between Trump support and industrial competition has given rise to a debate about the relative weight of racism and economic distress as journalists, professors, and pundits try to figure out what fueled his surprising 2016 victory.[3] As is often the case, there is less there than meets the eye. The difference is a matter of emphasis. The hostility to immigration that Trump articulated was triggered by years of industrial decline and rested on a base of racial animus that is deep-rooted and easily extended. There's some evidence, for example, that whites who are uncomfortable with immigration are also uncomfortable with American-born Blacks as the nation's demography gets more complicated. Studies and surveys reveal that white Americans don't distinguish between legal immigrants, undocumented immigrants, and native-born Latinos. As with so much else, white views about immigration are heavily racialized. These findings are broadly consistent with 50 years of research demonstrating that "ethnocentric suspicions of minority groups in general, and attitudes about Blacks in particular, influence whites' opinions about many issues."[4] This process has been developing for half a century, beginning when hostile reactions to the civil rights movement began to reorganize partisan politics and shape presidential elections. White attitudes toward Blacks were a major reason why the once-solid Democratic South has become an indispensable stronghold for the GOP. They fueled George Wallace's appeal to Northern white voters, Richard Nixon's claim to speak for the "silent majority," and Ronald Reagan's ability to whistle. Obama's election made attitudes about race even more salient to national politics and accelerated the Republican Party's turn toward an extreme racial conservatism. The GOP has now gone over to a more serious flirtation with white nationalism, exemplified by Trump's embrace of birtherism during his campaign, his attempt to ban the immigration of virtually all Muslims early in his first term, and much of his subsequent policy and rhetoric as president.

More was involved than Donald Trump's personal views. Republican voters and elected officials have become much more conservative about racial matters over the past few years. Trump stepped forward as their spokesman, performing best with voters who scored highest in measures of white ethnocentrism, hostility to immigrants, racial resentment, fear of Muslims, and more general measures of racial and ethnic intolerance. His explicit appeals to social anxieties grouped his targets together on a bedrock hostility to Blacks. They took the immediate form of insistent warnings about the advent of a non-white America. Strong feelings of white identity, a conviction that whites are treated unfairly, and fear of a non-white future came together to powerfully predict support for Trump and, more generally, for Republican candidates. When former Ku Klux Klan Grand Wizard and present white nationalist David Duke warned whites that voting against Trump was "treason to your heritage," he was articulating the unspoken fears of millions of people and trying to chart the future course of the Republican Party.[5] He may be right. The immediate future pits a white GOP against a coalition of Latino, Black, and Asian Americans who are gravitating toward the Democrats. The short-term result of this racial sorting is a nation whose politics will be more sharply defined by race than ever.[6]

Public policy has worked together with private prejudice for decades to produce America's racial hierarchy, a hierarchy that is facing serious demographic and economic challenges. Whiteness has long had a material value that has been generated and reinforced by private habits and political choices. Discriminatory housing markets, unequal educational opportunities, privileged employment networks, and intergenerational transfers of wealth have worked together for years to produce a set of material rewards that are recognized and defended by millions of voters. When white families of limited means were faced with pressure to integrate their neighborhoods, schools, and workplaces, they sought to safeguard their well-being and security with whatever means they had. Their homes held most of their wealth, their neighborhoods provided a valuable sense of community, their jobs delivered decent pay and an important measure of security, and their schools provided an escalator for their children's future. These benefits were tied up with skin color and they were reinforced by public assumptions and government policy. No wonder whites were unwilling to share. Given their assumption of a zero-sum environment, they figured they had a lot to lose if others were to move ahead. In the absence of commitments to broaden social welfare, it stood to reason that everyone's piece of the pie would be smaller if it were divided among more participants. "Whiteness" is a biological delusion to be sure, but it is a social fact that carries enormous value for the distribution of wealth, security, prestige, and opportunity. It has long been a material fact that goes far beyond a set of ideas of ideological categories. Race in America is, above all else, a matter of power and it is not clear that the United States can move past its racial history without provoking a rebellion from the working- and lower-middle-class whites who have benefited most directly from policies that protect them from competition in areas of housing, education, jobs, and status.

When economically and socially vulnerable white voters cast their ballots for a candidate who blames their troubles on Black and brown people and promises to alleviate their troubles by gutting affirmative action, eliminating welfare, and barring immigrants, they are translating their private worries into political facts. Appeals to racial grievance are far more than an upper-class ploy to distract the attention of virtuous, if misled, white voters. Many whites have been more than willing to serve as willing accomplices of racial animus because there are substantial material and psychological benefits to the color of their skin. They get treated better than others by the police, ordinary bureaucracies, and virtually every other public and private institution from schools and PTAs to hospitals, banks, and insurance companies; they are the beneficiaries of government-sanctioned discrimination in housing markets and school choice; their jobs, benefits, working conditions, retirements, and union protections benefit from substantial public support their neighborhoods are redlined by formal procedure and informal agreement; and even their farmers are preferentially entitled to access to government protection, loans from local banks, and protection from the dangers of global warming. The benefits extend to virtually every area of public and private life. They help shape the voting behavior of millions of voters, whose common desire to defend the advantages of whiteness defines the conservative coalition that now dominates American politics and anchors the political power of the Republican Party. But times are changing. The GOP's electoral strategy of racial polarization and base mobilization have brought Republican candidates many victories but are running straight into the country's rapidly changing demographics.

Some Republican leaders have tried to reconcile the party's dependence on older, rural, male, conservative, white Christian voters by guiding the party toward gradual immigration reform and a broader outlook on racial matters. George Bush's stance on immigration was worlds apart from Pat Buchanan's xenophobia and the social conservatives of the Tea Party, who openly yearned for an America that had returned to its imaginary white, Anglo-Saxon roots. Far more comfortable with diversity, bilingualism, and pluralism than his party's conservative base, Bush ran afoul of the Right's bitter resistance to reform and alarm at the proliferation of Spanish-speaking enclaves around the country. The Tea Party was largely a movement of older Americans, most of whom were relatively prosperous and thoroughly white. Unhappy with changing demographics and convinced that "their" country was being taken away from them, they were bitterly disappointed at Obama's election and the newer, younger, hipper, secular, sophisticated and diverse America that he represented. Whispered suggestions that Obama was a secret Muslim soon yielded to outraged shouts that his mysterious birth certificate, Kenyan father, and Arabic-sounding middle name signified a hostile takeover of the White House. Trump recognized their origin in the fused anxiety about race and immigration and was more than willing to take advantage of it. A broad commitment to defend the status quo in racial matters positioned him as the savior of a beleaguered white population. He had the enthusiastic backing of a substantial number of conservative voters who are threatened by changes they cannot stop. When recently asked whether the goal of politics is more about "enacting good public policy" or "ensuring the country's survival as we know it," nearly half of the Republican respondents said it's about survival.[7] They are animated by a conviction that the country is changing more rapidly than is tolerable, they are under siege, time is running out on them, white people are an endangered species, important institutions are in the hands of their enemies, the future is one of continuous threat, the past was better than the present, and their only option is a determined defense of what they have. Their fierce commitment to the status quo is what lay behind Trump's litany of grievances that he presented to the Republican National Convention and his self-important claim that "only I can fix it."

The "it" that has to be "fixed" is the demographic cliff that has become impossible to ignore. A growing conviction that the country's future requires limiting the political power of non-white citizens unites Republican voters and political leaders. It has become a Republican article of faith that an orderly, dependable, and safe political future means an orderly, dependable, and safe *white* political future. A high level of racial animus, a fierce commitment to defend the status quo, a fear of a non-white majority, and a rejection of a multiracial political order mark the beginning of the GOP's unmistakable transition from an organization of racial conservatives to a white nationalist apparatus. Restrictions on absentee voting, onerous identification requirements, shrinking voting times and places, politicized ballot-counting, uncontrolled gerrymandering, and reinforced partisan supervision of election processes – all of these measures, and more, chart Republican attempts to deal with the demographic cliff that threatens it. The attack on voting rights continues, fueled by an increasingly desperate sense that time is against its constituency. It is likely to work in the short run. For the moment, the GOP has solved the problem of consolidating a racially resentful base and mobilizing it to support leaders whose central policy objectives are reinforcing the plutocracy. Whether that achievement will last in a country that is rapidly diversifying remains to be seen.[8] A multiracial political democracy has become a serious threat to the Republican Party. The reverse is equally true: the Republican Party has become a serious threat to a multiracial political democracy.

The Voting Rights Act of 1965 marked the first time in American history that universal suffrage was the law of the land. After all, women were not able to vote until the Nineteenth Amendment was passed in 1920. From then on, a thicket of perfectly legal restrictions limited the franchise to whites in the Jim Crow South. An ingenious set of impediments, from residency requirements and poll taxes to literacy tests – supplemented by unofficial and official violence when needed – effectively disenfranchised Black citizens without explicitly violating the Fifteenth Amendment's clear statement that "the right of citizens of the United States to vote shall not be denied or abridged by the United States or by any State on account of race, color, or previous condition of servitude." The organs of the national government, from the Supreme Court to Congress and the presidency, cooperated in the fiction that Southern suppression of the Black vote was not in violation of the Constitution. From the late nineteenth century until 1965, voting in the South was a white monopoly that was used to organize the Jim Crow system of official, state-sanctioned white supremacy. It took years of struggle for the civil rights movement to win its great victory with the passage of the Voting Rights Act (VRA) and the attainment of full political democracy and formal equality in 1965. The Republican Party's assault on minority voting is an assault on the signature accomplishment of the most important democratic movement in recent American history. Until recently, the law's legitimacy was unquestioned. Even as it became more racially conservative, the GOP had not dared to directly attack the VRA. That's no longer true. Its contemporary assault on minority voting marks the beginning of its turn from a conventional racial conservatism to a nascent white nationalism.

The Republicans did not have to invent racial prejudice to benefit from it. It is permanently resident in the white population, and much of the country's history is the story of a back-and-forth between these attitudes and enterprising politicians willing to take advantage of it. It is relatively easy to activate it for electoral gain, and many seemingly unrelated policy issues are clustered around the more visceral issues of race. Obama's election did little to change this fundamental fact of American politics, and hopeful claims that the country had entered a "post-racial" phase of development were soon dashed on the bitter rocks of the country's history. Even as his campaign and later administration tried to minimize their importance, racial and ethnic attitudes turned out to be stronger predictors of voting behavior in 2008 and after than they had been in earlier elections. They persisted throughout his first term and powerfully influenced voting in 2010 and 2012. Obama's election created a broad spillover effect as unrelated issues like healthcare, votes for Congress, attitudes toward Muslims and Latinos, immigration reform, and economic recovery from the Great Recession were evaluated in overtly racialized categories. Republican districts that were already racially conservative became more intensely so after his election, and racial animus was a powerful reason for the "shellacking" the Democrats suffered in the off-year election of 2010. It powerfully contributed to the refusal of Congressional Republicans to cooperate with the Obama White House on virtually any issue, and it has contributed to the process by which the Republican Party has become the instrument of a radicalized white segment of the electorate. The Obama presidency saw the most racialized era in modern American history, and it certainly contributed to the vitriol and paralysis that gripped Washington for eight years. The fact that all of this happened during a period of relative racial peace is testament to its power.[9]

Its permanence notwithstanding, racial politics has had its ups and downs. The Republicans had used it to shatter the New Deal coalition. As they became experts at using the wedge issues of busing, affirmative action, crime, and open housing to pry millions of white voters from the Democrats, they illustrated the old political maxim that bigotry comes in clusters. Particular issues have spillover effects and often have a broader impact than the immediate issue under consideration. Trump's attacks on immigrants, his promises to defend white jobs and neighborhoods, his complaints that too many immigrants were coming from "shithole" countries like Haiti rather than from Norway, and an endless stream of verbal bigotry that his admirers applauded were all built on a foundation of anti-Black racial prejudice. That foundation predated his rise to prominence; his accomplishment was to weaponize it and use it to his advantage. Endless suggestions that Blacks no longer face much discrimination and their disadvantages stem mostly from a poor work ethic, implications that equality before the law means that they have only themselves to blame for their poverty and isolation, whispers that Democratic government policy ends up rewarding them for being Black rather than from their real accomplishments – all of these suggestions carry with them a visceral content that has driven conservative political movements to the far right. They were far more powerful predictors of political behavior than Tea Party positions about limited government, gun rights, religious fundamentalism, or authoritarianism. Racial attitudes have a more powerful effect on voting behavior than party identification, attitudes about the size of the federal government, health care reform, educational funding, and expansion of health care. The raging debate about health care that consumed the nation during Obama's first term was most powerfully affected by how thoroughly it became racialized.[10]

For all its skill in using race to its advantage, the problem facing the Republican Party will not go away. Even in the short term, it will only get worse. The white population is shrinking and that of all minorities is increasing.[11] Given the GOP's refusal to adapt to the country's changing demographics, there's only one path forward if it is to aspire to national influence. As the political environment continues to weaken it, the GOP must move toward permanent minority rule. Its motion comes with significant risks to American politics. Holding power against the wishes of a majority of citizens in a political democracy requires authoritarianism and disenfranchisement. These have become much more than policy choices. The Electoral College and Senate that are heavily weighted toward sparsely populated rural states, a nationwide campaign of voter suppression, a politicized Supreme Court, aggressive gerrymandering – these perfectly constitutional structures for imposing the will of the minority on the majority have been available to all political parties since the birth of the republic. Trump's campaign and presidency mark their transformation from available tools to strategic necessities.

Faced with profound demographic challenges that will only intensify, the Republican Party has become increasingly authoritarian and antidemocratic. Having closed off all alternatives save one, it has mastered the art of using the most antimajoritarian institutions of the federal government.[12] When it can't win elections, it is increasingly focused on altering the playing field to its advantage. Refusing to consider a sitting Democratic president's Supreme Court nominee, attempting to meddle with the census, passing restrictive voting laws, trying to overturn a free and fair presidential election, setting the conditions for future electoral challenges to contests it loses – all of these measures are attempts to cement permanent advantage into the party system for an apparatus that represents a declining segment of the population and is well on the way to abandoning the notion that elections are contests for the support of a majority of voters.[13] When Trump warned his listeners on *Fox & Friends* that Democrats were trying to organize levels of voting that "if you'd ever agreed to it, you'd never have a Republican elected in this country again," he was redefining the Republican strategy of voter suppression as a life-and-death matter rather than a policy option.[14]

Even before the election of 2020, Trump had been signaling that he would refuse to accept the results if he didn't win. When the results came in, the signals were translated into claims that results from minority precincts in Pennsylvania, Arizona, Wisconsin, Michigan, and Georgia had been tampered with, that a criminal conspiracy was trying to rob him and his voters of the victory they had won, and that Joe Biden's election was illegitimate. What he could not know is how many Republican voters would sign on to this renunciation of the most basic rule of democratic electoral politics. There merits of the case are far less important than the fact that the case is being made. The refusal of Republican voters, officeholders, and party officials to break with Trump's evident lies about his electoral loss are motivated by far more than personal cowardice or fear of the party's base. They are driven by a desire to preserve a weapon held in reserve. This will not be the last time that Republican politicians cry foul when they lose an election.

Even without their party's intense commitment to voter suppression and intimidation, claims that presidential elections are "rigged" against Republicans –

and, by more than implication, against white people – ignores who really benefits from the "rigging." The Constitution is a deeply antimajoritarian document. A minority of voters can choose a majority of the Senate, determine the composition of the Supreme Court and much of the federal judiciary, and even elect a president from time to time. These features of the American constitutional order help anchor Republican political power. The party's embrace of white minority rule has deep structural roots and will have a significant base of popular support. It's no surprise that the substantial number of Republicans who believe that Trump really won the 2020 election score very high on measures of racial animus, political authoritarianism, resistance to immigration, social intolerance, and reactionary worldviews.[15] For these voters, the stakes are very high. The survival of "their" republic is at stake. "I think this will be the last election that the Republicans have a chance of winning," said Trump during the 2016 campaign, "because you're going to have people flowing across the border, you're going to have illegal immigrants coming in, and they're going to be legalized … and be able to vote. Once all that happens you can forget it."[16]

This cluster of attitudes is not particularly new. Minority rule has characterized much of American political history, and so have its accompanying belief structures. A violent commitment to preserve slavery precipitated the secession of 11 Southern states whose leaders were unwilling to live with Lincoln's victory in 1860. After they lost the Civil War, Southern whites managed to sabotage the universal manhood suffrage required for their readmission to the Union for the better part of a century. From 1876 until the passage of the Voting Rights Act in 1965, unremitting violence, legal maneuvering, and national indifference permitted Southern whites to organize a Jim Crow system that made a mockery of democratic politics. And it wasn't until 1920 that women won the right to vote in the country as a whole. If universal suffrage is to be taken as democracy's indispensable characteristic, then the United States has been democratic for all of 57 years.

What used to be a Southern problem has become a national one. As the two major parties recomposed themselves under the pressure of the civil rights movement, Democrats became a coalition of different racial and ethnic groups while Republicans have become whiter, older, more Christian, rural, and much more conservative. The Democratic coalition is broad and less disciplined, while the Republican base is narrow and more cohesive. The same tendencies that manifested themselves in Dixie now characterize the national GOP and its white voters: a conviction that they constitute the nation's authentic and legitimate citizenry, that they deserve to govern, that an election is legitimate when they win and illegitimate when they don't. This is the operative definition of white nationalism. A substantial portion of the Republican base is now willing to sacrifice political democracy to preserve white Christian hegemony. They score high in measures of political authoritarianism and demonstrate intense levels of animosity toward Blacks, Latinos, Muslims, and other outgroups. Trump did not create these attitudes. He got elected by harnessing the prejudices of

> a renegade segment of the electorate, perhaps as large as one-third of all voters, which disdains democratic principles, welcomes authoritarian techniques to crush racial and cultural liberalism, seeks to wrest away the election machinery and suffers from the mass delusion that Trump won last November.[17]

Hostility to majority rule was part of Barry Goldwater's claims that the United States is a "republic, not a democracy" and signaled his opposition to the civil rights movement's attempt to curb the national power of a Southern minority. The Republicans developed that claim as they sought to organize an argument against the "activist" Warren Court's "one man, one vote" rulings during the Sixties. Ronald Reagan attempted with some success to build a majority coalition that could support Republican candidates and meant it when he talked about a party that included disenchanted Democrats, but that effort was dependent on his personal charisma and the party leaders abandoned it soon after his presidency ended. George Bush tried to broaden the GOP's base by reforming its positions about immigration, focusing on outreach to Latinos and trying to calm anti-Islamic bigotry after the 9/11 attacks – but at the same time he was elected after his campaign fomented the "Brooks Brothers Riot" in Florida that allowed the Supreme Court to determine the results of the election. Reagan's talk of a "big tent" and Bush's rhetorical commitment to a more inclusive party were replaced by attacks on "RINOS" as an ideological litmus test began to separate true believers from "Republicans in Name Only." Since then, an ideologically cohesive party has focused on reinforcing the electoral power of a declining white population. This is what lies behind its attempts to restrict the franchise and introduce partisan requirements about who gets to vote. As Republican officeholders become more reliant on a shrinking and intensely radicalized base, they have foregone the opportunity to build a majority coalition. It is noteworthy that two of the last three Republican presidential victories have been through the Electoral College rather than through the popular vote. The GOP has managed to retain considerable electoral power in the short run, but it is not clear how long it can manage to hold on given the set of strategic and demographic constraints that it faces. As it focuses less on assembling majority coalitions that can win elections and more on catering to a declining base of fervent supporters, it gets closer to embracing a white nationalist vision about who should be able to vote – and, equally important, who should not.

As important as the Trump administration's official racial animus was to the many members of the Republican voting base, its economic policy was essential to its few economic beneficiaries. His signature "Tax Cuts and Jobs Act" of 2017 accelerated the historic transfer of income and wealth to corporations and the rich that began with Reagan's presidency and has resulted in historic levels of inequality. Some of its provisions illustrate just how far the country has fallen from its earlier political regime. Where the corporate tax rate was 48 percent and the top individual rate was 70 percent during the 1970s, the Trump act lowered the corporate tax rate to 21 percent and slashed the top individual rate to 37 percent. These deductions have had their intended result. The share of income going to the top 1 percent has doubled, from 10 to 20 percent, since the pre-1980 period, while the share of wealth owned by the top 1 percent has risen from around 25 to 42 percent.[18] Despite the enormous Trump tax cuts, incomes for the middle and working class have stagnated and many taxpayers now pay a larger share of their pre-tax income in payroll taxes. Broad, systematic reductions in government regulation accompanied the administration's regressive fiscal and monetary policy and accelerated the entrenchment of the plutocracy that now dominates American economics and politics.

Encouraging racial animus and inflaming fears of a non-white future has created a mass base for a set of policies that benefit the very rich and the largest corporations. Millions of white voters got reassurance, nationalism, and racism while tax cuts, deregulation, and privatization appealed to corporations and the rich. Taken together, they provided the raw material for the massive upward transfer of wealth and income that has created a new American plutocracy. The Republican Party has been transformed by this process and is becoming an ultra-right formation that is isolated from the political center and can live only by pandering to racism, outrage, and division. It has fused right-wing populism and plutocracy with a set of policy positions that are strikingly out of touch with the interests of their base voters. As it organized a set of electoral appeals that were increasingly strident, alarmist, and racially charged, it learned how to use white identity and racial animus in the service of inequality. In this regard, American right-wing populism is strikingly different from its European counterpart. It shares its nativism, xenophobia, nationalism, hostility to immigration, and racism – but not its commitment to social protections. From the British Conservatives to France's Marine Le Pen and Italy's Northern League, the broad European Right remains committed to preserving the core institutions of the welfare state. But the United States is different. Our Republicans have coupled their populist turn with an unremitting, relentless attack on social welfare.

Racism has been central to this process. A series of empirical studies document the extent to which white voters reject social welfare programs when they perceive them as benefiting minority groups – even if they benefit from them as well. The perception that public money flows disproportionately to Blacks and Latinos is a powerful determinant of white hostility to these programs. Claims that government spending favors minorities at the expense of whites, that whites are generally victimized by public programs such as affirmative action, and that "reverse racism" drives the Democratic Party explains a good deal of the support for Trump. Studies that chronicle "last-place aversion" demonstrate that whites just above the cutoff for public assistance were most opposed to means-tested programs for the poor. The "psychological wage" of having someone below you accounts for a good deal of the white opposition to the welfare state's protection of minorities. It feeds into a general position that the white poor are deserving of help and the non-white poor are not. A widespread belief that the former are unlucky and the latter are lazy feeds into a story that the white poor are victims of forces beyond their control while the non-white poor are victims of their own disposition, failures, "culture," and choices. Fear of losing social status and political power is a powerful driver of white hostility to welfare.[19]

These attitudes were not invented by the Republican Party, even as its candidates benefited from them. As the GOP embraced plutocratic goals, it adopted increasingly hostile racialized appeals to its base voters. Appeals to resentful whites freed them to pursue long-standing policy goals as they responded to widespread fear of declines in social standing, political power, and economic security. As Trump articulated these fears, he repeatedly suggested that white backlash and hostility to immigrants could restore white privilege and power in a period of demographic and economic upheaval. His rhetoric gave many whites the illusion that he was speaking for and defending them after years of victimization, but it came with a heavy price tag. When health care programs were attacked, environmental regulations eviscerated, gun laws loosened, and social welfare programs cut back, the result was devastating for exactly those white people who were supposedly being helped. In the short run, it didn't seem to matter. The power of whiteness is demonstrated by the continuing popularity of these policies, and of Trump, even after his promises and claims unraveled.

None of this was inevitable. Many crucial choices were made along the way, and other paths were possible. But in the end, the allaince between leaders in thrall to plutocracy and their base of racially resentful voters has led the Republican Party to this point. Once its leaders decided to appeal to their most radical and angry constituents, they were forced to maintain the momentum if they wanted to hold on to their voters, respond to a rapid intensification of their racial animus, and have a chance at winning elections. The imperative to purify and intensify their base created a Republican electorate that is remarkably unified, loyal, and resentful. The key discovery was provided years ago by Lee Atwater: *racial animus made it possible to win the allegiance of poor Southern whites to an economic program that would benefit corporations and the rich.* One could package the plutocracy's desire for tax cuts, deregulation, and privatization into "abstract" talk that everyone knew was aimed at Blacks without saying so. It started in the South and spread to the rest of the country as Dixie became the great strategic reserve of the Republican Party. Social issues, the culture war, and racial resentment were packaged together to make possible the historic transfer of income and wealth that has shaped contemporary American politics. Many different studies, journalistic exposes, and everyday observations illustrate the basic fact of contemporary American life: we have become a society in which the breathtaking wealth enjoyed by the richest come at the direct expense of the vast majority.

The interplay between ideology and material reality makes it clear that they are mutually reinforcing. White identity has incorporated others that have become so important to the GOP: Christian, rural, conservative, male, gun owner, believer in traditional gender roles. They all became lumped together into a cohesive and unified whole whose disparate elements have made possible the explosion of wealth and income for those at the top and the corresponding stagnation of wealth and income for those below them.[20]

Forty years of a developing plutocracy have shaped both major political parties, but it has had the most dramatic effect on the Republicans. Until the Biden victory, the Democrats had largely stepped back from their traditional commitment to New Deal regulation and redistribution and championed tolerance and cultural pluralism as pale substitutes for social justice and economic equity. The Republicans have remained remarkably consistent in their orientation toward politics and economics. At virtually every opportunity, they have embraced plutocracy and attacked the welfare state. Where they used to be a responsible and conventional center-right party with an interest in governance, they have become an ultraconservative insurgency dedicated to obstruction and sabotage. In the process, the core principle of American civic nationalism is under severe stress. The Republican Party is coming closer than ever to renouncing the foundational position that formal citizenship is inclusive and that its benefits are offered regardless of race, religion, and other markers of identity. Its developing embrace of white nationalism rests on a denial that state's obligations extend to all and renounces the civil rights movement's great triumph: enshrining the principle that the privileges of citizenship are not determined by race or skin color.

Trump entered public life with his intervention in the case of the Central Park Five, but his "birther" slander of candidate Obama took his willingness to indulge in public racism to an entirely new level. His earlier foray into New York politics had been a fairly simple matter of pandering to hysteria and fear. But the birther matter was of a different order entirely, for it made explicit what he had been hinting at in earlier appearances. The claim that Obama was born outside the United States, that he had forged his birth certificate, and that he was an illegitimate president illustrated Trump's suggestion that citizenship is a matter of blood, race, and ethnicity rather than of naturalization or place of birth. His repudiation of the Fourteenth Amendment's clear definition of citizenship suggests that much more was at stake than his opponent's status. It lies at the heart of his claim that he really won the election of 2020, that he was denied victory only by massive electoral fraud, and that the courts should invalidate the ballots of hundreds of thousands of minority voters in Philadelphia, Atlanta, Milwaukee, Phoenix, and Detroit. Manifestly false claims that Biden is an illegitimate president have opened the door to the Republican Party's unmistakable position that it intends to deny the right to vote to millions of Americans on the basis of race or ethnicity. This is the core position that lies at the heart of its recent drive to restrict the franchise, rewrite electoral rules, and engage in grotesque gerrymandering to set in place the foundations of permanent white minority rule. The entire effort is to redefine what it means to be a full member of the national community – who is in, who is out, whose voice matters, whose does not, who can wield political power, and who must be subject to it.

All of this goes far beyond Trump. It is built on a mass base that predated his arrival on the national scene and will persist long after he is gone. Faced with the contradiction between its drive for power and the country's changing demographics, the Republican Party will continue to attack broad political participation and renounce the elementary democratic principle of majority rule. What was once a policy choice has become an iron necessity. Having refused repeated opportunities to reform itself, the party's leadership has doubled down on a resentful, fearful, and agitated base of white voters. This is what lies behind its claim that the Democrats stole the 2020 presidential election. Even as Trump continues to insist that he is still the president, endless Republican claims of voter fraud and electoral criminality will become the party's default response to future electoral losses. Underneath it all will be its foundational assumption that some voters matter more than others, that the majority cannot rule if it's not white, and that elections are legitimate only when Republicans win. Organizing this position has become the party's core project, its desperate attempt to confront the demographic cliff that awaits it and the economic turmoil that has ensnared millions of its voters. It unites a cynical and nihilistic GOP leadership with an embittered white voting base around a shared rejection of democracy's basic assumptions. It won't be long before American politics will feature more explicit ethno-nationalist position that some people simply matter more than others and that the interests of non-white members of society are corrupt, dangerous, and unworthy of legal recognition or political support.[21]

There is very little evidence that either the party's leadership or its rank and file is ready to move past Trump and return to a traditional understanding of citizenship or democracy.[22] Large numbers of Republicans are now willing to jettison historical commitments to democratic institutions and institutions in favor of a frankly ethnocentric orientation toward politics. Elementary commitments to the rule of law, the importance of elections, and the peaceful transfer of power are no longer widely shared as a substantial part of American society moves toward accepting violent and lawless solutions to political disputes. And it turns out that "the strongest predictor by far of these antidemocratic attitudes is ethnic antagonism – especially concerns about the political power and claims on government resources of immigrants, African-Americans, and Latinos."[23] A substantial part of the Republican electorate is driven by acute levels of ethnic and racial resentment that cluster together, are easily inflamed by political entrepreneurs, and set the conditions for a dramatic change compared to earlier periods. Racial and ethnic antagonism has driven the development of the American Right since Barry Goldwater convinced the Republican Party to go fishing where the votes were. The intensity of contemporary animus has produced a radicalized and racialized

Republican base that has become an active menace to democratic norms, procedures, and institutions. One of the country's most eminent social scientists summarized the results of a recent survey:

> The frailty of public commitment to democratic norms in the contemporary United States is illustrated by the responses of 1,151 Republican identifiers and Republican-leaning Independents interviewed in January 2020 to survey items contemplating transgressions of a variety of essential democratic principles, including the rejection of violence in pursuit of political ends and respect for the rule of law and the outcomes of elections. A majority of respondents (50.7%) agreed that "The traditional American way of life is disappearing so fast that we may have to use force to save it." A substantial plurality (41.3%) agreed that "A time will come when patriotic Americans have to take the law into their own hands." A near-majority (47.3%) agreed that "Strong leaders sometimes have to bend the rules in order to get things done." Almost three-fourths (73.9%) agreed that "It is hard to trust the results of elections when so many people will vote for anyone who offers a handout." In each case, most of those who did not agree said they were unsure; only 1 in 4 or 5 or 10 said they disagreed.[24]

The conjuncture of a large, resentful, and increasingly antidemocratic Republican base with political leaders ready to amplify and direct its animus sets the conditions for their relationship. Ever since his intervention in the case of the Central Park Five, Trump was more than willing to take advantage of already-existing racial anxiety and animus to advance his personal interests. Even as he happily intensified his followers' fears and resentments, he was also the vehicle for a constellation of beliefs that preceded him and will outlive him. As radical as was his willingness to truck in racism and prejudice, it was also the product of an environment that has been half a century in the making. This project is all the more dangerous because it is developing from the bottom-up *and* the top-down. There is a real mass base for it in the 85 percent of Republicans who demand that their candidates agree with Trump and the two-thirds who want him to run again for president in 2024.[25] The GOP is now dependent on a nativist, right-wing population – a dependence it shares with the European far right. No longer exclusively concerned with taxes and spending, it now speaks in Buchananite terms of "traditional morality" and a "national way of life." As its declining white Protestant base becomes angrier and more alienated, it will become even more radical, nihilistic, obstructionist, and destructive.

Its radicalism is born of a widespread conviction that white people are being victimized by hordes of undeserving minorities aided and abetted by corrupt Democratic politicians. People who are desperately trying to maintain their privileged position are increasingly convinced that they deserve it. Heightened levels of resentment accompany a loss of entitlement and prestige, and a defense of their privileged position is tantamount to a defense of civilization itself. Trump rode his story of humiliation, insecurity, and vulnerability to the White House. He convinced millions of aggrieved white voters that he offered a path back to what is normal. His ability to capitalize on insecurity led him to organize an administration that was designed to restore the country's proper social and political hierarchies. Constant attacks on the Republican political establishment and Democratic officials for negotiating "bad deals" helped him paint a picture of a weakened nation that was systematically disadvantaged by a failure of leadership. The country was being demeaned by corruption and incompetence, but he would "Make America Great Again." Through it all was the promise that he would use the power of the state to restore, strengthen, and maintain white dominance. Trump's appeals to discontented whites harkened back to a magical time when their supremacy was unquestioned and minorities knew their place.

The GOP used to have a coherent governing philosophy, but it has been drowned in a sea of anger, grievance, racism, and paranoia. It harbors a deep contradiction between an electoral base that is increasingly rural, Southern, white, and evangelical, on the one hand, and a set of policies that are those of the wealthy and the large corporations, on the other. The politics of race papered over the fissure for some time, and there is no sign that the party is prepared to move away from its reliance on white animus to win elections. As the conservative message of small government and individual freedom was swamped by the ethno-nationalist message of racial grievance and cultural loss, the GOP began to embrace white nationalism as a political program. As it did so, it also began to orient itself against many popular economic and social programs – even programs that will benefit many of its base voters.

The problem that the Republicans face is born of this contradiction. They have tried for decades to forge a coalition consisting of corporations and the rich on one hand and resentful lower-middle and middle-class whites on the other. Racial animus was an effective glue that held the coalition together for a time, but it's turned out to be an unreliable cement. The conservative coalition that Ronald Reagan put together looked very powerful for two elections, but it depended on his ability to unite the wealthy's desire for smaller government and lower taxes with white voters who were culturally conservative and wanted to be left alone. The problem was that large majorities of the GOP's base still supported most of the New Deal and much of the Great Society. They were not particularly interested in cutting back the regulatory state, reducing government spending, gutting the minimum wage, tying Social Security to the market, or turning Medicare over to the private insurers. Race did provide the disparate elements of the Republican coalition with a measure of common interest, but it remains an unstable arrangement. As the Republican Party moves toward white nationalism in an effort to paper over serious differences between the two important elements of their electoral and programmatic coalition, what was once a source of strength is becoming a weakness.

The long Republican project of strengthening plutocracy by appealing to racial animus still works with a substantial number of aggrieved white voters, but they remain a fringe. Their marginal status explains their extremism and intensifying hysteria. There's considerable evidence that the American population is getting more accustomed to racial diversity and cultural pluralism. Even as the Republican base has become more radically conservative about racial matters, the same is not true of the population as a whole. Opposition to Trump's obvious flirtation with white nationalism was widespread and there is no doubt that it contributed to his 2020 defeat. It's true that Trump did not invent this flirtation, that other Tribunes of Whiteness are ready to step forward, and that intense racial animus still drives the politics of a large part of the Republican base. But it's no less true that a substantial percentage of Americans believe that racism remains a powerful force, and an even larger percentage want something done about it. Similar findings indicate that substantial majorities were ready to welcome immigrants and decisively rejected Trump's attacks on ethnic diversity and racial equality.[26] The Republican coalition is inherently unstable, depending as it does on an alliance of those who want smaller government and lower taxes with those who are culturally and racially conservative but whose economic interests are fundamentally at odds with those of the corporations and the rich. Universal social and economic programs might be a way to break the conservative alliance that has dominated American politics for more than 40 years. Expanding Social Security, funding universal pre-kindergarten, making childcare affordable and available, redistributing wealth, protecting the environment, strengthening health insurance, instituting progressive taxation – all these programs would mobilize the broad middle and working classes against the inevitable opposition of key elements of the Republican coalition. It's worth remembering that even as they railed against Washington, tried to dismantle Obamacare, and vowed to "drain the swamp," the Tea Party militants were always careful to defend Medicare and Social Security. For all their nihilistic attacks on government, they wanted to safeguard the programs that worked for them.

A majority of Americans hold left of center views on most social and economic questions, but a system that empowers minorities often makes it difficult to translate broad consensus into policy. Differences of opinion about who gets to be an American and who should benefit from social welfare programs are still influenced by the country's racial past and present. They intensified during the Obama presidency and affected debate about the Affordable Care Act. While there was broad agreement that access to health insurance should be broadened, there was increasing polarization about who should benefit from that broadening. Broad sections of white voters were vulnerable to arguments that the social safety net should not be strengthened if benefits were to be shared with non-white citizens – even if they themselves would benefit from that strengthening.[27]

The Republican Party has long benefited from this situation and has skillfully exacerbated racial animus to clear the field for plutocracy. It has largely given up trying to attract a wider base of support, since it faces an electorate that does not support its economic agenda. Still reliant on a declining segment of the population, it is reduced to using an antimajoritarian political system to further the unpopular and narrow priorities of corporations and the rich. It is compelled to stoke outrage, to rely on the most extreme voices of grievance and to leverage white racial anxiety so it can win elections without wide support for its narrow set of policies. In a fair electoral system that accurately registered the preferences of the majority, they would have no future. The Democrats have successfully made a transition from their base in the South to becoming a national party that has become comfortable with being a multinational, multiracial coalition. The Republicans, on the contrary, have become the monolithic fortress of Confederate sympathizers, racial reactionaries, and unabashed plutocrats. This is what has driven their turn toward the structural tools that the Constitution makes available to a fringe party. A system that reinforces minority rule, rewards intransigence, and makes endless obstruction possible contains few incentives for them to refashion their plutocratic policy preferences or moderate their appeal to white racial anxiety. An entire political party is now organized around racial animosity and is uninterested in even pretending to represent the interests of the majority. As the GOP's base continues to shrink and becomes more radical, the party will align itself even more strongly against a multiracial democracy. As it becomes a minority of a minority, its base will still be systematically overrepresented in the national government and its desire to organize permanent white minority rule will only intensify.

But time is against them, and they know it. The country will continue to diversify despite their desperate attempts to maintain white minority rule. Even as the Republicans have moved radically to the right over the last 15 years, Democrats and independents have moved left on issues of racial equity and economic redistribution. This movement directly threatens an ultra-right party devoted to racial animus and plutocracy. While they have doubled down on the politics of racial outrage and are making their campaign against critical race theory the centerpiece of a national political strategy, they mirror the orientation of a white voting base that will remain resentful and determined to "Make America Great Again." But American society is becoming more cosmopolitan, secular, educated and integrated. Changing demographics, employment patterns, lifestyles, romantic attachments, and more are posing challenges that will restructure American society no matter what any political party may try to do. For all their efforts to close the country to immigrants and restore the old racial hierarchies, Republicans have been unable to shape the country's future. If they're not careful, they will continue their trajectory toward becoming a force that can only obstruct and delay, painting themselves into an ever-smaller corner as they resist doing anything about environmental collapse, accelerating inequality, or an endangered democracy. Dependent on ideological unity and purity, they will relegate themselves to protecting the interests of plutocracy in an environment that will only become more hostile.

American plutocrats want policies that elections won't provide. White nationalists want a return to a past that is disappearing. An obsolete and dysfunctional political system makes it possible to protect the interests of both for the moment, but time is against them. Their racially reactionary plutocratic party faces a future that will surely be an unkind one.

Notes

1 Heather Cox Richardson, *How the South Won the Civil War* (New York: Oxford University Press, 2020).
2 Carol Anderson, *White Rage: The Unspoken Truth of Our Racial Divide* (London: Bloomsbury, 2017).
3 See, among others, Jeffry Frieden, "The Political Economy of the Globalization Backlash: Sources and Implications" in *Meeting Globalization's Challenges*, eds. Maurice Obstfeld and Luis Catão (Princeton, NJ: Princeton University Press, 2019); J. Lawrence Broz, Jeffry Frieden, and Stephen Weymouth, "Populism in Place: The Political Economy of the Globalization Backlash," *International Organization*, 75:2 (2021), 464–494; Dani Rodrik, "Populism and the Economics of Globalization," *Journal of International Business Policy*, January 2018; and Lubos Pastor and Pietro Veronesi, "A Rational Backlash against Globalization," *Vox*, September 28, 2018.
4 Michael Tesler and John Sides, "How Political Science Helps Explain the Rise of Trump: The Role of White Identity and Grievances," *Monkey Cage* blog at the *Washington Post*, March 3, 2016.
5 Eliza Collins, "David Duke: Voting Against Trump is 'Treason to Your Heritage," *Politico*, February 25, 2016.
6 Marisa Abrajano and Zoltan L. Hijnal, *White Backlash: Immigration, Race, and American Politics* (Princeton, NJ: Princeton University Press, 2017).
7 "A Top GOP Pollster on Trump 2024, QAnon and What Republicans Really Want," The Ezra Klein Show, *New York Times*, March 26, 2021.
8 Thomas Edsall, "How Far Are Republicans Willing to Go? They're Already Gone," *New York Times*, June 9, 2021.
9 Michael Tesler, *Post-Racial or Most-Racial? Race and Politics in the Obama Era* (Chicago: University of Chicago Press, 2016).
10 See Jonathan M. Metzl, *Dying of Whiteness: How the Politics of Racial Resentment is Killing America's Heartland* (New York: Basic Books, 2019).
11 Sabrina Tavernise and Robert Gebeloff, "Census Shows Sharply Growing Numbers of Hispanic, Asian and Multiracial Americans," *New York Times*, August 21, 2021
12 Sanford Levinson, *Our Undemocratic Constitution: Where the Constitution Goes Wrong (And How We the People Can Correct It)* (New York: Oxford University Press, 2008).
13 Texas is a case in point. See Stephen Pedigo, "Texas Is the Future of America," *New York Times*, October 5, 2021.
14 Jon Queally, "Trump Admits 'You'd Never Have a Republican Elected in This Country Again' if Voting Access Expanded," *Salon*, March 31, 2020.
15 Thomas Edsall, "Trump True Believers Have Their Reasons," *New York Times*, October 6, 2021.
16 Ivan Kratsev, "The Apocalyptic Politics of the Populist Right," *New York Times*, November 13, 2020.

17 Thomas Edsall, "Trump's Cult of Animosity Shows No Sign of Letting Up," *New York Times*, July 7, 2021.
18 Emmanuel Saez, "Striking it Richer: The Evolution of Top Incomes in the United States" at https://eml.berkeley.edu/~saez/saez-UStopincomes-2015.pdf.
19 See Suzanne Mettler, *The Government–Citizen Disconnect* (New York: Russel Sage, 2018) and Jonathan Metzl, *Dying of Whiteness: How the Politics of Racial Resentment is Killing America's Heartland* (New York: Basic Books, 2019).
20 See, inter alia, Jacob Hacker and Paul Pierson. *Let Them Eat Tweets: How the Right Rules in an Age of Extreme Inequality* (New York: Liveright, 2020); Juliana Menasce Horowitz, Ruth Igielnik, and Rakesh Kochharand, "Trends in Income and Wealth Inequality," Pew Research Center, January 9, 2020 at www.pewresearch.org/social-trends/2020/01/09/trends-in-income-and-wealth-inequality/; George Lipsitz, *The Possessive Investment in Whiteness: How White People Profit from Identity Politics* (Philadelphia, PA: Temple University Press, 2018), p. 112; Emmanuel Saez, op. cit.
21 Nick Corasaniti, Jim Rutenberg, and Kathleen Gray, "As Trump Rails Against His Loss, His Supporters Become More Threatening," *New York Times*, December 8, 2020 and Jim Rutenberg and Nick Corasaniti, "An 'Indelible Stain': How the G.O.P. Tried To Topple a Pillar of Democracy," *New York Times*, December 12, 2020.
22 Lisa Lerer and Reid J. Epstein, "Abandon Trump? Deep in the G.O.P. Ranks, the MAGA Mind-Set Prevails," *New York Times*, January 21, 2021.
23 Larry Bartels, "Ethnic Antagonism Erodes Republicans' Commitment to Democracy," *Proceedings of the National Academy of Sciences of the United States of America*, July 10, 2020. At www.pnas.org/content/117/37/22752.
24 Ibid.
25 Charles M. Blow, "The G.O.P. Menace to Society," *New York Times*, August 1, 2021. See also Jacob Jarvis, "Donald Trump and His Allies Trapped by Doctrine of Conformity They Created," *Newsweek*, August 27, 2021.
26 Steven Levitsky and Daniel Ziblatt, "End Minority Rule," *New York Times*, October 23, 2020.
27 "Ezra Klein Interviews Lilliana Mason," *New York Times*, August 13, 2021. See also Metzl op. cit. and Heather McGhee, *The Sum of Us: What Racism Costs Everyone and How We Can Prosper Together* (New York: Random House, 2021).

BIBLIOGRAPHY

Books

Abrajano, Marisa and Zoltan L. Hijnal. *White Backlash: Immigration, Race, and American Politics*. Princeton, NJ: Princeton University Press, 2017.

Abramowitz, Alan. *The Great Alignment: Race, Party Transformation, and the Rise of Donald Trump*. New Haven, CT: Yale University Press, 2018.

Alberta, Tim. *American Carnage: On the Front Lines of the Republican Civil War and the Rise of President Trump*. New York: Harper, 2019.

Anderson, Carol. *White Rage: The Unspoken Truth of Our Racial Divide*. London: Bloomsbury, 2017.

Buchanan, Patrick J. *State of Emergency: The Third World Invasion and Conquest of America*. New York: St. Martin's Press, 2006.

———. *The Death of the West: How Dying Populations and Immigrant Invasions Imperil Our Country and Civilization*. New York: St. Martin's Press, 2002.

———. *Nixon's White House Wars: The Battles That Made and Broke a President and Divided America Forever*. New York: Crown, 2017.

Carter, Dan. *The Politics of Rage: George Wallace, the Origins of the New Conservatism, and the Transformation of American Politics*. Baton Rouge: Louisiana State University Press, 1995.

———. *From George Wallace to Newt Gingrich: Race in the Conservative Counterrevolution 1963–1994*. Baton Rouge: Louisiana State University Press, 1996.

Churchwell, Sarah. *Behold, America: The Entangled History of "America First" and "the American Dream."* New York: Basic Books, 2018.

Dionne, E.J. Jr. *Why the Right Went Wrong: Conservatism from Goldwater to Trump and Beyond*. New York: Simon & Schuster, 2016.

Edsall, Thomas and Mary Edsall. *Chain Reaction: The Impact of Race, Rights, and Taxes on American Politics*. New York: Norton, 1992.

Ehrenberg, John. *Civil Society: The Critical History of an Idea*. New York: New York University Press, 2017.

———. *Servants of Wealth: The Right's Assault on Economic Justice*. Lanham, MD: Rowman & Littlefield, 2006.

Fording, Richard C. and Sanford F. Schram. *Hard White: The Mainstreaming of Racism in American Politics*. New York: Oxford University Press, 2020.
Fountain, Ben. *Beautiful Country Burn Again: Democracy, Rebellion, and Revolution*. New York: HarperCollins, 2018.
Frieden, Jeffry. "The Political Economy of the Globalization Backlash: Sources and Implications" in *Meeting Globalization's Challenges* ed. Maurice Obstfeld and Luis Catão (Princeton: Princeton University Press, 2019).
Fraser, Steve and Gary Gerstle eds. *The Rise and Fall of the New Deal Order*. Princeton, NJ: Princeton University Press, 1990.
Goldwater, Barry. *The Conscience of a Conservative*. Shepherdsville, KT: Victor Publishing Company, 1960.
Hacker, Jacob and Paul Pierson. *Let Them Eat Tweets: How the Right Rules in an Age of Extreme Inequality*. New York: Liveright, 2020.
Hofstadter, Richard. *The Paranoid Style in American Politics and Other Essays* Cambridge, MA: Harvard University Press, 1952.
Honey, Michael K. *To the Promised Land: Martin Luther King and the Fight for Economic Justice*. New York: Norton, 2018.
Ignatiev, Noel. *How the Irish Became White*. New York: Routledge, 1995.
Jardina, Ashley. *White Identity Politics*. New York: Cambridge University Press, 2019.
Judis, John. *The Populist Explosion: How the Great Recession Transformed European and American Politics*. New York: Columbia Global Reports, 2016.
Kazin, Michael. *The Populist Persuasion*. Ithaca, NY: Cornell University Press, 1995.
Kendi, Ibram X. *Stamped from the Beginning: The Definitive History of Racist Ideas in America*. New York: Nation Books, 2016.
Key, V.O. *Southern Politics*. New York: Vintage, 1963.
Lesher, Stephan. *George Wallace: American Populist*. New York: Addison-Wesley, 1994.
Levinson, Sanford. *Our Undemocratic Constitution: Where the Constitution Goes Wrong (And How We the People Can Correct It)*. New York: Oxford University Press, 2008.
Lipsitz, George. *The Possessive Investment in Whiteness: How White People Profit from Identity Politics*. Philadelphia, PA: Temple University Press, 2018.
López, Ian Haney. *Dog Whistle Politics: How Coded Racial Appeals Have Reinvented Racism and Wrecked the Middle Class*. New York: Oxford University Press, 2018.
Lowndes, Joseph E. *From the New Deal to the New Right: Race and the Southern Origins of Modern Conservatism*. New Haven: Yale University Press, 2008.
Lucks, Daniel S. *Reconsidering Reagan: Racism, Republicans, and the Road to Trump*. New York: Beacon Press, 2020.
Maly, Michael T. and Heater M. Dalmage. *Vanishing Eden: White Construction of Memory, Meaning, and Identity in a Racially Changing City*. Philadelphia, PA: Temple University Press, 2016.
Mann, Thomas E. and Norman J. Ornstein. *It's Even Worse than it Looks*. New York: Basic Books, 2016.
Maxwell, Angie and Todd Shields. *The Long Southern Strategy: How Chasing White Voters in the South Changed American Politics*. New York: Oxford University Press, 2019.
Mayer, Jeremy D. *Running on Race: Racial Politics in Presidential Campaigns, 1950–2000*. New York: Random House, 2002.
McGhee, Heather. *The Sum of Us: What Racism Costs Everyone and How We Can Prosper Together*. New York: Random House, 2021.
Mettler, Suzanne. *The Government–Citizen Disconnect*. New York: Russell Sage, 2018.
Metzl, Jonathan M. *Dying of Whiteness: How the Politics of Racial Resentment is Killing America's Heartland*. New York: Basic Books, 2019.

Morgan, Edmund S. *American Slavery, American Freedom*. New York: Norton, 1975.
Norris, Pippa and Ronald Inglehart. *Cultural Backlash: Trump, Brexit and Authoritarian Populism*. New York: Cambridge University Press, 2019.
Parker, Christopher S. and Matt A. Barreto. *Change They Can't Believe In: The Tea Party and Reactionary Politics in America*. Princeton, PA: Princeton University Press, 2013.
Perlstein, Rick. *Nixonland: The Rise of a President and the Fracturing of America*. New York: Scribner's, 2008.
———. *Before the Storm: Barry Goldwater and the Unmaking of American Consensus*. New York: Nation Books, 2009.
———. *Reaganland: America's Right Turn 1976–1980*. New York: Simon & Schuster, 2020.
Phillips, Kevin. *The Emerging Republican Majority*. New York: Crown, 1969.
Porter, Eduard. *American Poison: How Racial Hostility Destroyed Our Promise*. New York: Alfred A. Knopf, 2020.
Richardson, Heather Cox. *How the South Won the Civil War*. New York: Oxford University Press, 2020.
Rieder, Jonathan. *Canarsie: The Jews and Italians of Brooklyn Against Liberalism*. Cambridge, MA: Harvard University Press, 1985.
Roediger, David R. *The Wages of Whiteness: Race and the Making of the White Working Class*. London: Verso, 1999.
———. *How Race Survived US History: From Settlement and Slavery to the Obama Phenomenon*. London: Verso, 2008.
Sandbrook, Dominic. *Mad as Hell: The Crisis of the 1970s and the Rise of the Populist Right*. New York: Anchor Books, 2011.
Skocpol, Theda and Vanessa Williamson. *The Tea Party and the Remaking of Republican Conservatism*. New York: Oxford University Press, 2012.
Stephens-Dougan, Lafleur. *Race to the Bottom: How Racial Appeals Work in American Politics*. Princeton, NJ: Princeton University Press, 2020.
Stevens, Stuart. *It Was All a Lie: How the Republican Party Became Donald Trump*. New York: Knopf, 2020.
Sugrue, Tom. *The Origins of the Urban Crisis: Race and Inequality in Postwar Detroit*. Princeton, NJ: Princeton University Press, 2005.
Sykes, Charles. *How the Right Lost Its Mind*. London: Biteback, 2019.
Tesler, Michael. *Post-Racial or Most-Racial? Race and Politics in the Obama Era*. Chicago: University of Chicago Press, 2016.
Viguerie, Richard. *The New Right: We're Ready to Lead*. Viguerie Company, 1981.
Warren, Donald. *The Radical Center: Middle Americans and the Politics of Alienation*. South Bend, IN: University of Notre Dame Press, 1976.
Wilentz, Sean. *The Age of Reagan*. New York: Harper, 2008.
Wuthnow, Robert. *The Left Behind: Decline and Rage in Rural America*. Princeton, NJ: Princeton University Press, 2019.
Zelizer, Julian E. *Burning Down the House: Newt Gingrich, the Fall of a Speaker, and the Rise of the New Republican Party*. New York: Penguin Books, 2020.

Articles

Acharya, Avidit, Matthew Blackwell, and Maya Sen. "The Political Legacy of American Slavery," *Journal of Politics* 78:3 (July 2016), accessed on October 23, 2019.
Allen, Joe. "When George Wallace Came to Town," *Jacobin* January 6, 2017.
Anderson, Carol. "The Policies of White Resentment," *New York Times* August 5, 2017.

———. "Republicans Want a White Republic. They'll Destroy America to Get It," *Time* July 17, 2019.

"A Top GOP Pollster on Trump 2024, QAnon and What Republicans Really Want," The Ezra Klein Show, *New York Times* March 26, 2021.

Badger, Emily and Nate Cohn. "White Anxiety, and a President Ready to Address It," *New York Times* July 20, 2019.

Baker, Peter. "Trump Fans the Flames of a Racial Fire," *New York Times* July 14, 2019.

Balmer, Randall. "The Real Origins of the Religious Right," *Politico* May 27, 2014.

Banks, Antoine. "Anger Makes Ethnocentrism among Whites a Stronger Predictor of Racial and Immigration Policy Opinions," *London School of Economics* at http://bit.ly/2uhO8yk.

Bartels, Larry. "Ethnic Antagonism Erodes Republicans' Commitment to Democracy." *Proceedings of the National Academy of Sciences of the United States of America* July 10, 2020.

———. "Ethnic antagonism erodes Republicans' commitment to democracy," *Proceedings of the National Academy of Arts and Sciences* August 31, 2020.

Baum, Dan. "Legalize It All," *Harper's* April 20, 2016.

Beauchamp, Zach. "Donald Trump's Victory Is Part of a Global White Backlash," *Vox* November 9, 2016.

Beinart, Peter. "The Republican Party's White Strategy," *The Atlantic* July/August 2016.

———. "The Harsh Truth Exposed by the Midterm Elections," *The Atlantic* November 7, 2018.

Bjork-James, Sophie and Jeff Maskovsky. "When White Nationalism Became Popular," *Anthropology News* May 18, 2017.

Black, Derek R. "What White Nationalism Gets Right About American History," *New York Times* August 19, 2017.

Blow, Charles M. "The White Rebellion," *New York Times* April 26, 2018.

———. "The G.O.P. Menace to Society," *New York Times* August 1, 2021.

Bouie, Jamelle. "Government by White Nationalism is Upon Us," *Slate* February 6, 2017.

———. "White Elephant," *Slate* September 1, 2017.

———. "Trump's America is a 'White Man's Country,'" *New York Times* July 15, 2019.

Broz, Lawrence J., Jeffry Frieden, and Stephen Weymouth. "Populism in Place: The Political Economy of the Globalization Backlash," *International Organization* 75:2, (2021), 464–494. doi:10.1017/S0020818320000314.

Bunyasi, Tehama Lopez. "The Role of Whiteness in the 2016 Presidential Primaries," *Perspectives on Politics* 17:3 (2019), 679–698.

Burghart, Devin and Leonard Zeskind. "Tea Party Nationalism: A Critical Examination of the Tea Party Movement and the Size, Scope, and Focus of its National Factions," Institute for Research and Education on Human Rights, 2010. www.irehr.org/2010/10/12/tea-party-nationalism-report-pdf/.

Burns, Sarah. "Why Trump Doubled Down on the Central Park Five," *New York Times* October 17, 2016.

Chait, Jonathan. "Donald Trump's Race War," *New York Magazine* April 4, 2017.

Chinoy, Sahil. "What Happened to America's Center of Gravity?" *New York Times* June 26, 2019.

Carnes, Nicolas and Noam Lupu. "It's Time to Bust the Myth: Most Trump Voters were not Working Class," *Monkey Cage* June 5, 2017.

Chait, Jonathan. "Donald Trump's Race War" *New York Magazine* April 3, 2017.

Coates, Ta-Nehisi. "The Case for Reparations" *The Atlantic* June 2014.

———. "The First White President" *The Atlantic* October 2017.

Cobb, Jelani. "In Trump's World, White Are the Only Disadvantaged Class," *The New Yorker* August 4, 2017.

———. "What Is Happening to the Republican Party?" *The New Yorker* March 8, 2021.

Collins, Eliza. "David Duke: Voting Against Trump Is 'Treason to Your Heritage,'" *Politico* February 25, 2016.

Coppins, McKay. "The Man Who Broke Politics," *The Atlantic* November 2018.

Corasaniti, Nick, Jeremy W. Peters, and Annie Karni. "New Trump Ad Suggests a Campaign Strategy Amid Crisis: Xenophobia," *New York Times* April 10, 2020.

Corasaniti, Nick, Jim Rutenberg, and Kathleen Gray. "As Trump Rails Against His Loss, His Supporters Become More Threatening," *New York Times* December 8, 2020.

Corn, David. "How Republicans Normalized Donald Trump's Racism," *Mother Jones* January 12, 2018.

Craig, Maureen A., Julian M. Rucker, and Jennifer A. Richeson. "The Pitfalls and Promise of Increasing Racial Diversity: Threat, Contact, and Race Relations in the 21st Century," *Current Discussions in Psychological Science* 27:3 (2018), 188–193.

Edsall, Thomas. "The Peculiar Populism of Donald Trump," *New York Times* February 2, 2017.

———. "Donald Trump's Identity Politics," *New York Times* August 24, 2017.

———. "White-On-White Voting," *New York Times* November 16, 2017.

———. "Trump Wants America to Revert to the Queens of His Childhood," *New York Times* April 12, 2018.

———. "Why Don't We Always Vote in Our Own Self-Interest," *New York Times* July 19, 2018.

———. "The Trump Legions." *New York Times* November 1, 2018.

———. "Trump is Changing the Shape of the Democratic Party, Too," *New York Times* June 19, 2019.

———. "How Racist is Trump's Republican Party?" *New York Times* March 18, 2020.

———. "Trump Reaches Back into His Old Bag of Populist Tricks," *New York Times* April 22, 2020.

———. "Trump Hasn't Given up on Divide and Conquer," *New York Times* April 29, 2020.

———. "Trump Wants a Backlash. Can He Whip One into Shape?" *New York Times* July 1, 2020.

———. "'I Fear That We Are Witnessing the End of American Democracy,'" *New York Times* August 26, 2020.

———. "White Riot," *New York Times* January 13, 2021.

———. "Trump's Cult of Animosity Shows No Sign of Letting Up," *New York Times* July 21, 2021.

———. "How Far Are Republicans Willing to Go? They're Already Gone," *New York Times* August 9, 2021.

———. "Trump True Believers Have Their Reasons," *New York Times* October 6, 2021.

Ehrenfreund, Max. "Researchers Have Found Strong Evidence That Racism Helps the GOP Win," *Washington Post* March 3, 2016.

"Ezra Klein Interviews Lilliana Mason," *New York Times* August 13, 2021.

Farrell, John A. "Breaking the Grip of White Grievance," *The New Republic* April 16, 2020.

Fea, John. "Evangelical Fear Elected Trump," *The Atlantic* June 24, 2018.

Gerson, Michael. "Trump Is Evangelicals' 'Dream President.' Here's Why," *Washington Post* May 15, 2017.

———. "Trump's Nixonian White-Grievance Strategy Doesn't Have to Define the GOP," *Washington Post* August 17, 2020.

Gerstle, Gary. "Radical Republicans: The Radicalization of the Republican Party," *Die Zeit* November 2017.
Gilbert, Greg. "UW Professor Got It Right on Trump. So Why Is He Being Ignored?" *Seattle Times* June 14, 2017.
Glickman, Lawrence. "How White Backlash Controls American Progress," *The Atlantic* May 21, 2020.
Greenfield, Jeff. "Trump Is Pat Buchanan with Better Timing," *Politico* September–October 2016.
Graham, David A., Adrienne Green, Cullen Murphy, and Parker Richards. "An Oral History of Trump's Bigotry," *The Atlantic* June 2019.
Green, Emma. "It was Cultural Anxiety that Drove White, Working-Class Voters to Trump," *The Atlantic* May 9, 2017.
Green, Jon and Sean McElwee. "The Differential Effects of Economic Conditions and Racial Attitudes in the Election of Donald Trump," *Perspectives on Politics* October 29, 2018.
Greenberg, David. "Dog-Whistling Dixie," *New York Times* November 20, 2007.
———. "What Roger Ailes Learned from Richard Nixon," *New York Times* May 18, 2017.
Grohsgal, Dov and Kevin M. Kruse. "How the Republican Majority Emerged," *The Atlantic* August 6, 2019.
Hannah-Jones, Nikole. "It Was Never about Busing," *New York Times* July 12, 2019.
Hasan, Mehdi. "Time to Kill the Zombie Argument: Another Study Shows Trump Won Because of Racial Anxieties – Not Economic Distress," *The Intercept* September 18, 2018.
Herr, Jeet. "How the Southern Strategy Made Donald Trump Possible," *The New Republic* February 18, 2016.
———. "Pat Buchanan Is a Bigot, Just Like Donald Trump," *The New Republic* May 9, 2017.
Herriot, Michael. "How the Republican Party Became the Party of Racism," *The Root* July 23, 2018.
Hofstadter, Richard. "The Paranoid Style in American Politics," *Harper's* November 1964.
Horowitz, Juliana Menasce, Ruth Igielnik, and Rakesh Kochharand. "Trends in Income and Wealth Inequality," *Pew Research Center* January 9, 2020, at www.pewresearch.org/social-trends/2020/01/09/trends-in-income-and-wealth-inequality/.
Illing, Sean. "A Princeton Sociologist Spent 8 Years Asking Rural Americans Why They're So Pissed Off," *New York Times* March 13, 2018.
Inglehart, Ronald F. and Pippa Norris. "Trump and the Populist Authoritarian Parties: The Silent Revolution in Reverse," *Perspectives on Politics* 15:2 (June 2017), 443–454.
———. "Trump, Brexit, and the Rise of Populism: Economic Have-Nots and Cultural Backlash," *Harvard Kennedy School* August 2016.
Ingraham, Christopher. "Trump's 'Offensive and Prejudicial Rhetoric' Skews How White People View Minorities, Research Finds," *Washington Post* October 31, 2018.
Jacobs, Tom. "How White Identity Shapes American Politics," *Pacific Standard* March 25, 2019.
———. "A New Study Confirms (Again) That Race, Not Economics, Drove Former Democrats to Trump," *Pacific Standard* April 29, 2019.
Jardina, Ashley, Sean McElwee, and Spencer Piston. "How Do Trump Voters See Black People?" *Slate* November 7, 2016.
Johnson, Theodore R. "How the Black Vote Became a Monolith," *New York Times* September 16, 2020.
Jones, Robert P. "Trump Can't Reverse the Decline of White America," *The Atlantic* July 4, 2017.

Kindred, Chris. "The Nationalist's Delusion," *The Atlantic* November 20, 2017.
Krastev, Ivan. "The Apocalyptic Politics of the Populist Right," *New York Times* November 13, 2020.
Laugland, Oliver. "Donald Trump and the Central Park Five: The Racially Charged Rise of a Demagogue," *The Guardian* February 17, 2016.
Leonhardt, David. "No, It Wasn't Just Racism," *New York Times* October 23, 2019.
Lerer, Lisa. "Moving Beyond MAGA?" *New York Times* June 11, 2020.
Lerer, Lisa and Reid J. Epstein. "Abandon Trump? Deep in the G.O.P. Ranks, the MAGA Mind-Set Prevails," *New York Times* January 21, 2021.
Leonhardt, David and Ian Prasad Philbrick. "Donald Trump's Racism: The Definitive List, Updated," *New York Times* January 15, 2018.
Levitsky, Steven and Daniel Ziblatt. "End Minority Rule," *New York Times* October 23, 2020.
Lieberman, Robert C., Suzanne Mettler, Thomas B. Pepinsky, Kenneth M. Roberts, and Richard Valelly. "The Trump Presidency: A Historical and Comparative Analysis," *Perspectives on Politics* 17:2 (October 29, 2018), 470–479. doi:10.1017/S1537592718003286.
Lithwick, Dalia. "Everyone Is Biased (Except White People)," *Slate* August 7, 2017.
Lopez, German. "The Past Year of Research Has Made It Very Clear: Trump Won Because of Racial Resentment," *Vox* December 15, 2017.
Marcotte, Amanda. "It Wasn't Abortion That Formed the Religious Right. It was Support for Segregation," *Slate* May 29, 2014.
———. "Heading Into GOP Convention, Trump Goes All-in on Ugly White Grievance Politics," *Slate* August 19, 2020.
Martin, Jonathan, Maggie Haberman, and Katie Rogers. "As Public Opinion Shifts on Racism, Trump Digs In," *New York Times* June 11, 2020.
Masciotra, David. "Trump Won on 'White Fright': Why Identity Politics Win Elections," *Salon* July 27, 2017.
McCarthy, Michael A. "The Revenge of Joe the Plumber," *Jacobin* October 26, 2019.
McElwee, Sean and Jason McDaniel. "Anatomy of a Donald Trump Supporter: What Really Motivates This Terrifying Political Movement," *Salon* May 16, 2016.
———. "Economic Anxiety Didn't Make People Vote for Trump. Racism Did," *The Nation* May 8, 2017.
McFarland, Melanie. "'The Reagans' Shows How the Gipper Paved the Way for Political Actors Pretending They Aren't Racist," *Salon* November 16, 2020.
Mudde, Cass. "Stephen Miller Is No Outlier. White Supremacy Rules the Republican Party," *The Guardian* November 16, 2019.
Mutz, Diana. "Status Threat, Not Economic Hardship, Explains the 2016 Presidential Vote," *Proceedings of the National Academy of Sciences* March 26, 2018.
Oberhauser, Ann M., Daniel Krier, and Abeli M. Kusow. "Political Moderation and Polarization in the Heartland: Economics, Rurality, and Social Identity in the 2016 Presidential Election," *The Sociological Quarterly* April 12, 2019.
O'Toole, Fintan. "The Trump Inheritance," *New York Review of Books* February 25, 2021.
Packer, George. "We Are Living in a Failed State," *The Atlantic* June 2020.
Pastor, Lubos and Pietro Veronesi. "A Rational Backlash against Globalization," *Vox* September 28, 2018.
Payne, Charles M. "The Whole United States Is Southern!: *Brown v. Board* and the Mystification of Race," *Journal of American History* 91:1 (June 2004), 83–91, https://doi.org/10.2307/3659615.
Pedigo, Stephen. "Texas Is the Future of America," *New York Times* October 5, 2021.

Perlstein, Rick. "Exclusive: Lee Atwater's Infamous 1981 Interview on the Southern Strategy," *The Nation* November 13, 2012.
———. "I Thought I Understood the American Right. Trump Proved me Wrong," *New York Times* April 11, 2017.
Porter, Eduardo. "Whites' Unease Shadows the Politics of a More Diverse America," *New York Times* May 22, 2018.
Posner, Sarah. "Amazing Disgrace," *New Republic* March 20, 2017.
Queally, Jon. "Trump Admits 'You'd Never Have a Republican Elected in This Country Again' if Voting Access Expanded," *Salon* March 31, 2020.
Rapoport, Ronald B., Alan I. Abramowitz, and Walter J. Stone. "Why Trump Was Inevitable," *New York Review of Books* June 23, 2016.
Rauch, Jonathan. "How American Politics Went Insane," *The Atlantic* June 20, 2016.
———. "It's George Wallace's World Now," *The Atlantic* April 26, 2020.
Reny, Tyler T., Loren Collingwood, and Ali Valenzuela. "Vote-Switching in the 2016 Election: How Racial and Immigration Attitudes, Not Economics, Explain Shifts in White Voting," *Public Opinion Quarterly* May 21, 2019.
Reuters Staff. "Trump to Give $5 Million to Charity if Obama Releases Records," *Reuters* October 24, 2012.
Riley, Dylan. "American Brumaire?" *New Left Review* January–February 2017.
Risen, Clay. "How the Party of Lincoln Became the Party of Racial Backlash," *New York Times* March 31, 2018.
Rodrik, Dani. "Populism and the Economics of Globalization," *Journal of International Business Policy* January 2018.
Rosenberg, Paul. "'The Long Southern Strategy': How Southern White Women Drove the GOP to Donald Trump," *Salon* July 1, 2019.
Ross, Janell. "Donald Trump's Doubling Down on the Central Park Five Reflects a Bigger Problem," *Washington Post* October 8, 2016. Roudman, Sam. "Pat Buchanan Is 'Delighted to Be Proven Right' by 2016 Election," *New York Magazine* November 1, 2016.
Rovere, Richard. "The Campaign: Goldwater," *The New Yorker* September 26, 1964.
Rutenberg, Jim and Nick Corasaniti. "An 'Indelible Stain': How the G.O.P. Tried to Topple a Pillar of Democracy," *New York Times* December 12, 2020.
Saez, Emmanuel. "Striking it Richer: The Evolution of Top Incomes in the United States," at https://eml.berkeley.edu/~saez/saez-UStopincomes-2015.pdf.
Saletan, William. "What Trump Supporters Really Believe," *Slate* August 29, 2017.
———. "The President's Racist Base, By the Numbers," *Slate* August 29, 2017.
Schaffner, Brian F., Matthew Macwilliams, and Tatishe Nteta. "Understanding White Polarization in the 2016 Vote for President: The Sobering Role of Racism and Sexism," *Political Science Quarterly* March 25, 2018.
Schermerhorn, Calvin. "Racial Divides Have Been Holding American Workers Back for More Than a Century," *Washington Post* December 15, 2017.
Server, Adam. "White Nationalism's Deep American Roots," *The Atlantic* April 2019.
Serwer, Adam. "Trumpism is 'Identity Politics' for White People," *The Atlantic* October 25, 2018.
———. "White Nationalism's Deep American Roots," *The Atlantic* April 2019.
———. "The Coronavirus Was an Emergency Until Trump Found Out Who Was Dying," *The Atlantic* May 8, 2020.
———. "Birtherism of a Nation," *The Atlantic* May 13, 2020.

Shepard, Steven. "Study: Views on Immigration, Muslims Drove White Voters to Trump," *Politico* June 13, 2017.
Smith, Rogers M. and Desmond King. "White Protectionism in America," *American Political Science Association* May 13, 2020.
Sorkin, Amy Davidson. "Donald Trump and the Central Park Five," *New Yorker* June 23, 2014.
Stevens, Stuart. "We Lost the Battle for the Republican Party's Soul Long Ago," *New York Times* July 29, 2020.
Taibbi, Matt. "The War in the White House," *Rolling Stone* May 3, 2017.
———. "Why Trump Can't Quit the Alt-Right," *Rolling Stone* August 21, 2017.
Taub, Amanda. "Behind 2016's Turmoil, A Crisis of White Identity," *New York Times* November 1, 2016.
Tavernise, Sabrina and Robert Gebeloff. "Census Shows Sharply Growing Numbers of Hispanic, Asian and Multiracial Americans," *New York Times* August 21, 2021.
Touré. "White People Explain Why They Feel Oppressed," *Vice* September 17, 2015.
Tesler, Michael. "Economic Anxiety Isn't Driving Racial Resentment. Racial Resentment Is Driving Economic Anxiety," *New York Times* August 22, 2016.
Tesler, Michael and John Sides. "How Political Science Helps Explain the Rise of Trump," *Monkey Cage* March 3, 2016.
Trump, Donald. "Central Park Five Settlement Is a Disgrace," *New York Daily News* June 21, 2014.
Vance, J.D. "How Donald Trump Seduced America's White Working Class," *The Guardian* September 10, 2016.
Wade, Peter. "75 Percent of Republicans Say White Americans Are Discriminated Against," *Rolling Stone* March 9, 2019.
Wagner, Alex. "The Republican Party Moves from Family Values to White Nationalism," *The Atlantic* June 22, 2018.
Waldman, Paul. "Why White People Think They're the Real Victims of Racism," *The Week* October 25, 2017.
———. "The Cycle of Republican Radicalization," *American Prospect* December 2, 2014.
Walt, Stephen M. "America's New President is Not a Rational Actor," *Foreign Policy* January 25, 2017.
Weiner, Jon. "Eric Foner: White Nationalists, Neo-Confederates, and Donald Trump," *The Nation* August 17, 2017.
Westneat, Danny. "UW Professor Got it Right on Trump. So Why Is He Being Ignored?" *Seattle Times* June 14, 2017.
Wheaton, Sarah and Michael D. Shear. "Blunt Report Says GOP Needs to Regroup for '16," *New York Times* March 18, 2013.
Wood, Thomas. "Racism Motivated Trump Voters More than Authoritarianism," *Washington Post* April 17, 2017.
Yamahtta-Taylor, Keeanga. "The Bitter Fruits of Trump's White-Power Presidency," *The New Yorker* January 12, 2021.
Yglesias, Matthew. "Why I Don't Think It Makes Sense to Attribute Trump's Support to Economic Anxiety," *Vox* August 15, 2016.

INDEX

abortion 54
affirmative action 38, 44, 58, 59, 60
affirmative policies 29
Affordable Care Act 86, 87, 123
agriculture, industrialization of 14
"America First" program 83
American Dream 7, 67
antidemocratic attitudes 120
Apprentice, The 95
Arpaio, Sheriff Joe 100
Atwater, Lee 48, 66, 118
auto industry 27, 28, 37, 53, 54
"Aztlan Strategy" 80–1

Bakke case 60
bankers 84
Biden, Joe 113, 119
"birtherism" 10, 94
birthrate 82
Black Lives Matter 11
Black migration North 23, 28
Black music 72
Black neighborhoods 33, 69, 71
Black progress at the expense of whites 43
Black rights, North and South 14
Black violent crime, fear of 93
Blackmun, Justice Harry 60
Blacks: blaming 32; exclusion from housing market 33; migration to Democrats 39; and orderly society 32; as scapegoats 33, 34; as trustworthy 102
blaming the poor 33

Bronx, the 68–9, 70
Brown v Board of Education (1954) 9, 15, 17–18, 59, 60, 107; objections to 16, 17
Buchanan, Pat 64, 65, 76, 77–8, 80, 88; campaign 77, 78; ideas of the future 79, 81–2, 83
Bush, President George H W 23–4, 66, 67, 77, 96
Bush, President George W 4, 10, 79–80; reaction to trump speech 104
busing 33, 35, 36, 37, 44

California's growth 50
Carter presidency 44–5, 49, 52
census, meddling with 113
Central Park Five 5, 69, 70, 93–4, 121
Charlottesville 95, 96, 101
city decline 28, 53
city violence 27, 30, 68
Civil Rights Act (1964) 3, 20; opposition to 2, 8
Civil Rights Bills: (1957) 36; (1964) 16
civil rights era, end of 37
civil rights legislation 29; declining to enforce 43–4, 91; objections to 43, 48 *see also* Civil Rights Act, Voting Rights Act
civil rights movement 2, 3, 22, 34, 115; backlash 18, 19, 22; end of 107; hostility to 43, 47
Civil War 115
Clean Air Act (1963) 39

Index

Clinton, Hillary 70; debates with Trump 95
Clinton, President Bill 66, 67–8, 72, 76, 77
"colorblind" racial policy 38, 44, 58, 59, 60, 61
Conscience of a Conservative, The 17, 18
conservatism based on white resentment 31–2
Constitution 17, 115
construction industry 29
"Contract with America" 74, 75
corporate tax rate 117
corporations and the rich, rewards to 7, 8
crack epidemic 61, 68, 70–1
cultural conservatism 21
cultural erosion 82
"culture of dependency" 34
"culture of poverty" 69
"culture wars" 35, 38

deindustrialization 54, 99, 108
Democratic Leadership Conference (DLC) 66
Democratic National Convention 15
democratic norms 121
Democratic supremacy, foundation of 3
Democrats and Black voters 14–15
Democrats move away from redistribution 76–7
deregulation 44, 52
desegregation plans 36
desegregation of schools 16, 36, 38
deserving and undeserving 84, 85, 118
Detroit 27, 53
Dilulio, John J 69
diseases from immigrants 79
disinvestment 99
Dixie (Southern United States) 13
Dixiecrats 15; rebellion 8
dog whistles 20, 48; Clinton 68; Nixon 38, 40; Reagan 47, 48, 49, 51, 54, 61; Wallace 27
Dole, Senator Bob 70
drug market 68, 69, 71
drugs, criminalization of 40
Dukakis, Michael 66
Duke, David 95, 96, 109

economic distress 108
economic inequality 7
elections, "rigged" 114–15
Electoral College 113, 116
electoral losses, future 120

Employment Retirement Security Act (ERISA) 36
enemy inside 82
Energy Policy and Conservation Act 36
Environmental Protection Agency (EPA) 39
Equal Rights amendment, opposition to 74
equality before the law 20, 61
Erlichman, John 29, 40
ethnic antagonism 120

family breakdown 69
Federal Housing Act (1934) 14
Federal Housing Administration (FHA) 22–3, 37
Federal Housing Agency 14
financial institutions 84
Food Stamp program 38
Ford, President Gerald 36, 37, 41
Fourteenth Amendment 2, 11, 17, 85, 119

"gangsta rap" 71, 72
gerrymandering 111, 113, 119
GI Bill (1944) 14
Gingrich, Newt 64, 65, 72–6, 88; policies 73–4
Giuliani, Rudy 72
globalization 108
Golden Age of American capitalism 7; end of 44–5, 53
Goldwater, Barry 2, 6, 17, 22, 65; Black vote 36; campaign 8, 12, 13, 18–19, 31, 45; views of 16, 17, 18; white vote 15
GOP (Grand Old Party) 2, 6, 73, 76, 90, 118; base 116, 124; electoral strategy 110; profiting from racial tensions 102; refusal to adapt 112–13; Southern White voters 29; values 119; and white nationalism 16, 17, 109, 111; *see also* Republican Party
governmental interference 46
Graham, Lindsey 11
Grand Old Party *see* GOP
Great Migration 107
Great Recession 5, 97
"Great Society" programs 31
"Growth and Opportunity Project" 87

Haldeman, H R 38, 40
Hayes, President Rutherford B 15
Hayes-Tilden compromise 13, 15
health care debate 112

herrenvolk 10, 102
hip-hop 70–1, 72
homelessness 69
homeownership 14, 22–3, 32; non-white exclusion 14
Horton, Willie 66, 93, 95, 96
hostages in Tehran 44, 56
House of Representatives 72
housing complexes 14
housing segregation 23, 32, 46, 47

immigrants 78–9; hostility to 108; Mexicans 78, 94; under Reagan 62; Trump's preference 94
income 7, 99, 117
income tax 117
industrial core, evisceration of 54, 99, 108
industrial unions 13
inequality, historic levels of 98, 116–17
inflation 52, 53
inner city collapse 69
integrated education 17, 18; backlash 22
integration, abstract support but no reality 57–8

Japanese competition 28
Jim Crow 8, 9, 112, 115; after 1965 27; defense of 35; opposition to 12–13, 16
Johnson, President Lyndon B 27, 40

Kennedy, President John F 17
Kennedy, Senator Edward 49, 52
Kennedy, Senator Robert 19
Keynesianism 12, 44, 57
King, Martin Luther 10, 28, 36, 60
Ku Klux Klan 109; murders 99

Latinos 97, 108
legislation, punitive 69
Levittown 14
Lincoln, Abraham 115
Lott, Trent 51

"magic of the market" 10, 57
"Make America Great Again (MAGA)", Trump promise 2, 97, 122
manufacturing jobs, loss of 27–8, 53
mass incarceration policy 68, 69
McCain, John 4, 98
Medicaid 39, 57
Medicare 38, 39, 57, 84
Meili, Patricia 93
Mexican immigrants 78, 94

"middle Americans" 30
middle whites, exploitation of 21
Milliken v Bradley 36
minority population, increasing 112
miscarriage of justice 93–4
Mississippi Freedom Summer 51
Moore, Roy 99–100
moral panics 61, 69, 70
mortgages 23
Moynihan, Daniel Patrick 39
music genre 70–1
Muslims 96, 97; ban on 94, 95, 109; Obama as 85, 111
Myrdal, Gunnar, report 12

Nazis 96
neighborhood ratings 37
"neoliberal consensus" 68
New Deal 13, 14, 15, 22, 28, 38; break up of 3, 9–10, 30–1, 34, 40, 66
"new Democrats" 67
Nineteenth Amendment 112
Nixon, President Richard 3, 27, 28, 36, 38–9; appeal to white voters 35; black vote 36; campaigns 9, 26, 29, 35–6, 38, 40, 41; on civil rights enforcement 37, 38, 43–4; on culture 39; and the economy 35, 39; policies of 3, 39; promises 37, 43; on racial issues 9, 16, 36, 39; silent majority 35; views of 30, 57

Obama, President Barack 4, 5; birth certificate 10, 85, 94, 95, 119; election 111, 112–13; hostility to 84, 100; as a Muslim 85, 111; racial backlash 92; Tea Party reaction to 86; and Trump 94–5; white voters for 83
Obamacare 84, 108
Occupational Safety and Health Administration (OSHA) 39
oil boycott 44
open housing 22, 28, 33, 35

parasitic rich and poor 9, 21
Parks, Rosa 12
partisan warfare 74, 75, 76
patriotic values 82
Phillips, Kevin 30–1, 34, 35, 39, 40, 55
plutocracy 7, 119
political movements to the far right 112, 113
populism 9, 21, 30, 52, 117
pork-barrel spending 75

Powell, Congressman Adam Clayton 36
privatization 41, 44, 52

racial animus 2, 108
racial grievance, appeals to 110
racial hierarchy 3
racial politics 22, 27
racializing insecurities 26
racism: intentional 59–60; overt, 19; "reverse" 92
rap 71, 72
Reagan, Nancy 61
Reagan, President Ronald 3, 46, 47, 50, 99; anti-statism 3, 56–7; appeal to Californians 45, 46, 47; campaigns 49, 51, 53, 54, 55, 56; and civil rights movement 43, 52; conservative coalition 122; deregulation 52; immigration under 62; new conservatism 42, 65; policies 10, 65; privatization 52; refusal to enforce legislation 58; on school segregation 58; speech 62; and taxes 48, 52, 56; and welfare state 10; and white fears 45, 46, 53; white voters 4, 99
"Reaganomics" 57
"real Americans" 10, 24, 85
recession 52
regulation, reductions in 117
regulatory agencies 39
Republican National Committee (RNC) 4, 87
Republican Party 7; antiestablishment 75; authoritarian and undemocratic 113; base 118, 120, 121; demographic problem 79–80; effect of plutocracy 119; *see also* GOP
Republicans in Name Only (RINOS) 116
residential segregation 23, 32, 46, 47
rewards to privileged groups 98–9
Reyes, Matias 93, 94
Reynolds, William Bradford 58, 59
rich at the expense of the poor 56
right-wing populism, American and European 117
Roberts, Chief Justice John 58, 59, 60
Roe v Wade 52
Romney, Senator Mitt 87, 98
Roosevelt, President Franklin D 13
Rove, Karl 80
Rumford Fair Housing Act (1963) 46, 47
Russell, Richard 16

school desegregation 16, 36, 38
segregated occupations 64
segregation, residential 23, 32, 46, 47
segregation of schools 58
"silent majority" 9, 21, 26, 27, 29, 35
slavery days 100
slavery, preserving 115
social disorder 69
social protections 117; white opposition to 118
Social Security 38, 39, 57, 84; exemptions 14
Social Security Act 13
social welfare, attacks on 117
society, changing 124
Souljah, Sister 68, 108
Southern Manifesto 16
Spencer, Richard 96
"stagflation" 44, 52, 56
stagnation of wealth and income 119
state regulation, attacks on 56–7
"States' Rights Democratic Party" (Dixiecrats) 8, 15
steel industry 53–4
student unrest 50
"superpredators" 69, 70, 72
Supreme Court 59, 115

Taft-Hartley Act (1947) 28
"Tax Cuts and Jobs Act" 116–17
tax dollars, misuse of 54
Tea Partiers 84, 85–6, 111
Tea Party 4, 64, 65, 74, 75, 86–7; reaction to Obama 86
teenagers 71–2
Tenth Amendment 15, 16, 17, 20
threats from within 82
Thurmond, Senator Strom 15, 16
Truman, President Harry S 15
Trump, Donald (The Donald) 1, 2, 5, 91, 93, 99; and Democratic congresswomen 95; falsehoods 94, 113; and Hillary Clinton debates 95; global warming denial 96; and immigrants 1–2, 8, 10; and Obama 10, 94–5, 119; policies 101–2, 116; racial attitudes 8, 11, 91, 94–6, 97; "shithole countries" 5, 10, 94, 112; and white nationalism 5, 10, 123
Trump, Donald, campaign 91–2, 97, 98, 103, 104, 105; appeal to white anxieties 1–2, 5, 24, 100–1, 103, 122; defeat 123; "only I can fix it" 5, 92; policies 95; racism in 95; support for 117; targets

during 5, 97; Tribune of Whiteness 91; victory 91, 97, 116; voters 8, 97, 98
Trump, Donald, presidency 91–2; announcement of candidacy for 90; inaugural address 103, 104; racism in 95; refusal to accept he didn't win 113, 115, 116, 119, 120

unions, industrial 13
University of Mississippi, resistance to integration 17
urban crisis 32, 69
urban decay 44, 68–9
urban uprisings 29

victimization, white sense of 60, 83, 92
voter suppression 113
voters: Latino 80; white 6–8, 26, 32, 35, 48, 120; working and middle class 7, 26, 35
voting behaviour (in 2010 and 2012) 112
voting, impediments to 112
Voting Rights Act (1965) 3, 20, 27, 112; attack on 112; *see also* civil rights legislation

Wagner Act 13
Wallace, George 2–3, 6, 18, 19, 51, 65; campaigns 8–9, 13, 19–21, 22, 24; economics 22; legacy 24; racism 9, 26–7; supporters 23
"War on Drugs" 40, 61, 71
wars in Afghanistan and Iraq 84

Watts Rebellion 24–5, 27, 45, 46
wealth: creators 21; downward redistribution 50; at the expense of the majority 118–19; and politics 7; share of 117; transfer up 4, 7, 44, 53, 56, 65, 116–17
welfare and parasitism 34
"welfare queen" 54
welfare state: attacks on 44, 106; expansion of 36, 40
white fears 3, 21, 86, 111
white grievance 91, 92, 103–4; winning elections 41
white nationalism, definition 115
white people: defender of 62; lower-income 4, 109; middle- and working-class 40, 68
white population, declining 112, 116
white privileges 13–14, 64, 110
white resistance to Black advancement 107
white supremacists 95
white victimization 60, 83
"wilding" 69, 70, 93
"Wire, The" 71
Wise, Korey 93
Wright, Jim 75
wrongful imprisonment 93
Wygant v Jackson Board of Education 59, 60

X, Malcolm 13

Yarborough, Senator Ralph 24